HIGHER EDUCATION AND OPINION MAKING
IN TWENTIETH-CENTURY ENGLAND

T0316015

Previous books include:

Expectations of Higher Education: Some Historical Pointers (with P. Silver) (1981)

Education as History: Interpreting Nineteenth and Twentieth Century Education (1983)

A Liberal Vocationalism (with J. Brennan) (1988)

Education, Change and the Policy Process (1990)

A Higher Education: The Council for National Academic Awards and British Higher Education (1990)

An Educational War on Poverty: American and British Policy Making 1960–1980 (with P. Silver) (1991)

Good Schools, Effective Schools: Judgements and their History (1994)

Students; Changing Roles, Changing Lives (with P. Silver) (1997)

Researching Education: Themes in Teaching and Learning (1999)

Innovating in Higher Education: Teaching, Learning and Institutional Cultures (2000)

HIGHER EDUCATION AND OPINION MAKING IN TWENTIETH-CENTURY ENGLAND

HAROLD SILVER

University of Plymouth

Routledge
Taylor & Francis Group

LONDON AND NEW YORK

First published in 2003 by
FRANK CASS PUBLISHERS
and
WOBURN PRESS

This edition published 2014 by Routledge
2 Park Square, Milton Park, Abingdon, Oxon OX14 4RN
711 Third Avenue, New York, NY 10017

Routledge is an imprint of the Taylor & Francis Group, an informa business

British Library Cataloguing in Publication Data

Silver, Harold, 1928–
Higher education and oinion making in twentieth-century
England
1. Education, Higher – England – History – 20th century
I. Title
378.4'2'0904

ISBN 0-7130-0231 X (cloth)
ISBN 0-7130-4049 1 (paper)
ISSN 1462-2076

Library of Congress Cataloging-in-Publication Data

A catalog record for this book is available
from the Library of Congress

Typeset by Cambridge Photosetting Services, Cambridge and in 10.5/12.5 Times

CONTENTS

LIST OF ILLUSTRATIONS

1. Lord Haldane with Albert Einstein.
2. 'The Project of a University College at Hull', by the Principal, *University Bulletin* (University College, Hull), 1930.
3. Abraham Flexner.
4. Ernest (Lord) Simon.
5. 'A Redbrick Tea-Party', by 'Bruce Truscot', *Universities Review*.
6. 'Introducing Universities Quarterly', 1946.
7. Sir Walter Moberly speaking on the television programme 'Viewpoint' about changes in the Church in his lifetime.
8. A.D. (Lord) Lindsay, c. 1950.
9. Eric (Lord) Ashby, 1979, Salt Lake City.
10. 'Lone Voices: Views of the "Fifties"', by Kingsley Amis, *Encounter*, July 1960.
11. Lionel (Lord) Robbins.
12. 'Spring too far behind for Lord Robbins', the *Guardian*, 12 December 1963.
13. 'The Council for National Academic Awards', *Reports on Education*, June 1966.
14. 'University Development in the 1970s', by The Committee of Vice-Chancellors and Principals of the Universities of the United Kingdom, April 1970.
15. 'The Development of Higher Education into the 1990s', by the Secretary of State for Education and Science and the Secretaries of State for Scotland, Wales and Northern Ireland, p. 4.
16. Ron (Lord) Dearing.

ACKNOWLEDGEMENTS

I am indebted to the archivists and staff of the following institutions for invaluable assistance: the University of London Institute of Education (for the Moot papers); the University of Birmingham (for the Student Christian Movement); the University of Liverpool (for the E. Allison Peers/'Bruce Truscot' and Sir James Mountford papers); the Royal Society (for Sir Eric [Lord]Ashby); the Special Collections Library, Queen's University of Belfast (for Sir Eric Ashby); the John Rylands University Library, University of Manchester (for Sir Walter Moberly); the Modern Records Centre, University of Warwick (for the Committee of Vice-Chancellors and Principals); the University of Keele (for the A.D. [Lord] Lindsay papers); Manchester Archives and Local Studies (for Ernest [Lord] Simon).

I would also like to acknowledge the following: Professor Michael Ashby, for help concerning sources for Eric Ashby; Professor Leslie Clarkson, for help with sources regarding Eric Ashby at Queen's University, Belfast; Sir John Moberly, for help regarding Sir Walter Moberly; Professor Ann Mackenzie, for encouragement in pursuit of 'Bruce Truscot'; Stephen Court for help regarding E. Allison Peers's membership of the Association of University Teachers.

Crucial help was provided from other sources: The Nuffield Foundation, from whom a Social Sciences Small Grant made possible many of the visits essential for this research. The Rockefeller Foundation and its Bellagio Study Center, Italy, which provided, after ten years, a much appreciated second period of residence and the ideal working conditions in which some of the chapters were drafted. The University of Plymouth, its Faculty of Arts and Education and particularly Professor Andrew Hannan, for support that a visiting professor may not always receive, but which in this case has been forthcoming and warmly welcomed. Professor Peter Gordon, for important encouragement and help.

Pam, as always.

Versions of the chapters on Bruce Truscot and Eric Ashby have appeared in *History of Education*, vols 28 (1999) and 32 (2002) respectively.

Oxford, 2003

ABBREVIATIONS

ATTI	Association of Teachers in Technical Institutions
AUBC	Association of Universities of the British Commonwealth
AUT	Association of University Teachers
C&IT	Communications and Information Technology
CAT	College of Advanced Technology
CDP	Committee of Directors of Polytechnics
CNAA	Council for National Academic Awards
CVCP	Committee of Vice-Chancellors and Principals
DES	Department of Education and Science
DfEE	Department for Education and Employment
DSIR	Department of Scientific and Industrial Research
EHE	Enterprise in Higher Education
FDTL	Fund for the Development of Teaching and Learning
HEF	Higher Education Foundation
HEFCE	Higher Education Funding Council for England
IIIC	International Institute of Intellectual Co-operation
ILT	Institute for Learning and Teaching
NACEIC	National Advisory Council on Education for Industry and Commerce
NCIHE	National Committee of Inquiry into Higher Education
NCTA	National Council for Technological Awards
NUS	National Union of Students
OU	The Open University
PCFC	Polytechnics and Colleges Funding Council
PGCE	Postgraduate Certificate of Education
RAE	Research Assessment Exercise
SCM	Student Christian Movement
SISTER	Special Institution for Scientific and Technological Education and Research
TES	Times Educational Supplement
THES	Times Higher Education Supplement

TLTP   Teaching and Learning Technology Programme
TQA   Teaching Quality Assessment
UFC   Universities Funding Council
UGC   University Grants Committee

Archive references

(N.B. It has not always been possible to identify date of publication, page number or other detail of press cuttings in some collections, for example the E. Allison Peers papers.)

FCMA   University of London Institute of Education, Moot papers deposited by Sir Fred Clarke (the code is that used by W. Taylor in 'Education and the Moot', in R. Aldrich (ed.) *In History and in Education* (London: Woburn Press, 1996), p. 183.
JM   Sir James Mountford papers, University of Liverpool archives.
LP   Lord Lindsay Papers, University of Keele Library.
MRO   Modern Records Office, University of Warwick, records of the Committee of Vice-Chancellors and Principals.
PP   E. Allison Peers Papers, University of Liverpool archives.
QUB   Queen's University, Belfast, Special Collections, and papers collected from uncatalogued archives by Professor L. Clarkson.
SCM   Student Christian Movement archives, University of Birmingham Westhill campus.
SP   Lord Simon Papers, Manchester Archives and Local Studies Library.
UMJRL   University of Manchester John Rylands Library: archives. V: Vice-Chancellor's files. C: C Series.

FOREWORD

This book should be read by anyone who cares about English universities and their future. Why? Because it reminds us of important truths about our past.

Too many current commentators on and self-styled advocates for UK higher education give the impression that they are engaged on two fronts simultaneously. In one direction they are locked in a battle for resources with their political masters. Meanwhile, more philosophically, they debate with the ghost of Cardinal Newman as if nothing had been said since. As Harold Silver's masterly study demonstrates, the funding battle is hardly new, and the philosophical argument is a much longer and more nuanced story.

In this story there are several consistent themes. These include tensions between 'liberal' and 'vocational' priorities for the curriculum, between teaching and research, between regional and national needs, and between state direction and institutional autonomy. There are also perennial concerns about the definition of a university 'community' (for example, the extent to which it has to be residential), the role of higher education in inculcating 'citizenship', and the ability of its representative bodies (notably the CVCP) to get their act together. Another ongoing trap is that of comparing all aspects of provision to those enjoyed by (and at) Oxford and Cambridge. Compared to the history of our late-medieval foundations, the creation of a twentieth century system was extraordinarily rapid and uneven, with major spurts of growth and of institutional transformation. Towards the very end of the century, Lord (then Sir Ron) Dearing very sensibly refused to allow discussion of Oxbridge when his National Committee of Inquiry tackled any of the pressing generic issues facing UK Higher Education.

Equally, there are some important things which have changed. Much of the value-system, and certainly the language, of Silver's key group was that of evangelical Christianity, now a minority presence on British campuses. As it has grown, the system has also declined in esteem (unlike the experience in the United States). Such declension can be measured both by the cultural salience of Vice-cancellerian spokesmen (yes, invariably men) and the general popular view of universities. Meanwhile, in the wake of Eric Ashby's 'climacteric' (the point after the Second World War when the state took a majority stake in the enterprise), the planning and accountability cycles have become progressively tighter and the 'felt' investment meaner. On the more positive side Silver is right to celebrate the recent emergence of an authentic 'practitioner' voice.

Bridging the gap between Newman and today is thus a valuable and revealing exercise. I offer just three examples. Walter Moberly's 'chaotic' university significantly anticipates Ron Barnett's musings about 'supercomplexity'. Similarly, there is a startling modernity to many of Eric Ashby's tips on how to manage change in a framework of consensual governance. About all, Silver has disinterred the wonderful 'inside-out' critique of Bruce Truscot. Truscot was the pseudonym of E. Allison Peers, who despite an intensive academic manhunt (and unlike the author of *Primary Colors*) was able to take his secret to the grave. Then there are the cases of genuinely mould-breaking innovation, like A.D. Lindsay's 'foundation year' at Keele (the victim of a subsequent round of central cost-cutting) and Jennie Lee's Open University (now re-inventing itself for a much younger and instrumentally-inclined student clientele).

Critically, Silver's achievement is to reaffirm the importance of thinking about thinking about higher education. The contemporary social–scientific term for this exercise is 'sense-making'. He is correct that we have no contemporary figures to put up against Ashby, 'the last of the twentieth century's major advocates', with his understanding of and response to audiences both inside and outside the academy. Anyone wishing to fill this gap – to contribute a new 'practical vision' or 'equilibrium' – would do very well to start with this cautionary tale.

David Watson
Brighton
February 2003

Professor Sir David Watson is Vice-Chancellor of the
University of Brighton.

PART I

SYSTEM MAKING

1

PRELUDES

Perhaps every decade, even every year, of the twentieth century was in some important sense one of transformation for higher education, and a succession of writers described it in this or similar vocabularies of crisis, change or transition. The present study approaches some of these higher education trans-formations and their interpreters in England, with a time scale that begins with the opening of the twentieth century. This is not simply convenient arithmetic, since the new century demonstrated vital new developments, opportunities, directions and meanings. The particular phases and characteristics of these developments will be considered in the chapters below, but here it may help to set out briefly some of the unfolding changes in attitudes towards and ideas about the patterns of higher education that emerged.

The nineteenth century in England had seen the creation of a university in Durham, in the mould of Oxford and Cambridge, and one in London in the mould of Scottish and continental universities. 'University colleges' had emerged in the penumbra of the University of London, their students taking its degrees. One of them, Mason College, Birmingham, was to become the twentieth century's first new university, in 1900, and others (some science or medical colleges, some growing out of the University Extension Movement from 1892) were to become universities at different points in the twentieth century – in Southampton or Exeter, Reading or Hull. Owens College Manchester, however, was the focus of the creation of the third nineteenth-century university, after London and Durham – the federal Victoria University of Manchester, which incorporated colleges in Liverpool and Leeds. Created in 1888, Victoria University was in 1903 to be dissolved and become three separate universities (in the same year as the nineteenth-century Welsh colleges were grouped within the University of Wales). The ground for development was therefore laid in the nineteenth century, but the first decade of the new century marked the beginning of a new momentum of development.

The grounds of debate laid out in the nineteenth century were to change rapidly with the designation of the new provincial universities around the end of the century. Early in the nineteenth century lines were drawn not only between the 'modern' University of London and the ancient universities of Oxford and Cambridge, but also between the secular University College and the Christian King's College that were united as the University of London in 1836. The pamphleteering and journal disputations gave way later in the century to more fundamental, alternative conceptions not of institutional rivalries but of what constituted a university and a university education. Prominent on one 'side' were Cardinal Newman, John Stuart Mill and Matthew Arnold, and on the other the most prominent was Thomas Huxley. The core of the debate included the nature of a liberal education, knowledge as useful or as an end in itself, and therefore the place of science and practical subjects in university curricula. Newman's view in 1852 was encapsulated in such statements as:

> I am asked what is the end of University Education, and of the Liberal or Philosophical Knowledge which I conceive it to impart ... the end cannot be divided from that knowledge itself ... there is a knowledge worth possessing for what it is, and not merely for what it does ...Liberal Education, viewed in itself, is simply the cultivation of the intellect as such, and its object is nothing more or less than intellectual excellence ... If then I am arguing, and shall argue, against Professional or Scientific knowledge as the sufficient end of a University Education ...

A university did, however, teach law or medicine, geology or political economy, but in a context from which those who taught them gained 'a special illumination and largeness of mind'. A 'cultivated intellect' was useful in the sense that it was 'a good in itself' and brought with it 'a power and a grace to every work and occupation'. At the heart of his view of the university was the conception of knowledge as an end in itself and the profound difference between subjects as taught in the university and elsewhere.¹ Fifteen years later, when Mill gave his famous inaugural address as Rector of the University of St Andrews (immediately widely available in a 'People's Edition'), he asserted in terms that became central to the controversy:

> [a university] is not a place of professional education. Universities are not intended to teach the knowledge required to fit men for some special mode of gaining their livelihood. Their object is not to make skilful lawyers, or physicians, or engineers, but capable and cultivated human beings ... What professional men should carry away with them from an University, is not professional knowledge, but that which

should direct the use of their professional knowledge, and bring the light of general culture to illuminate the technicalities of a special pursuit.

It was wrong, in Mill's view, for a university to teach modern languages for example, when the only languages and literature it should teach were those of Greece and Rome.[2]

T.H. Huxley, in the 1860s and 1870s, rejected the kind of argument propounded by Mill, and after him by Matthew Arnold. Huxley acknowledged the advances made, including at Oxford and Cambridge, in incorporating science, but there remained major obstacles and academic resistance to overcome. In the 1860s the ancient universities still did not have modern studies as did the German universities, which strove 'to represent and embody the totality of human knowledge, and to find room for all forms of intellectual activity'. He vigorously criticized the view that 'culture' was obtainable only by a liberal education defined as 'synonymous, not merely with education and instruction in literature, but in one particular form of literature, namely, that of Greek and Roman antiquity'. Both an exclusive literary and an exclusive scientific training would be 'lop-sided', and Huxley set out the forms of knowledge that an ideal university would offer, ranging from logic and psychology through moral and religious philosophy and the natural and social sciences.[3] Although 'sides' were not taken in the same way in the twentieth century, the ideas at stake continued to be reflected in much of the writing about and advocacy of higher education in immensely changing circumstances.

The nineteenth century had laid the basis not only for institutional but also other developments that took place early in the new century. The first government grants to the universities were made in 1889, a national advisory committee 'on grants to university colleges' was created in 1906 and eventually led to the establishment of the University Grants Committee in 1919. A Royal Commission on the University of London was appointed in 1909. Oxford and Cambridge had had measures of reform in the nineteenth century, and though there was much debate about them in the early twentieth century it was not until 1919 that a further Royal Commission on Oxford and Cambridge was appointed. Nevertheless, as an article on 'The needs of Oxford' in *Blackwood's Magazine* made clear in 1903, 'after two decades of comparative neglect by the public, recent events have combined to rivet attention on the University of Oxford'.[4] An article on 'Oxford in the new century' in 1906 (by 'a junior member of the classical staff') portrayed a daily widening breach between Oxford and its critics.[5] (Berdahl points out 'in what a very limited sense the term "university system" was appropriate in the 1920s'.)[6]

From 1903, therefore, developments that could ultimately lead to a 'system' were taking shape. What would eventually become the university 'system' at this time simply meant the intermittent proliferation of universities and colleges that struggled to become universities. In these and later decades the mounting issues were those of funding, political and public recognition of the university's purposes – purposes being defined beyond those shaped in earlier centuries. The universities and university education, and then a broader pattern of higher education, became the target of increasingly complex and controversial interpretation, ensured by the changing contexts of industry and the professions, technology and the state and the impacts of war. By the Second World War, in fact, all of these had continued to help shape debate and decisions, and the 'system' was itself responding with greater explicitness to the momentum of change. Oxford and Cambridge were not immune from the processes of change, but they were less touched by major underlying structural and systemic pressures – theirs were mostly slow changes, given the commitment to retaining the collegiate and other basic features of both universities.

The University Grants Committee (UGC), which had itself been part of the transformations produced by the First World War, was in the late 1930s more pointedly interpreting its buffer role between government funding and the universities. It defined itself as protecting the latter against the spectre that greater state financial support had raised of possible state control, interference or failure to understand and accept the particular nature and mission of the university. By the outbreak of the Second World War the Committee of Vice-Chancellors and Principals, which acted informally as proxy for the universities, had positioned itself for increased and more vocal roles. The Association of University Teachers (AUT) and its journal, The *Universities Review*, the National Union of Students (NUS), individual vice-chancellors and academics, as well as foreign onlookers, were more and more seriously welcoming growth and change, or seeing them as inevitable and weighing their effects. They also, therefore, sounded alarms about the resource and other implications of growth, confusion over aims, and the uncertainties of transformations past, present and argued about or anticipated. The anxieties and the debates also featured more and more strongly in the internal debates of the institutions.

The Second World War and its aftermath produced sharpened attention to national policy and system, as the universities (including new and smaller ones) saw their futures as increasingly dependent on the fast-flowing currents of change in the pattern and dimensions of public education generally. The numbers of university students increased, small though the percentage of the English age group was in contrast to those now regularly cited for some other countries, notably the United States. Student numbers were an element in what was debated at many levels as the real or expected democratic, technocratic, economic, scientific or demographic changes in society. Student welfare, health, success and failure were on the agenda. Into the 1950s the universities felt the pressure of national demands for specific kinds of trained personnel, and from the 1950s they were aware also of alternative higher education routes being sought for the preparation of experts and professionals – particularly but not only in technology.

Outside the universities the transformations were being shaped after the Second World War most prominently by government, industry and commerce, and within education not only by the universities but also by the visible potential of technical and further education. Change and its directions were being recorded in the 1950s in government white papers and other policy documents, but also in the creation of the National Council for Technological Awards (NCTA) and its new 'degree equivalent' award of the Diploma in Technology at selected technical colleges. Higher education was the focus of more resonant speeches of prominent vice-chancellors and others, a variety of pronouncements, analyses and debates in professional and academic journals, including the new *Universities Quarterly* from 1946, other academic publications and publicity machineries, and the national and local press. From the end of the 1950s, pressures for and the emergence of new 'green fields' or 'plate glass' universities, as well as persuasive demands for a commission to review the widening and more complex system amid signals of dissent and alarm about the wisdom of expansion, led to the appointment of the Robbins committee. Its terms of reference and its report on *Higher Education* in 1963 crystallized the new vocabulary. 'Higher education' was inclusive of the new, predominantly technological institutions, the colleges of education and other aspirants to a status once reserved only for the universities. The NCTA was replaced by the Council for National Academic Awards (CNAA), 'higher education' became a bifurcated, 'binary' system with the universities on the one hand, and on the other hand the CNAA conferring the degree and other awards to students in the new pattern of polytechnics and colleges of higher education.

Since government funding now formed a large majority of university finances, national economic crisis also meant higher education crisis. International economic competition meant pressure on higher education to contribute to economic growth. Political attention to 'the age of majority' in the 1960s fed back into the universities questions about their traditional roles 'in loco parentis'. The patron state was increasingly in evidence and transformations in the 1960s and subsequent decades derived more and more from national policy, including funding that was conditional, given, withheld, promised or uncertain, or targeted on desired developments or expectations of efficiency and 'productivity'. The UGC as buffer was replaced by bodies that operated much more as quasi-government direction or surveillance organizations. Ever-growing increases in student numbers were regulated or induced by financial controls. The core changes in the universities and the remainder of higher education in the last three decades of the century concerned the relationships between the institutions and the operation and expectations of the world that had once been their context, but had now become part of their daily lives. The graduate labour market, employers' expectations, student employability and skills came towards, and often into, the centre of curriculum planning – for the first time in many universities. They had to respond to nationally managed schemes and criteria for quality assurance and assessment and the application of performance indicators and productivity concerns to their research and other activities. Adjusting to new situations, including above all those of expanded student numbers and the decline in the 'unit of resource', institutions adopted modular structures, were compelled to look for non-governmental sources of finance, and restructured, 'slimmed down' and centralized their administration and decision-making procedures. Every aspect of university life – teaching and learning, research, libraries, services, administration – had to respond to the priorities of the computer and other new technologies, using resources often dependent on national availability and at the same time deeply affecting the balance of resource allocation within institutions.

In the last decade of the century the binary groupings of institutions were combined into a single constituency of universities, although a single system was far from meaning the removal of major differences of status and operation. By the end of the twentieth century the well-established public grants had been replaced by loans and student poverty was a significant issue. Institutions, including the 'elite' universities, felt their finances, amenities and futures looking increasingly threadbare. The century ended with concerns and battles over the future of funding for institutions and their students, but these concerns influenced and to a large extent suppressed any vigorous and sustained debates about the identities and aims of higher education amidst changes of such magnitude.

ADVOCATES AND OPINION

Writers who have acted as advocates for higher education provide important insights into the nature and purposes of expansion and change in higher education and they form a crucial part of the framework of this study. They represent a significant thread in the story of higher education in England in the twentieth century, a story in many respects unlike that of any other country. Other parts of the United Kingdom have traditions and features that have shaped debate over different issues. Although the focus here is change and continuity in the higher education specifically of England, there are points at which developments or ideas in other parts of the United Kingdom – such as the period of Sir Eric Ashby's vice-chancellorship of the Queen's University of Belfast in the 1950s – are important for the English story. As states internationally acquired a greater stake in the 'performance' of their higher education, it became more necessary to see English and UK higher education in relation to national policy and opinion elsewhere. Analyzing some notable contributions to the literature of higher education, particularly in the first three-quarters of the century, means addressing salient issues in higher education itself and their importance at different times. It also means determining the audiences that writers appeared to address and whose voice for higher education as it is or as it might be they attempted to represent. The writers were influenced by, as well as influencing, changes in higher education and in the outside worlds to which it related. It is rarely possible unequivocally to determine the direction and process, even the existence, of influence. In some cases the pursuit of happenings or trends means taking account of a scatter of contributors over a given time, in others it means detailed attention to a significant voice at a decisive moment or process of reappraisal and change. For example, 'Bruce Truscot', Walter Moberly and Eric Ashby are three very different voices of the 1940s and 1950s chosen for detailed discussion in relation to the themes with which they can be most associated. The selection of such advocates makes it possible at key stages to explore the derivation of ideas and proposals, the use made of them, the forums in which they were pursued, their translation into print, their reception and possible influence on action. Other major players, such as A.D. Lindsay, Ernest Simon and Tony Crosland, also addressed, with varied resonances and outcomes, paramount themes at different times. The target here, therefore, is the inter-connections of important aspects of the higher education story and the aims of those who sought to influence opinion and promote the creation, development and change of institutions and the system.

Such advocates are, or aim to be, opinion makers, promoting change, speaking from a range of positions of authority and power. 'Opinion makers' is, of course, shorthand for those who target the sources of power and change, from inside or outside. 'Opinion' is therefore here taken to be the views, attitudes and aspirations of the audiences these writers intended to address and influence. They were enthusiasts who, in addition to their writing, also had the power and influence to take part in commissions, exert or arrange pressure in high places, talk to meetings of professionals (the like-minded and the needing-to-be-persuaded), and acted as champions and publicists. They targeted opinion through pamphlets and books, research and articles, speeches that got into print or were reported, with important differences of emphasis

and target, across parts of the century. They reflected on things as they were
– and moved them on, were committed and persistent, took advantage of
opportunities. These were their intentions and this is how they operated. The
outstanding exception in this discussion is 'Bruce Truscot'. Writing in the
Second World War pseudonymously, but with great impact, from his profes-
sorship in a redbrick university, he shared the aims but – apart from his books
– none of the other characteristics of these advocates.

There is no way of tracing precisely how, and to what extent, advocates
affect or are affected by opinion, but it is helpful to know to whom they wish
to speak, their roles in formal processes, the creation of organizations, their
'popularity ratings' with appropriate bodies as indicated by presidential or
inaugural addresses, the direction of their philanthropy, the nature of the
authority they possess locally or nationally. 'Opinion' makes or prevents
change, and is beyond the reach of measurement. It is the will to command
change or to maintain a status quo, it works in the interest of an idea, a
policy, an ideology. It is newspaper headlines and leading articles, book
reviews and conference agendas, but it is intangibly wider than these. It is the
expression at important times, even moments, of constituencies striving to
have their own voice, or responding to that of others, part of the play of power.
In these instances advocates may have a variety of subtly different roles,
representing, clarifying and harnessing opinion. One of the key figures in this
study, Sir Walter Moberly, writing about Plato, refers to the 'knowledge' of
the expert and the precarious 'opinions' of the amateur, a distinction Plato saw
as fundamental. 'The characteristic of opinion', in Moberly's formulation, 'is
that it is inexact, incoherent and imperfectly grounded. Even if it happens to
be correct in given conditions, it is unreliable as soon as they change.' Plato's
own description of opinions is that they 'run away out of the human soul and
do not remain long, and are not of much value until they are fastened by the
tie of the cause'.[7] Higher education in the twentieth century, in England as
elsewhere, vividly illustrates how rapidly both opinion and those who seek to
reach out to it find that the onslaught of complex changes makes both the
target and the cause 'run away'.

Influence is not exerted and opinion formed exclusively by writers, or even
writers who also operate from other points of leverage in the patterns of power
and decision making. There are politicians and political activists, Church
people and scholars, demagogues and visionaries of many kinds, who propel
ideas and cause ripples, and leave behind memories and traces and reputa-
tions. The writers are a kind of continuing presence, not necessarily of more
importance but telling complex and inter-related tales. They offer important
opportunities for points of entry into the long narrative of higher education in
the twentieth century. Their writings speak of their own origins and their
intended outcomes, their own and higher education's relationships to wider

social worlds. In this study they speak amidst the early college and university foundations that had origins in local initiative and national political advocacy and campaigning. The story moves to the final decades of the century, however, when advocacy has to be defined amidst government mechanisms for operation and direction setting, when government itself assumed more directly the role of advocate. From the expansion of the early 1960s, and especially from the 1970s, ideas and opinion became less a matter of a 'literature' of higher education and its possible influence than the ways in which governments sought to define the future roles of higher education, and the ways in which higher education itself sought to find a direction and a voice amidst transformations, difficulties and uncertainties.

The advocacy, the means of communication, the operation of opinion, the purposes – all remained partly identifiable within a longer tradition of higher education, but they also became radically different. The higher education world of the 1980s and 1990s was as different from that of the mid-twentieth century as the 1900s were from the beginning of the nineteenth century. Although books and articles never ceased to be written or speeches to be made, the constant hazards of the fight for survival and adjustment to change in the late twentieth century inhibited serious and sustained debate. From the 1970s in particular the ways in which opinion was influenced and expressed were determined with increasing force by contexts that can be seen to have changed continually throughout the century, but which now to a dramatic extent altered the nature of debate and the lives of the institutions themselves. While advocacy of change in higher education had become most firmly held in the hands of government and its agencies, writers on higher education had become more concerned with explaining and understanding the sources and implications of often unwelcome and always difficult effects of change or of crisis. In a limited sense the vocabularies of the early decades of the twentieth century remained on the agenda – including growth, recruitment, funding and standards. It was their meanings, amidst the rapids of change, that were unreliable and 'ran away out of the human soul'.

NOTES AND REFERENCES

1. Newman, Cardinal J.H., *On the Scope and Nature of University Education* (London, 1943, orig. pub. 1852), pp. 93–4, 104–6, 113, 157–60.
2 Mill, J.S., *Inaugural Address Delivered to the University of St Andrews* (London: Longmans, Green, Reader & Dyer, 1867), pp. 4–5, 11–12.
3. Huxley, T.H., 'A liberal education and where to find it' (1868), 'Universities: actual and ideal' (1874), 'Science and culture' (1880), in *Science and Education: Essays* (London, 1899), pp. 103–7, 141–2, 153–4, 206–7, 212.
4. 'Academicus', 'The needs of Oxford', *Blackwood's Magazine*, March 1903, p. 419.

5. Zimmern, A.E., 'Oxford in the new century', *Independent Review*, October 1906, pp. 95–104.
6. Berdahl, R.O., *British Universities and the State* (Berkeley, CA: University of California Press, 1959), p. 40.
7. Moberly, W., *Plato's Conception of Education and its Meaning for To-Day* (London: Oxford University Press, 1944), p. 10.

2

EARLY DECADES: 'UNEQUAL AND INADEQUATE'

'The general attitude of the public towards the universities', wrote a contributor to the *Nineteenth Century* in 1901, 'is that they are more or less of luxuries, to diffuse a smattering of general culture and to give a tone to, or label with a degree, a favoured few of our countrymen'. American public opinion had 'awakened to the enormous importance of the development of universities', and the future of England depended on a similar awakening.[1] At the end of the nineteenth century England had its handful of universities, and a few more were about to appear. Luxuries for the favoured few were not just a perception. At the end of the 1920s the Principal of the University of Birmingham could write that 'the average citizen of to-day has very hazy ideas of what a university is and what it ought to be'.[2]

Growth there was in these initial decades of the century, but the literature on the universities addressed primarily the importance and potential of the small number of recent university and college foundations, plans and ideas for more, and proposals for the reform of Oxford and Cambridge. Luxuries and hazy ideas do not accurately describe the aims and practices of all the universities in this period, or the notions of all 'average citizens'. There were no echoing pronouncements of the kind associated with Newman, Mill or Huxley in the previous century. The voices of higher education in the first three decades of the twentieth century were carried through published speeches, articles, pamphlets – the ephemera of politics and advocacy. They spoke out of the processes of plotting and planning, local reports and national politics. There were also the brief and often self-congratulatory early accounts of the 'new' universities and biographies of their founding fathers, as well as addresses on how they were addressing 'the university problem'. Bristol, for example, engendered two such publications in 1906 and 1918; Liverpool one in 1903, three in 1907. Birmingham published a collection of lectures, including one on the history of the university and its parent institution, in 1911. Speeches by vice-chancellors and others had echoes in their local press, and articles and pamphlets celebrated anniversaries of, for example, medical or dental schools, faculties or libraries. The universities and university colleges themselves produced campaigning literature, in their search for national or local political or financial support or enhanced status or, in the case of colleges, university status. Reading, for example, became a university in 1926, and Leicester and Hull became university colleges in 1927.

More comprehensive accounts of the early years of these colleges and universities and their predecessor institutions began to appear particularly in the 1920s, for example at Leeds and Liverpool universities and Nottingham University College. The University of London was the subject of a variety of publications, as it had been in other periods since its foundation, and the early twentieth-century literature included accounts of commissions and legislation, buildings, founders and associated figures. A three-volume account of its reconstruction was published between 1905 and 1912 and an account of its origins also in 1912. Reports on its past, present and future opportunities appeared in 1922–23. In 1930, however, it was still possible to complain that there was no authoritative history of university education, although 'special histories of separate institutions, of course, exist in abundance'.[3]

All of this kind of literature could be described as the invention of tradition (in the case of Oxford and Cambridge its defence or critique). In the first three decades of the century a crucial location for commentaries on university education in general was the large number of serious, prestigious periodicals. Sidney Webb, pioneer and advocate of educational and social causes, published articles on the University of London in the *Cornhill Magazine* and the *Nineteenth Century and After* in 1903, both incorporated into a chapter on the University in his book *London Education* the following year.[4] Sir Richard Jebb, former professor of Greek and MP for Cambridge University, published an article on 'Some aspects of a modern university education' in *Macmillan's Magazine* (an address given at the University of North Wales, Bangor), also in 1903. In it he declared that 'we have entered a new period in the history of our higher education', evidence for which was the creation of the University of Wales, the University of Birmingham and the universities being created out of the federal Victoria University, and the project for a new University of Sheffield.[5] Barrister J.E.G. de Montmorency, who had published *State Intervention in English Education* in 1902, wrote an article on 'Local universities and national education' for the *Contemporary Review* in 1909. He was later to work part-time for *The Times* and direct its attention to education, resulting in the launch of the *Times Educational Supplement*.[6] R.B. (Lord) Haldane's many supporting and advocacy activities for the universities included among his pamphleteering and other writings an article on 'The civic university' in the *Hibbert Journal* in 1913. In this 'address delivered to the citizens of Bristol' he argued for the chance of a university education to be offered to the 'average' as well as to the 'exceptional'.[7] The first journal dedicated exclusively to university issues began as the *University Bulletin* published by the Association of University Teachers in 1922, and it became the *Universities Review* in 1928.

'THE MULTIPLICATION OF UNIVERSITIES'

This range of literature was concerned with the internal priorities and policies of the new institutions, as well as with wider issues of provision and the modernization of the universities. In 1903, alongside the journal literature, a book on education contained a chapter on 'higher education' by Halford Mackinder, Reader in Geography at the University of Oxford and Principal of the new University Extension College, Reading (forerunner of the University). In 1903 he became Director of the London School of Economics. His argument was basically for the modernization of existing institutions. Oxford and Cambridge had been 'compelled to an effort of defensive energy' by the invasion of the territory that was 'claimed but not effectively occupied in all parts by the older universities'. The Victoria University had been created as a federal university because of 'a certain timidity, a fear lest an increase in the number of degree-giving bodies should reduce the value of degrees'. 'Assimilation' of the older and newer universities was taking place to some extent: 'there is forming a group of national universities, all tending in certain essentials to one type. They will all be located in single seats', have examinations that followed teaching without controlling it, and conduct the research that was important for the efficiency of the teacher and 'the atmosphere of the place'. Like other protagonists, he saw the future of the universities as bound up with improved secondary education: 'the nation must learn to believe in education'.[8]

Given his cross-boundary experience, Mackinder foresaw the co-ordination of the institutions in what he called 'the outer, newer zone' of these national universities.[9] From the 1920s in particular the foundation and distribution of university institutions made it possible to see this development as a whole in more descriptive and analytical terms. H.G.G. Herklots, writing on *The New Universities* in 1928, explained the book's origins in a commission set up by the National Union of Students some 18 months before, to 'consider its positions in the universities of England'. The commission had found it necessary first to discuss 'the more fundamental problems of the universities themselves, and especially the more modern universities'. Although Herklots opposed the creation of more new universities, he saw the existing ones as a revolution that 'hardly anybody noticed'.[10] Abraham Flexner, an American enthusiast for clear university goals, comparing his country's universities in 1930 with those of England and Germany, thought the English provincial universities, like the American state universities, were 'an amazing achievement within a brief period'.

Writers were therefore now pondering the variety of institutions in existence, particularly the strengths and weaknesses of the new ones. In 1933 Edwin Deller, Principal of the University of London, talked of universities 'increasing in public esteem and respect', and subject to 'criticism, not generally unfriendly, from the outside'. In their defence, he pointed to 50 years of accomplishment: new chairs, new curricula and faculties, significant discoveries in their laboratories, and their role in raising the level of education in the country's schools.[11] Other commentators were less sanguine. By the mid-1930s, however, the phenomenon of the new and the critical scrutiny of the old had generated extensive debate about liberal education and its relationship to vocational and professional developments, as well as about the internal balances and operations of the universities, their responsibilities and responsiveness to external pressures. A clear example in the mid-1920s was the way University College, Southampton, felt it necessary to present its BA degree in terms reminiscent of the mid-nineteenth century but adapted to the twentieth:

> A Degree in Arts should ... primarily be valued for its own sake, and in an ideal system of education would, as it once did, precede the narrower vocational studies. But under the stress of modern conditions, few students are fortunate enough to be able to take a University course without some definite vocational aim ... the teaching profession ... the Ministry of one or other of the Churches ... a preliminary to reading for the Bar... But a sound training in 'humane' studies is an advantage not only for the so-called professions, but for every form of work in the State. Studies which develop both intellect and character cannot but increase efficiency in any vocation, and for the higher posts in business houses the tendency is rightly to demand not only men of special technical qualifications, but men of general knowledge, intelligence and character.[12]

Traditions were being continued and being adapted.

A vital focus for the writers on the universities was the emergence and distribution of new institutions in different parts of the country. They spoke of what was happening and what needed to happen further. Sidney Webb, in a forthright statement in 1903 described the nation as being engaged 'on no small scale, in the business of making universities. We are evidently going, during the next few years, to endow each part of England with its own local university ... It is not a demand for additional Oxfords or new Cambridges, but for something essentially different.'[13] At the same time, Jebb's account of modern university education focused on 'this growing multiplication of centres for training of the university type ... The great fact which determines the character of the whole movement is the extraordinary development of local interest and energy in this direction.'[14] Webb spoke as a reforming socialist, Jebb as a Conservative member of parliament. Local patriotism, given clearer shape from the 1880s by changes in local government, was one reason for 'the whole movement'. Increasing industrial and commercial awareness of the economic benefits of a local university presence was another. For the first quarter of the century the issue of the local and regional map of university provision was a prominent one. Filling out the map meant for all of these early-century writers the proliferation of new colleges and universities, and for some like Mackinder the aspiration for these institutions to become part of a national system – either of universities or of education as a whole. A 'national' system was also related to the roles that universities could play locally and regionally. De Montmorency wrote of 'the part which a modern University, created for the purpose of serving a restricted area, may play in the too-long delayed elaboration of a national system of education'. The phrase 'local university' did not mean 'provinciality of culture ... the University, when it appears, represents local feelings and local needs, and is a living thing, carrying in its heart the essential life of the area'. Like other writers he was aware that universities built on the expansion and local coherence of other parts of education, and he visualized the university as 'the *brain*, so to speak, of the local system which it crowns; the machinery that places in *thinking* connection with each other all the various parts of the system'.[15] Through the 1910s and 1920s this message of the importance of what had been achieved and what was still needed in other localities was carried in the journals, intended for an audience with some experience of or thoughtful interest in the universities.

Of critical importance in this 'whole movement' was the prolonged championship of new universities by Lord Haldane. He collaborated with Sidney and Beatrice Webb over the improvement of higher technological education in London, notably by fashioning the South Kensington science and technology institutions into a major new entity (the Haldane Committee was appointed in 1904 and proposed their amalgamation). He was active in promoting the grant of a charter for the University of Liverpool, and in 1912 became Chancellor of the University of Bristol. While holding senior government appointments he chaired a royal commission on university education in London from 1909 to 1913, bringing to fruition his work to obtain a teaching university for London. Haldane derived from his public

1. Lord Haldane with Albert Einstein. (Courtesy of the Bodleian Library,
University of Oxford.)

service a vision of the relationship between the universities and education
generally and the state, the development of which was the end to which the
state itself and its members had to strive, together with all the 'higher ends of
life'. The role of the universities was of especial importance, developing both
insight and 'the gift of organisation' essential to a modern society.[16] He later
qualified his view of the relationship by emphasizing that it was not for the
state to focus on the quality of the university or its atmosphere. In fact in 1920
he devoted an address to 'The nationalisation of the universities', dismissing
the meaning of nationalization in its ordinary sense, and using it to describe
a machinery to ensure that universities 'should be available for the nation in
a much larger degree than they are at present'. It was no good 'swamping'
the universities with students, but instead the university must 'go to the
democracy', by extending the experiments in extramural work conducted by
the Workers Educational Association and the university tutorial movement.
The state was now called upon 'to assume responsibility for providing the
chance of education, of higher education ... for the adult worker'. The
University of London should be more than 'a local institution in a great city'
and become 'the chief centre of learning in the entire Empire, perhaps ... for
the entire world'.[17]

In 1918 the *Journal of Education* commented that of all Haldane's many
interests none had 'so completely absorbed his intellectual energy as the
development of our University system ... He recognized ... that a University

is an intellectual focus of civic life.' The old Universities no longer had the monopoly of higher education, but provision nationwide was 'unequal and inadequate'. Claimants to combat this inadequacy now included Nottingham, Exeter and Southampton.[18] Three years later Haldane's presidential address to the inaugural meeting of the British Institute of Adult Education, reported in the *Journal*, defined education as not 'the monopoly of any class ... The well-to-do send their children to the university. It is very unfair that they alone should do so. It deprives the nation of a reservoir of untapped talent.'[19] This was a vocabulary that presaged key debates of the 1950s and 1960s. When he died in 1928 an obituary in the first issue of the *Universities Review* began: 'Bristol has lost its Chancellor, who had held office for sixteen years.' It spoke of his 'championship of the new universities in which he always had a profound belief'.[20] The national distribution of local universities was something that Haldane consistently saw as providing a chance of higher education for all, and he believed that the future of the system depended on a degree of specialization amongst the new universities. It was not always an easy battle to conduct, given opposition to the proliferation of universities and fears about a decline in standards.[21] However, he consistently argued the case for the improvement of and access to all levels of education – including adult education – and he was a mainstay of efforts to enable the new universities to become the pinnacle of the educational system.

Across these decades the emphases placed by Webb, Haldane and others on the establishment of local and regional universities continued to be widely expressed, although they diminished as the gradual extension of the map of new universities became more of an accepted fact. Herklots, in 1928, saw strengths as well as weaknesses in placing a university in a city, but of great importance was the 'more continuous and closer interaction of thought and life, of theory and practice than is possible in more secluded places'.[22] In this vein, as in Haldane's view of the university as 'an intellectual focus of civic life', the new universities and university colleges often promoted themselves in such language. Hull University College, for example, in a pamphlet entitled *Why a University at Hull*, described its anticipated future status in almost apocalyptic terms that echo an important theme in the movement for university expansion. A university could become a 'driving force':

> It is the centre of the intellectual and cultural life of the community which it serves. It is the channel through which new intellectual vigour is constantly sweeping to irrigate the city and its district. It is a guarantee against stagnation. Its importance as an inspiration to the younger generation cannot be over-estimated ... the College will ... irradiate the whole of the community with the rays of its influence. Hull can never again be what it was before that lamp was lit.[23]

THE UNIVERSITY BULLETIN

The Project of a University College at Hull

FOR several years Hull has talked of establishing a University College, but it was only in 1925, when the Right Honourable T. R. Ferens gave a sum of two hundred and fifty thousand pounds as the nucleus of an endowment fund that the idea began to take shape. The subsequent decision of the Hull Education Authority to make substantial capital and maintenance contributions took the matter a step further; and now the project is definitely under way.

An Organizing Board is in charge of affairs until such time as the University College is formally incorporated with the usual governing bodies, Court and Council, to which in due course Senate will be added as the staff is appointed. It is hoped that incorporation, for which application is now being made, may not be long delayed. The funds and lands now held in trust for the College will then be legally vested in the College itself.

In starting a new venture of this kind one is conscious of the critical gaze of the existing University institutions of the country, but all evidence goes to show that if the onlookers are critical they are extremely sympathetic. The University College of Hull takes for granted its right to existence, but it is not unmindful of the need to proceed with the utmost circumspection. On merely selfish grounds the new College must not undertake what it cannot reasonably hope to carry through, and it must also bear in mind from the very start and all the time that in appealing for admission to the academic comity of the country it assumes a grave responsibility.

The first principle which is guiding policy is the need of confining activities strictly within the limits of practicable performance. There are many things the College would like to do and many things Hull wants the College to do, but the proposal is to start with only two Faculties—Arts and Pure Science. The Faculty of Arts will comprise the usually recognized departments which necessity dictates, and will probably include a department of Commerce. It will doubtless be necessary to rest content with a certain variability of level. Some departments which in a fully developed University would be represented by professors may be in charge of lecturers. Circumstances, which will be mainly financial, must develop before details can be determined. The present intention

I

2. 'The Project of a University College at Hull', by the Principal, *University Bulletin* (University College, Hull), 1930.

In more temperate terms the following year the College described itself as 'becoming more and more a centre of culture and knowledge for the city and district, and those who have been responsible for its establishment are surprised by the rapidity with which its influence is spreading'.[24] Such 'irrigation' and 'spreading influence' as a 'centre of cultural life' was central to the social philosophy of the campaigners for these new institutions.

Supporters and advocates like Haldane and Webb, particularly in the early decades of the century, were often critical of the limited expansion taking place, and they looked forward to continued expansion for a cluster of reasons. The 1901 article on 'The pressing need for more universities' responded to 'the lack of trained brains' and the emigration of parts of the chemical industry to Germany: 'the race is no longer to the strong, but to the wise. Intellectual supremacy means now commercial supremacy.'[25] Webb, in 1903, was equally insistent that the continued provision of new universities was 'imperative' because other nations were 'rapidly increasing both the number and propor-tion of their citizens equipped with the highest scientific and professional advantages'.[26] The increase in the number of universities was described in 1909 as partly due to the failure of Oxford and Cambridge to widen their fields of studies, but even more to the general spread of education and the growing wealth of the country.[27] The increase was not viewed as a temporary phenomenon. The British Science Guild was told by its president in 1918, as many others had been told before, that in proportion to its population Scotland had more than three times as many university students as England, Germany nearly three times as many, and the United States more than twice as many.[28] Viscount Bryce, who had chaired the Royal Commission on Secondary Education which reported in 1895, and who had recently returned from a period as Ambassador to Washington, told the Conference of Educational Associa-tions in 1914 that the salient educational issues included 'the multiplication of universities'. These needed to provide, like American universities, such subjects as political economy, commercial geography and the elements of finance. Having too many universities, however, was dangerous for standards and it was 'better to have a few strong than many weak seats of learning'.[29] By the early 1930s the reasons offered for expansion had not fundamentally changed, but the climate was different. 'For good or ill', the AUT was told in 1932, 'the country is irrevocably committed to the policy of fostering provincial universities', though it was not without problems – for example, students in the provincial universities did not have sufficient diversity of peers: 'the root of the trouble with our local universities is that they are so intensely local'.[30] By the late 1930s, technical education, industrial depression and its social implications had moved high on the public agenda.

In this period of development, however its speed was interpreted, such commentators welcomed it as progress towards a national distribution of access to university education, and they promoted the idea of nationwide provision for reasons in which 'intellectual and commercial supremacy' played a major, but not the only part. Their messages related to particular institutions or the prefiguring of a 'system', serving their localities and regions. The writing and reporting frequently arose out of addresses to scientific, educational and other professional associations, of which the speakers were sometimes the president and in other cases visiting politicians or well-known public figures. In 1925 Sir Michael Sadler spoke at the first congress of the National Union of Students, with an emphasis that was to be of growing importance in decades of international tension, competition and conflict – not just the provision of higher education, but its relationship to external pressures and needs. He 'struck boldly at the intellectual lethargy of the universities in regard to external affairs ... not pulling their weight, intellectually and politically, in the movement for the adjustment of educa-tion to new national needs'.[31] the *Journal of Education* supplemented the prestigious political and cultural periodicals, providing a limited forum for a different audience, and from the late 1920s the *Universities Review* became a means of addressing the widening university audience.

'SYSTEM'

It was rare in these early decades of the century for any vision of a system of higher education to incorporate Oxford and Cambridge – they were present but off limits for discussion of integration or co-ordination. In the campaign-ing literature under discussion here they were at the margins except when their 'reform' was a target. Adapting their academic and social traditions was a slow process, and in neither size nor the composition of their student body were there major changes. The author of the 1903 article on 'The needs of Oxford' pointed to the possibility from the previous year of 'a grand trunk staircase from the basement to the upper platforms' of English education, as a result of the 1902 Education Act on secondary education. Oxford, however, was 'largely, if not exclusively, open to the sons of the aristocracy, the sons of the governing and upper middle class', and the author suggested that it needed to convince the nation that it wished 'to recruit undergraduates also from the students for whom the grand trunk staircase is mainly being built'.[32] In the following years demands for reform of Oxford's administration, curriculum and student recruitment were persistent, and in 1907 an article in the *Nineteenth Century* commented: 'to such opinion expression has lately been given in the columns of the daily press'.[33] Debate focused also on the relative poverty of Oxford and Cambridge universities as distinct from the wealth of their constituent colleges. In the 1920s some poorer students benefited from the existence of a system of state scholarships and county awards, and the two universities from receipt of public funds through the University Grants Committee. Although colleges for women were created in both universities in the late nineteenth century, neither of them admitted women students to degrees until the twentieth. The percentage of women in Oxford's slow growth actually fell in the 1920s. In both universities the issue of the admission of women as students and as entitled to graduate remained alive; in 1921 Cambridge rejected the right of women students to graduate (and this remained the position until 1947). To students from other than public or independent school backgrounds the two universities remained a strange land. A reviewer of Herklots's *The New Universities* in 1929 accused him of idealizing the older universities: 'the future lies with the modern universities already extant, and with those which the near future will see incorporated'.[34] In 1956 Arnold Kettle, a professor at the University of Leeds, recalled that as a Cambridge undergraduate in the 1930s he was not aware of 'the existence of the modern universities':

> ... because I lived in the south of England and had been to a public school they did not in any serious sense impinge on my consciousness. I remember hearing with some surprise in a lecture that there was a reputable School of History at Manchester ... I remember learning with astonishment that if you read English at Leeds you had to do Anglo-Saxon.

Such ignorance was not uncommon. As an undergraduate he had only some scraps of information suggesting that there were 'a number' of universities in Britain.[35]

By 1930 the elements of a system were in place, with increasing numbers of institutions, government funding to the universities and university colleges and scholarship support for a limited number of students. Nevertheless, commentators still found it difficult to see a 'system': in one 1930 typology Oxford and Cambridge were 'of respectable antiquity', London was a century old, and the other six in England (even Durham, created at roughly the same time as London) were 'modern'.[36] From his American background Flexner, in the same year, could not see how the disparate entities of the federal University of London could be said to be 'a university at all'. He described the provincial universities, as we have seen, as 'an amazing achievement', but they had not yet 'impaired the tremendous prestige' of the ancient universities.[37] In 1930 the vice-chancellors also took a step that was to make theirs a more resonant voice. Lord Eustace Percy, Conservative MP, who had recently ceased to be President of the Board of Education (the nearest England could devise at the time to a Ministry), wrote to *The Times* in January complaining that the universities could not give a lead on various aspects of neglect because 'they have no adequate machinery for joint consultation'.[38] Coincidentally, two days later a subcommittee of the Universities Bureau of the British Empire adopted a report that led to the establishment of the Committee of Vice-Chancellors and Principals (CVCP). The Bureau, superseding previous groupings, had been set up in 1912, and a Standing Subcommittee of Vice-Chancellors and Principals had followed in 1918. The 1930 report proposed replacing this with a new body, the CVCP, with a formal constitution, 'for the purpose of mutual consultation'.[39] Although the CVCP aimed to speak for the universities it remained what one of is future members described as 'no more than a club'.[40] Its creation was, however, a contribution to the further crystallization of the university system, and with the Second World War the CVCP was to be heard more strongly and clearly amongst the voices concerned with higher education.

The journal literature on the universities continued into the early 1930s, though with somewhat different concerns. The *Universities Review* addressed a range of British and international issues, including one article that discussed 'What is wrong with the modern universities?' and saw their main weakness lying in the rapid expansion and competition for students that had resulted in the absence of 'close personal relations between teacher and student'. The only solution it could see was 'a considerable reduction in the number of students ... the smaller the numbers in a university or a department, the better the chance of establishing effective contacts'.[41] Although this was an extreme (and possibly isolated) version of the argument, other writers bemoaned the modern universities' lack of resources, their difficulty in maintaining tutorial relationships and the congestion of the science curriculum in particular.[42] An article in the *Political Quarterly* in 1931 (based on an address to students) considered 'The purpose of a university', the definition of which involved 'pursuing in a liberal spirit the various sciences which are a preparation for the professions or higher occupations of life'. One of its most distinctive modern features was the inclusion of technology.[43] There was no further discussion of higher education in this *Quarterly* until 1944.

Letters to *The Times* about higher education were a regular feature, and a particular flurry occurred in 1929–30. One topic under discussion was education for careers in commerce, the demand for graduates and the best way of meeting it. The Vice-Chancellor of the University of Birmingham thought that after '20 years of slowly dissolving scepticism' he could see a complete change in the attitude of business, 'now pressing us to supply it with university-trained men and women'.[44] From the outset, the new universities had been engaged in preparation for an increasing number of professionalizing occupations, and business and industry were to become important in the changing relationship of universities with the employment market for their graduates. Part of the discussion in *The Times* focused on the issue of retention of 'honours schools', and as one correspondent explained:

> I have been responsible during the last 25 years for the employment of some hundreds of university men for service in a world-wide business. The experience leaves me with no doubt that it is from the university Honours Schools that we find the men best fitted for these tasks.[45]

The Principal of Hull University College argued strongly in this correspondence in favour of degrees in commerce, or diplomas for graduates who had specialized in other subjects.[46] Lord Percy disagreed since, as a strong supporter of technical and commercial colleges, he thought they were the best place in which to situate such courses, leaving the universities free to concentrate on post-graduate schools of business administration.[47] Diversification, vocationalism and standards were becoming focal points of higher education debate. All of these debates called into question the university ideal, which had surfaced regularly in the United States, particularly since Veblen's attack, in *The Higher Learning in America*, on the influence of business on the universities. A.N. Whitehead, British mathematician and philosopher, at the time a professor in the United States at Harvard, in 1929 opened his reflections on the international expansion of universities with a warning of the dangers that could result:

> this growth of universities, in number of institutions, in size, and in internal complexity of organization, discloses some danger of destroying the very sources of their usefulness, in the absence of a widespread understanding of the primary functions which universities should perform in the service of a nation ... The modern university system in the great democratic countries will only be successful if the ultimate authorities exercise singular restraint, so as to remember that universities cannot be dealt with according to the rules and policies which apply to the familiar business corporations.[48]

What exactly the functions of the universities and their response to the 'service of the nation' should be was already exercising British writers. The issues would become even more central to debate as social concerns, the threat of war and its advent intensified attention to them. The question of 'restraint' by 'ultimate authorities' was to surface more and more critically after the Second World War, as the role of government-as-paymaster became critical.

Three contributions to the literature of the early 1930s illustrate the range of serious analysis of the development of higher education. In his *Universities: American, English, German* in 1930, Flexner was in pursuit of universities

3. Abraham Flexner. (Courtesy of the Archives of the Institute for Advanced Study, Princeton.)

that met the needs of the modern age, while he saw reconstruction being hampered in all countries by 'history, traditions, vested interests'. He distinguished a university from both a research institute and a technical institute. In the University of London he found much that was inappropriate and an organization that obstructed change and improvement:

If it be the purpose of a modern university to promote the search for truth and the training of men competent to advance and interpret knowledge, would one regard the University of London as well designed for this purpose? Whatever else one may say as to its usefulness, this question I venture to answer in the negative.

Oxford and Cambridge, in spite of their distinguished past and present merits, had responsibilities 'not ... just now fully discharged'. They were 'largely advanced secondary schools; they still abound in prejudices and customs apparently calculated to interfere with their being institutions of learning'. The provincial universities were 'unpretentious', lacking in the resources that would enable them to recruit good staff, and focused (with important exceptions) mainly on undergraduate studies. His most important criticism, however, was of their curricula:

The provincial universities sprang from the soil; they obtain part of their support by heeding local needs. Thus technological activities, varying with the locality, are highly, in places, too highly developed, and, for a university, too highly specialized ... diplomas and certificates can be obtained for work that is largely technical in character.

In this latter connection he cited programmes in commercial studies, photographic technology, brewing, dyeing, glass technology and other subjects – including such 'excrescences' as librarianship, journalism, civic design and automobile engineering. Slight though these developments were by comparison with those he denounced in America, they were 'none the less deplorable'.[49]

Flexner's analysis of English higher education was a piece of pioneering scholarship. It combined a description of the basic features of the universities with critical insights and helped further to move public debate beyond the need not just to establish universities but also to construct (or reconstruct) them in ways that preserved their academic integrity and at the same time met modern needs. The position of technical and technological, commercial and other applied studies, the focus of *The Times* correspondence, was of major concern to Flexner also. Whatever reservations reviewers might have on particular aspects of his account, they welcomed it. The reviewer in *The Universities Review*, for example, found it a 'remarkably interesting book', and although 'we may not agree with every suggestion the author makes ... he combines breadth and sanity of outlook with the highest ideals of scholarship'.[50] A review in the *Journal of Adult Education* also called it 'a remarkable book' and applauded its 'courteous and well-informed' criticism, but rejected, among other things, Flexner's failure to understand the appropriateness of British university extra-mural studies.[51] If influence could be measured by citations, Flexner in and after the 1930s would qualify significantly!

In 1930 Lord Eustace Percy also contributed as writer (including the above letter to *The Times*). As President of the Board of Education Percy had pursued policies that highlighted the raising of the school leaving age and technical education. In an article in the *Journal of Education* in the same year he affirmed his strong belief in the importance of part-time higher education (by which he here meant all post-elementary education). He attacked 'the superstitious reverence for full-time schooling which we owe to a hereditary governing class ... the assumption that all education must take the form of a continuous school and university life'. We had therefore 'despised the idea of part-time education', and one of his solutions was that the last two years of schooling (from 15–16) could take place part-time in continuation schools.[52] Percy's 1930 *Education at the Crossroads*, however, was his main contribution, and though he had much to say about schools and indicated some of the weaknesses of the universities, most relevant here was his dedication to an enhanced future for the technical colleges, which he saw as an example of national waste. He believed that they could become institutions of paramount importance, and they and the universities could do more to teach students to think, currently prevented by over-specialization. The technical colleges, he underlined, were widely viewed with suspicion because they were municipal in character and did not have the same independence as the universities. Instead of creating new university colleges, therefore, independent, local technical colleges seemed to him the solution. In a chapter on 'Universities and local colleges as partners', Percy indicated that the converted technical colleges would set standards for the schools, serve the growing needs of industry and provide higher education opportunities for their students: this 'requires ... the co-operation of the universities'. Joint arrangements with the universities would be needed: it was not desirable for the colleges to 'resign all higher work to the universities or ... regard a university degree as the natural goal of the work of their more promising students', though the colleges should be closely associated with university technological and science departments.[53]

Percy's programme for technical and local education was not worked out in detail, and he left open the precise forms of collaboration with universities. What he was pointing to were the same national trends that underpinned letters to *The Times* and that caused Flexner to criticize vocational trends in the universities. In 1933 Edwin Deller, from inside the University of London, stressed that the primary duty of a university remained the promotion of learning and research, but that it was being besieged by other duties: 'it may reflect the concerns, loyalties and politics of the greater society of which it forms part. It may not only reflect them, it may sometimes anticipate them. Sometimes also it can stand aside and refuse to be a full participator'. Growth had been necessary; to some this was 'a cause of unmitigated delight', to others a source of 'misgivings and doubts'. There were dangers that could be avoided, such as teaching that was 'directed towards imparting skills rather than fundamental principles'. There were dangers of undue specialization, overloaded curricula and inappropriate demands on the university. He referred to Flexner's book as 'the most important and the most significant that has appeared for years'. Deller expressed disagreements with Flexner but 'no one can read his work without being under deep obligation to him; no writer has set up a higher standard of scholarly or scientific excellence'. He commended it for having indicated that there was no agency comparable to the university for examining the problems, facing the truth, training for the attitudes needed to confront and re-shape the world. Deller suggested, as we have seen, growing public esteem in which universities were held, as well as just criticisms of them, and he saw their freedom as central to their existing and changing roles.[54]

The central issues faced by writers from different backgrounds were becoming acute. They were united in recognizing them, though not in the potential solutions. Industry, technology and the universities' structures and programmes for responding to them; their relationships with other levels and types of education; the primary responsibilities of the university – these were significant and often controversial features of what the writers of the 1920s and early 1930s were beginning to treat as crucial to an emergent 'system'. The scholarly book, the teased-out programmes of politicians, the analysis by the educational journals – these signified both heightened debate within the system and a different range of audiences from those addressed in the periodicals and pamphlets of the first two decades of the century. Although echoes of Newman and others can be detected, the priorities for attention were changing markedly.

Other issues had gathered momentum by the 1930s, and indicated other audiences to be addressed. The issue of women's education surfaced in a number of ways. In 1927 Oxford Congregation decided to limit the number of women students in the University. Cambridge excluded women from full membership until after the Second World War, awarding them 'titles' instead of 'degrees'. What future, asked the *Journal of Education*, was there for the university education of women? The civic universities could not fully meet the need. Was a 'women's university' or more university colleges like Royal Holloway, London, the answer? Perhaps, it suggested, various types of university institution should cater for women students.[55] A writer in *The Universities Review* in 1933 strongly deplored the lowly position of the married woman on university staffs: although there were important exceptions, 'to all intents and purposes ... the profession is still closed to her'.[56] The conception of a 'system' had begun to bring such issues more clearly to centre stage.

Adult education had also achieved sustained prominence across these decades. In 1919 the well-known Final Report of an Adult Education Committee of the Ministry of Reconstruction, chaired by Arthur L. Smith, the Master of Balliol College, Oxford, pointed out that the provision of higher education for adult men and women had 'come to play an increasing part in the work of British universities'. Though the committee was aware that there were objectors who saw this movement as taking the university beyond its 'proper sphere of work', it felt that there was general support for it. The committee recommended the establishment of a 'department of extra-mural adult education' at each university.[57] This Adult Education Committee remained in existence and one of its publications was *Adult Education and the Local Authority* in 1933 – at which time its membership contained a dozen people who were either academics or people actively engaged in the adult education movement. Four of them had the title of professor and four that of doctor, plus others such as G.D.H. Cole and Barbara Wootton. In 1927, reviewing an American book on adult education, the *Journal of Education* considered adult education to be 'one of the major problems of our time in this country', something 'we well know'.[58] In his argument for local technical colleges Percy also believed that adult education could be brought into the sphere of the colleges. Adult education had been fostered by the universities over the previous 20 years, and 'the influence and prestige of the universities is as necessary as ever to the soundness and success of that movement'. Adult classes should also find a home in the local college, 'except, no doubt, in university cities where the university can itself provide a home for them; but the universities should continue to play a leading part in guiding their development.'[59] Deller thought the growth of extramural teaching to be 'one of the things of which English universities have cause to be proud'.[60] Reviews of Flexner took him to task for failing to see the importance and relevance of this university provision.

By the early 1930s the university landscape had changed to the point at which it could be perceived as at least a proto-system. The issues that writers treated as important addressed not only diversities in the landscape and the conditions specific to types of institution, but also the relationships between past and future university development and wide areas of economic and social concern. Two related aspects of these relationships were to be of paramount concern in the period ahead – the contribution universities could be expected to make to economic growth, and the values that they needed most strongly to espouse. Both of these were profoundly affected by international events, and attention to the internal working of universities was to an increasing extent in response to the tensions generated in the panoramic changes outside.

NOTES AND REFERENCES

1. Starling, E.H., 'The pressing need for more universities', *Nineteenth Century*, vol. 49, 1901, pp. 1032–7.
2. Robertson, C.G., *The British Universities* (London: Benn, 1930), p. 4.
3. Ibid., p. 3.
4. Webb, S., *London Education* (London: Longmans, Green, 1904).
5. Jebb, R.C., 'Some aspects of modern university education', *Macmillan's Magazine*, August 1903, pp. 268–9.
6. De Montmorency, J.E.G., 'Local universities and national education', *Contemporary Review*, vol. 95, 1909, pp. 609–18; Simon, J., 'Promoting educational reform on the home front: *The TES* and *The Times* 1940–1944, *History of Education*, vol. 18, p. 211.
7. Haldane, R.B., 'The civic university: an address delivered to the citizens of Bristol', *Hibbert Journal*, January 1913, pp. 233–54.
8. Mackinder, H.J., 'Higher education', in Wilkinson, S. (ed.) *The Nation's Need: Chapters on Education* (London: Constable, 1903), pp. 238, 243, 252, 258.
9. Ibid., p. 252.
10. Herklots, H.G.G., *The New Universities: An External Examination* (London: Benn, 1928), p. 3.
11. Deller, E., *Tendencies in University Education* (London: Oxford University Press, 1933), pp. 16–17.
12. University College, Southampton (no title, prospectus?). c. 1924, p. 14.
13. S. Webb, 'The making of a university', *Cornhill Magazine*, April 1903, p. 530.
14. Jebb, 'Some aspects of modern university education', p. 269.
15. De Montmorency, 'Local universities and national education', pp. 609–10, 616.
16. Haldane, R.B., *Universities and National Life: Three Addresses to Students* (London: Murray, 1910), pp. 67–8.
17. Haldane, R.B., *The Nationalisation of the Universities: An Address Delivered before the Old Students' Association of the Royal College of Science* (London: Lamley, 1921), pp. 3–13.
18. *Journal of Education*, article on Lord Haldane, September 1918, p. 527.
19. Haldane, R.B., Presidential address, British Institute of Adult Education, *Journal of Education*, September 1921, p. 555.
20. *Universities Review*, obituary of Lord Haldane, vol. 1, 1928, p. 43.
21. Ashby, E. and Anderson, M., *Portrait of Haldane at Work on Education* (London: Macmillan, 1974), ch. 4.
22. Herklots, *The New Universities*, p. 59.
23. Hull University College, *Why a University at Hull* (The College, 1929), p. 1.
24. Hull University College, *The University of Hull: What it is and What it Does* (The College, 1930), p. 1.
25. Starling, 'The pressing need for more universities', pp. 1028–9.
26. Webb, 'The making of a university', p. 531.
27. 'New universities', *Journal of Education*, August 1909, p. 530.
28. Sydenham, Lord, report of presidential address, British Science Guild, *Journal of Education*, July 1918, p. 395.
29. Bryce, Viscount, 'Salient educational issues', address to Conference of Education Association, *Journal of Education*, February 1914, p.140.

30. McLean, R.C., 'University uniformity', *Universities Review*, vol. 4, p. 114.
31. Sadler, M., Address, congress of National Union of Students, *Journal of Education*, vol. 57, 1925, p. 292.
32. 'Academicus', 'The needs of Oxford', *Blackwood's Magazine*, 1903, p. 433.
33. Marriott, J.A.R., 'Oxford and the nation', *Nineteenth Century*, 1907, p. 677.
34. Jones, F.C., review of Herklots, *The New Universities* in *Universities Review*, vol. 1, 1929, pp. 139–42.
35. A. Kettle, 'Leeds: impressions of a provincial university', *Twentieth Century*, no. 159, p. 153.
36. Hetherington, H.J.W., 'The history and significance of the modern universities', in Barker E.W. et al., *The Life of a Modern University* (London: Student Christian Movement Press, 1930), p. 9.
37. Flexner, *Universities: American, English, German*, pp. 231, 247–9.
38. Percy, E., 'What is a sound education?', letter to *The Times*, 9 January 1930.
39. MRO, CVCP [Taylor] 18 September.1984; MRO, CVCP, Special Sub-Committee, 11.January.1930.
40. Ashby, E., 'A voluntary club', *Times Higher Education Supplement*, October 1989, p. 17.
41. Dodds, E.R., 'What is wrong with the modern universities?', *Universities Review*, October 1931, pp. 14–15.
42. 'The problem of science in universities', *Universities Review*, April 1934, pp. 130–43.
43. Alexander, S., 'The purpose of a university', *Political Quarterly*, vol. 2, 1931, pp. 337–8.
44. Robertson, C.G., 'The average graduate', letter to *The Times*, 31 December 1929.
45. Cohen, R.W., 'The Honours Schools', letter to *The Times*, 6 January 1930.
46. Morgan, A.E., 'General degree courses', letter to *The Times*, 4 January 1930.
47. Percy, 'What is a sound education?'.
48. Whitehead, A.N., 'Universities and their function', first published in *Atlantic Monthly* in 1928, in his *The Aims of Education and other Essays* (London: Benn, 1950, orig. pub. 1930), pp. 136, 150.
49. Flexner, *Universities: American, English, German*, pp. 35, 255–7, 264–5.
50. Gough, J.W., review of Flexner, *Universities Review*, April 1931, pp. 134, 139.
51. Cavenagh, F.A., 'The idea of a modern university', review of Flexner, *Journal of Adult Education*, vol. 5, 1931, pp. 282–93.
52. Percy, E., 'A policy of higher education', *Journal of Education*, October 1930, pp. 743–4.
53. Percy, E., *Education at the Crossroads* (London: Evans, 1930), pp. 57–87, 91–104.
54. Deller, *Tendencies in University Education*, pp. 6–19.
55. Note on Oxford and Cambridge, *Journal of Education*, July 1927, pp. 493–4.
56. Neville, E.H., 'The misdemeanour of marriage', *Universities Review*, October 1933, pp. 5–8.
57. Ministry of Reconstruction Adult Education Committee, *Final Report* (London: HMSO, 1919), pp. 92–8.
58. Review note on adult education, *Journal of Education*, June 1927, p. 463.
59. Percy, *Education at the Crossroads*, p. 93.
60. Deller, *Tendencies in University Education*, p. 16.

3

1940s: 'A NEW CRISPNESS'

By the late 1930s any consideration of how to portray universities as they were and how to reassess their roles in the light of new conditions had to take account of acute dangers. An international student discussion of 'Education in the modern university', held a year before the outbreak of war, heard its rapporteur general, Dutch theologian Dr Visser 't Hooft, warn of two reefs – that of superficial discussion and that of unduly philosophical discussion.[1] There were other reefs of which everyone concerned with higher education was only too well aware – economic depression, Nazism and Fascism and the threat of war. The central issue was how universities could strike a balance between the traditional values of scholarship and resistance to the attack on humanitarian values represented by totalitarian regimes. Anyone writing about universities or education generally in the period leading up to war in 1939, and then when war had arrived, knew that Nazism and Fascism had presented an inescapable challenge to 'liberal education' everywhere. The advent of Soviet communism and the impact of economic depression on living conditions in the industrialized countries had already begun to undermine settled understandings of the roles of universities in modern conditions.

Writing of the literature on the English universities in the1940s Sir James Mountford described what he called 'a new crispness in the academic air'.[2] Writers had moved from such positions as Flexner's advocacy of appropriate curricula and Percy's advocacy of local technical education. Theirs became a 'crisp' concern with the momentous issues that now had to be confronted in times of war and in preparation for a post-war world that would need to be fundamentally different from the pre-war world of profound and agonizing social and political failures. Basic to the discussions from the late 1930s was an awareness that the university had become incapable of responding, it had become fragmented into specialisms to the point at which it no longer represented a whole or a general culture – an issue that dominated the international student discussion of 1938. A Swiss delegate there described the university as having 'lost all idea of creating and elaborating a comprehensive view of the world (except where tradition watches over the preservation of the empty form)',[3] and this was a view that underpinned a great deal of the analysis and discussion of the 1940s. Emergent issues of values related to how the university perceived its roles, how it interpreted the presentation and pursuit of knowledge and understanding, and how it defined its own strengths and weaknesses as an academic community situated in a changed and changing world. The vocabularies of culture (liberal, general or scientific) and the crisis of the world and social order and of faith increasingly sat alongside those of survival, planning and relationships with the state and with other beneficiaries of higher education, its research and its graduates.

WAR

The universities themselves were directly affected in many ways by preparations for war and by the war itself. Reflecting in 1948, the UGC described academic life in 1938–39 as 'gravely overshadowed by the impending threat of war', and the CVCP as beginning to undertake 'new and important responsibilities as a central body acting for the universities in their dealings with Government Departments'. Under government pressure the CVCP prepared plans for co-operation in the conditions of war, and these were put into effect when war came. The universities expanded their contacts with one another and with other organizations, 'widening the horizons both of teachers and students', and the UGC considered that such co-operation with other institutions would become permanent features of university life. The roles of the universities also markedly changed:

> The contributions which the universities were able to make in many fields of war-time activity won for them a new prestige and a place in the national esteem which it will be their ambition to retain in the period of reconstruction ... in a struggle in which brains counted no less than brawn, the universities did not fail to supply what those in authority expected of them.[4]

The new, sustained relationship of the universities with government and other bodies therefore put the CVCP and the universities generally on a different footing. Their graduates were in demand for science, technology and public administration. The expectations and requirements of both university and state determined new priorities, but also new methods of working. In a memorandum to the Chancellor of the Exchequer regarding the parliamentary grant for 1936–37, the CVCP asked him

> to recommend Parliament still further to increase the amount of its assistance to University education ... on their present resources they cannot hope to make the full contribution to national life and national welfare of which they believe themselves to be capable.

Student and staff numbers had increased by this time, more research was taking place, accommodation needed to be improved, and 'additional highly specialist teachers' were needed to cope with the growth of 'knowledge itself'. All of this was necessary if the universities were to contribute to medical science and practice and social problems.[5] Sir Walter Moberly, chairman of the UGC, chaired a joint meeting with the CVCP in 1944, and commented that 'certain of the universities already had arrangements for consultation between themselves', though further such development seemed necessary, and there were proposals from various quarters for the establishment of some form of 'universities council'[6] – something which never materialized. The war clearly, however, strengthened the CVCP as a voice for the universities in the developments that were establishing new levels of dialogue between them and the UGC and government. The CVCP was 'destined to parallel the U.G.C. in growth of influence and responsibility ... the scene was set for the dramatic transition to positive state leadership in higher education after 1945'.[7] Not everyone, of course, gave the direction in which this transition was pointing an unmitigated welcome. Throughout the century, filling out the system had been seen as necessarily involving public finance, and this now meant a high level of national government support or involvement. The implications were of mounting concern.

Precisely what this might mean and the possible dilemmas for the universities and their relationships had never been perceived as clearly as they were amid the stresses of the pre-war years and those of post-war planning and reconstruction. These concerns, international tensions and war had considerable repercussions on the literature of education in general and on public opinion. Reflecting in 1944 in *Education in Transition*, covering the period since the outbreak of war, H.C. Dent began with a clear, representative statement of the mood regarding education:

> It is broadly true to say that up to the outbreak of the present war the average English man or woman was not interested in education. Today the reverse is the case; there is throughout the country the keenest interest. It would be idle to pretend that this is yet universal; but it is undeniably widespread, it is found among all sorts and conditions of

people, and it grows daily in extent and intensity. With the growth of interest there is emerging a broader and deeper conception of the meaning, the purpose and the scope of education.

The relationship between education and the social order was being recognized, and 'consequently if we desire a new order of society one of the inescapable conditions is a new order in education'. Proposals and planning were taking shape, with the aim of relating 'the entire educational process to the social context in a manner and to a degree hitherto unknown in this country or any other'.[8] In 1943 Sir Richard Livingstone, in a book typically entitled *Education for a World Adrift*, opened his analysis of the same phenomenon, equally clearly but with a different emphasis:

> England has probably never been so interested in education as to-day. There are many reasons: the obvious and increasing importance of knowledge to life; a sense of the great possibilities of modern civilisation and of its disorders and dangers; the perception that our democracy is ill-educated; a realisation that in foreign politics between 1919 and 1939 we have thrown away a great victory with a rapidity and completeness perhaps unexampled in history and that this has been partly due to political ignorance; the need of extending education if equality of opportunity is to be more than a phrase. These considerations have interested all classes in education and forced it into the foreground.[9]

These analyses justly highlight the origins, nature and implications of the interest in education. A similar phenomenon occurred in the United States, described in an introduction to the Harvard *General Education in a Free Society* in 1945: 'The war has precipitated a veritable downpour of books and articles dealing with education.' There was, however, an important difference, since the American 'downpour' encompassed publications on the liberal arts colleges ('a subject of widespread discussion both within and without the academic walls'), universities and groups such as the Association of American Colleges.[10] Although discussion of university education in England took place at several levels it did not encompass higher education to the same extent. Publicly expressed aspirations and proposals were largely for urgent reform of the school system. The CVCP and the UGC, as we have seen, were engaged in what can best be described as strategic planning, and towards the end of the war national committees were addressing university-related issues such as scientific and technological manpower and teacher education. The most significant debate about the future of the universities, as we shall see, took place mainly behind closed doors.

THE SOCIOLOGICAL STANDPOINT

Amidst its news, reviews and articles on such topics as examinations and lectures, the *Universities Review* published an article entitled 'A citizen challenges the universities', based on a speech given by E.D. Simon at an AUT Council meeting in 1936. This was a discussion of the relation of the universities to the depressed areas, and asked: 'are universities fulfilling their function of educating citizens who will give a wise lead to their fellows in the great effort [needed to eliminate] weak spots in our public life, and to build a better social order?'[11] The notion of the universities' social responsibility had not previously surfaced with such directness in the writings of, say, Sidney Webb or Lord Haldane. They and others had seen the local need for universities, often expressed in economic and developmental terms. Simon's formulation, however, was important, coming at a time when a sociology of education – though not explicitly of higher education – was beginning to take significant shape. Also important was the fact that Ernest Simon, later Sir Ernest and then Lord Simon, was at that time Governing Director of the family-founded Simon Engineering Group, he had long been active on the Manchester City Council – notably in connection with housing – had been Lord Mayor, had been member of the Council of the University of Manchester from 1915, its Treasurer from 1932 and from 1941 would be its Chairman for 16 years. He was at the time a leading Liberal and, of some importance here, from 1935 Chairman of the Association for Education in Citizenship.[12] It was through this Association that after the war he created *Universities Quarterly*, a forum in which – as well as at the University of Manchester and in the House of Lords – he was to continue to relate prominently to higher education. While he was in this not unlike Webb or Haldane, he was unlike them in the industrial base from which he could also criticize and advocate.

It was *Education and Social Change* by Fred Clarke, Director of the University of London Institute of Education, published in 1940 that more than any other offered the public statement of a sociology that was to influence thinking about education in general in the following years. Clarke's book combined the sociology with a Christian concern for social and educational values, and with a strong sense of social and economic history, a combination that was to be important in a time of war and across the rest of the 1940s and after. Reflecting subsequently on the origins of the book, Clarke pointed to the heightened awareness of social realities in the 1930s. English theorizing about education in the twentieth century had become 'much too speculative, too much bound to the findings of purely individual biology and psychology. So it tended to take for granted the actualities of society when it did not ignore them completely.'[13] Clarke owed much to Karl Mannheim, who had left Germany in 1933 and in the same year became a lecturer in sociology at the

4. Ernest (Lord) Simon. (Courtesy of Local Studies Unit, Manchester Archives and Local Studies.)

London School of Economics. While still at the LSE he worked part-time at the Institute of Education in London from 1940, became Professor of Education at the Institute in 1946, and died a year later. Without naming Mannheim as the author, Clarke introduced *Education and Social Change* with the statement that

one of the profoundest and most acute of contemporary students of modern society has given expression to the view that 'no educational activity or research is adequate in the present stage of consciousness unless it is conceived in terms of a sociology of education'.

A quotation that others were to use.[14]

Mannheim's enormous range of interests included education as a pivotal social activity, and he was widely involved with a range of educational thinkers and innovators, including A.D. (Lord) Lindsay, Master of Balliol College, Oxford, who had corresponded with Mannheim about the latter's *Ideology and Utopia* (first published in England in 1936). Lindsay was influenced by Mannheim's sociology and consulted him on the plan to create the University College of North Staffordshire (the future Keele University).[15] Mannheim's *Diagnosis of Our Time*, a collection of wartime essays published in 1943, discussed two of his important themes – 'militant democracy', which he saw as a third way between laissez-faire and totalitarian systems, and 'social awareness', which included an approach to modern educational practice. Dent thought Mannheim's sociological analysis of the problems of education 'easily the most brilliant and profound essay on the place of youth in modern society'.[16] Sharing Mannheim's view that education had to be seen as fundamental to society, Clarke also saw a historically rooted sociology of education as crucial to framing post-war educational and social reconstruction:

> ... we propose to accept unreservedly what may be called the socio-logical standpoint ... we are to attempt an interpretation, conscious and deliberate, in terms of a social economic history, and then, in the light of that interpretation, to estimate the capacity of the English educational tradition to adapt itself without undue friction or shattering to the demands of a changed order.

He pointed to the need for new educational structures that would advance social justice and sought to explain and overcome the class distinctions that underlay English education. English writers, he complained, had shown little awareness of the social presuppositions of their ideas. He advocated increased state intervention in education and did not share the anxieties often associated with it, because such intervention had hitherto not led to uniformity in county provision of education.[17]

Clarke was led to believe that his book 'had some influence on the course of events'.[18] It is important for the discussion here that Clarke, conducting a broad analysis of changed conditions, was also aware of his audience: 'This book ... may therefore properly be addressed to the ordinary citizen rather than more exclusively to professionals. Its interest is centred in national policy rather than classroom technique.' None of the writers previously discussed here had been so explicit in defining such an audience. Many had delivered addresses to precise scientific or other gatherings, and Haldane had addressed 'the citizens of Bristol' – doubtless those associated with the University. Clarke, with a very different mission, was addressing a concerned public, one that looked back on the pre-war years as a condemned past, and one that was soon to make Sir William Beveridge's plans for post-war social security a bestseller. In approaching policy and the general public Clarke confronted two issues relevant here. First, he entered the debate about the position of science in a liberal education, and although he did so with direct reference to schools, his emphasis is revealing. He characterized the liberal–humanist tradition as vocational, as an appropriate *training* for *rulers* (both are his words). In the modern world a balance had to be struck with science, which he described in a memorable passage:

> not as a mysterious and highly complex cult, pursued by highly special-
> ized 'scientists'; not as a many-sided magician producing wonders for
> the populace and profits for the enterprising; nor yet as a technical
> necessity of modern life for which, however reluctantly, any self-
> respecting school must make some provision. It is rather *modern life
> itself* in one of its most fundamental aspects, and therefore an essential
> basis of a modern education for everybody. Not the whole basis by any
> means, but an essential part of the whole.

Responding in this way not only to social but also to modern curricular realities, Clarke was offering a comprehensive guide to educational develop-ment, one that was quite different from those of his nineteenth-century predecessors. He explained that the universities were omitted from his discussion as they needed separate treatment, and the only reference to universities was not directly to these issues, but to the relationship between them and the schools. He thought that change in the universities would be determined 'even more by developments in the general school system than by an independent play of social influences upon them' – not a view that some of his sociological contemporaries would have shared. He focused on the content, not on the provision, of university education. Unlike in earlier decades, and now under the impact of war, his silence would suggest that the expansion of provision was so accepted as not to need discussion. After the sociology he turned, at the end of the book, to religion. These, he concluded, were 'days of social experiment on a vast scale and under conditions of extreme pressure', but doctrines of social cohesion now 'being subjected to test' could not be taught by a scheme of social studies, however valuable. Social cohesion could only be the product of 'faith and love'. The terms, he explained, 'look empty enough until they receive their proper content … It can be given only by life and sound education and the grace of God.'[19]

At this point public and private communication met. Clarke was a member of two inter-connected groupings, the Christian Frontier Council and the Moot (which is discussed further in a later chapter). In both he was regularly involved in discussion with fellow Christians, and in the latter body particularly with sociologists and others who shared in a search for the translation of appropriate values into the processes of a democratic society.[20] Mannheim attended almost every meeting of the Moot.[21] Sir Walter Moberly, chairman of the UGC and a leading figure in the CFC also rarely missed a meeting. In both organizations Clarke and others contributed and discussed papers on a range of topics, including in education sub-groups. For example, in August 1939 Clarke presented a paper to a Moot education group, of which Mannheim, Moberly and Sir Richard Livingstone (classicist and educationist, former Vice-Chancellor of Queen's University, Belfast, and later in the war to become Vice-Chancellor of the University of Oxford) were also members. Clarke's paper addressed educational institutions in relation to '"planning for freedom" in the coming collectivized regime',[22] and gave a historical–sociological interpretation of a paper by Mannheim on 'Planning for freedom'. This was a key concept promoted by Mannheim and readily taken up by many of his associates in these discussions (Mannheim in return commented on Clarke's paper). The symbiosis was a crucial element in the elaboration of Clarke's ideas and the structure of the resulting book. This was all part of a continuing confrontation of the devastating impact of developments in Europe, and then war itself, on all aspects of society, including assumptions about university education as addressed by Moberly at the time and then in *The Crisis in the University* at the end of the decade.

UNIVERSITIES AND SOCIAL ORDER

In February 1940 the Moot discussed two papers on the universities, by Moberly and Adolf Löwe, of the University of Manchester. Moberly's paper was in many ways a precursor of *The Crisis in the University*, the major book he was to publish in 1949. Löwe's paper was published without alteration as a book, *The Universities in Transformation* in 1940, the same year as Clarke's *Education and Social Change*, to which Löwe expressed his debt – as he did also to Mannheim. Clarke's approach to the 'historical determinants of English education' undoubtedly pointed Löwe and Moberly in important directions for their discussion of the universities.

Löwe was a Jewish refugee from Germany, an economist, critical of the weakness of the response to Nazism by the Western democracies. *The*

Universities in Transformation did not have in mind a popular audience such as Clarke defined, and did not have the same impact, though the book was grounded in the same sociological approach. It began with a section on 'the sociological background' and announced its intention to take a sociological view. A system of education could only be approached 'against the background of the social order in which it operates ... education always serves a social purpose'. The university was therefore 'a social agency', and its success would be measured by its 'social achievements, that is to say, by the degree to which it solves its threefold task' of general or cultural education, vocational or technical education and an increased amount of education. Such a synthesis had been possible in the nineteenth century, given a wide sharing of values by the university – especially the ancient universities, the 'leading schools', family life and the dominant manners and ethics in the society from which the universities drew their staff and students. The university had fed on existing attitudes, but it was now suffering from a 'social lag' (a concept he quoted from Flexner): 'the universities have failed in many important respects to take cognisance of decisive changes in their social environment'. They had been affected by the increasing demand for 'professional specialists', a new stratification of the student body, and a consequent change in most students' educational background and outlook. The universities were 'no longer educating a leisured class but are primarily regarded as agencies for social ascent and as training schools for remunerative professions'.[23]

If the sociological approach had directed Löwe's critical analysis, it also, he emphasized, had to frame the search for solutions. These could be found only by

> defining our educational aims in terms appropriate to the new society in formation ... to discover the criteria for a modern university education we must, first of all, form a general idea of the social order we are heading for, and of the position which the 'educated man' is to hold in it.

In this can be glimpsed the debates of the Moot, most of whose members were committed Christians, and outstandingly Mannheim's approach to post-war society and planning. Mannheim's view of 'planning for freedom' or 'a planned democracy' – his 'third way' between laissez-faire democracy and the rigidities of a totalitarian state, was a guiding force in much of the debate in the Moot, and Löwe was indebted to it. He saw the need for new social integration in a period of radical social change, which would require 'collective guidance and rational planning', at least for a period of transition lasting more than a generation. For such a 'planned democracy' the administrators would be important, regardless of the social strata from which political leaders would be recruited. Administrators would need 'qualities very different from the professional routine mind', and would have to be educated in the universities. From this starting point Löwe looked at ways in which specialization and vocational study could be related to 'the cultural process as a whole' and he looked across broad aspects of the university curriculum and the parts that might be played in the new 'cultural education which is both to balance and to underpin vocational education'. There could be no forced, accepted values, and the university and the student alike would need to accept the fact of competing ideologies in their work. What he was seeking was a reorganization of the universities on the basis of 'cultural education', possibly through an introductory two-year course, but there was also the alternative of 'humanistic specialisation', in which the vocational subject 'forms the centre from which scientific advances are being made into the bordering fields of study', including the humanities, psychology and economics (a view that Eric Ashby was later to take and to elaborate). No social agency was in more need of putting its house in order than was higher education:

> Yet at this point we come up against the greatest obstacle to a speedy all-round change: the lack of a sufficient number of university teachers who would be able and willing to carry out the cultural reconstruction of university education ... the conditions for a successful career in the universities, have less and less encouraged the 'synthetic' minds. The vocational trend, the incessant rise of new scientific specialisms and the emphasis on research, have deterred especially the young scholar from taking a real interest in the wider cultural aspects of his subject.

To solve this problem of narrowness on the part of university teachers, Löwe suggested a post-graduate school, an 'experimental college', in which groups of 'synthetically minded' specialists would prepare for university teaching, and the courses would reflect the cultural studies that he posed as the basis of a reorganized university education. It would mean preparing a 'progressive minority', a 'university within the university'.[24]

This was not only an attempt to promote discussion of practical possibilities for the transformation of the university, it also reflected one of the threads that ran through discussion in the Moot – how a small group of enthusiasts might exercise an influence. This was also a vital element in discussions in the related Christian Frontier Council, in the Student Christian Movement (SCM) and in the conferences and other discussions that they sponsored. They recognized that one realistic way of exercising influence was through the impact of such a minority movement, one that would send ripples through important organizations and the wider society. Löwe was therefore not appealing, like Clarke, to a concerned citizenry. He was appealing to those academics who might take part in such a movement to regenerate the universities, and also those who were concerned about the detail of university purposes, organization and planning. He was in a sense translating Mannheim's sociology and the values of a group whose members, whether or not Christians, similarly saw the outlines of the contemporary dilemma, into a very different approach to the modern university from the approaches of earlier writers. The result was the promotion of a kind of education for leadership, based on cultural values and social science. The experience of German totalitarianism, the exigencies of war, the emergence of a concept of planned democracy, and debates about the future directions of education generally, had combined to produce a new kind of higher education message. It was a message that was obviously directed at Löwe's fellow university teachers. He thought them to be among the best in the world, but a beginning now had to be made to prepare a generation of teachers who could carry out the cultural task he defined.

We shall in a later chapter consider Moberly's paper and discussion in relation to his ideas and the publication of *Crisis in the University*. Löwe is reported as suggesting in the discussion that 'there was nothing intrinsically wrong with the universities, but there was a "social lag" which made them out of harmony with the needs of society. Hence no frontal attack was either required or possible. The 19th century synthesis of vocational and general education was a lodestar.'[25] Löwe's presentation of this paper at the Moot helped to situate the universities in debates, limited in scale but conducted actively and with great commitment, and contributing in various ways to the literature of higher education in the next few years. He was one of the people who redirected the agenda towards the values, purposes and internal working of higher education. When he emigrated to the United States shortly after the outbreak of war he ceased personally to have any involvement in the debate, but the book had some reverberation in the circles for which it was primarily intended, being used for example in SCM study sessions and widely referred to in ensuing literature and debate. His intended audience was not so much the universities themselves as those in influential positions within them who could help with forms of reconstruction that would embody principles enunciated more generally by Mannheim and Clarke.

One author whose published work predated by a year that of Clarke and Löwe was David Paton, acknowledging how much he owed to the latter and to Moberly, both of whose ideas he knew through the SCM. Paton had also read in manuscript Brian Simon's *A Student's View of the Universities*, a Marxist view that was not to be published until 1943. Paton had been a student at Birmingham in 1936–39, and he dedicated his small book, with gratitude, to the members of that university. His *Blind Guides?* was not specifically about Birmingham (though he did mention three happy years there) or any other university. His focus was entirely on the roles there of Christianity and Christians. His historical diagnosis and beliefs were aimed at seeing 'some way through the confusion'. Few students had 'compelling convictions', and since they lived mainly at home were not members of a university community. Universities gave no consideration to truth and 'its relation to learning and knowledge', and their gospel was that truth 'cannot be reached, save scientifically'. It was now for Christians in the university, not the university itself, to preach 'the Gospel of God'.[26] Paton's book was different from the other Christian publications on the university that were to follow, in focusing its discussion on the theology and the Christian responsibility, and not, as he indicated at the outset, the history and other aspects of the university as he had experienced it. It did, however, indicate the ripples that were emanating from some of those who were active in the Moot and the Christian Frontier Council, and who were to have a continuing impact on the SCM after the war.[27]

The Moot and the educationists and sociologists prominent within it had established an agenda that was illuminated in most cases by their Christian faith, and that they continued to pursue in their discussions and in other contexts. It was assumed by all that the Moot was to be treated as a private gathering, and public outcomes derived from or informed by the discussions were silent on its existence and influence. In 1940 Clarke and Löwe made no reference to it in their books, nor did Mannheim in 1943 or Moberly in 1949. By the time it ceased to meet, when Mannheim died in 1947, and for some years afterwards there are important ways in which it contributed to a new generation of ideas about education. Reflecting the times in which they met, the members of the Moot helped to crystallize debate not only about the issues of provision, structural reform and access but also about values underpinning education as the crucial factor in social regeneration.

VERSIONS OF CULTURE

The UGC reflected after the war that 'even before the end of the war, much public attention had begun to be focussed upon the part which the universities would need to play in the post-war structure of society'. In the later years of the war two arguments pointed towards university expansion. The first was the experience of war itself, which had demonstrated 'the essential value to the community of university trained men and women', the pre-war output having been 'disconcertingly low'. The second was a conviction that the wartime equality of sacrifice should be matched by 'a much greater measure of social and educational equality than had existed before the war'.[28]

Discussions in the Moot did not focus directly on the issue of expansion, and this was true also of discussions in places where their kinds of concerns were raised. 'Public attention', as postulated by the UGC, was of course wider than these writers and these organizations, encompassing the reconstruction ideas of parties and churches, governmental and non-governmental agencies, business and trade unions, and individuals who contributed 'attention' from a variety of directions, including from the universities themselves. Under wartime difficulties of depleted numbers of staff and students, the government and military use of university buildings, shortened courses, bombing and the unending problems of modern war, the universities did look ahead to post-war expansion. In 1943, for example, the CVCP asked the UGC to review the financial implications of the expansion which 'national policy would require the universities to undertake' in the immediate future and over the next ten or twenty years.[29]

If there was no doubt about post-war expansion, there was also the extensive discussion about the nature of the social order in which it would take place and the values that the universities would represent. Increasing pressures for an expansion of science and technology had begun to intensify concerns about the strong tradition of the universities as a focus of liberal culture, though there had also been voices suggesting that with wise leadership the new could in one way or another be accommodated to the old. Löwe and Moberly both emphasized the virtues of Oxford and Cambridge traditions, notably Oxford Greats and the importance of college residential experience, but they also defined these traditions as belonging to a former age and not transferable to the modern universities in the same forms. The position at Oxford and Cambridge and at the nineteenth- and twentieth-century foundations had raised serious questions before the war, and in Britain as well as in the United States a concerned literature aiming at the defence of liberal education had emerged. This culminated in the Harvard Committee report of 1945 on *General Education in a Free Society*, a report that was widely discussed in the United States, especially in the colleges and universities themselves. The report's recommendations for a balanced general undergraduate education, which included science (but not technology, which was part of postgraduate professional programmes), were ones to which British discussions referred for many years. In Britain it was not until the 1950s and movements towards a wider acceptance of technology in the universities' curricula that the relationship between technological studies and a liberal education became a focus of extensive debate.

Discussions of the relationship between the protean meanings of 'culture' and the universities also began a trajectory during the war that led to more intensive attention, and controversy, in the 1950s. Any such discussion inevitably had to address three difficult areas. First, issues of purpose and meaning in relation to universities did not seem amenable to generalization, given the diverse identities of institutions and categories of institutions that had already emerged. Second, disciplines were widely interpreted as having their own culture, with changing frontiers as the fragmentation of knowledge and interdisciplinary subject areas emerged, and as research increasingly became their identifying signal. Third, issues of culture encompassed the range of external interests to which the work of the universities related – including government and employers, political parties and other branches of education. In some cases writers crossed over different approaches, and all were impelled by some sense of the destinations that the university would need to try to reach in the post-war world. The first set of issues were those that many members of the Moot wished to address, relating the diffuse pattern of universities and their fragmentation to questions of faith and values. Contributors to discussion of the second set of issues came largely from within the academic disciplines, not always sensing that these were problems, given what they saw as the coherent modes of thought and communication within their subject boundaries. The third approach was one of a definition of universities past and future from the starting point of political and ideological interpretations of the place of the university in the social order. For approaches to the university and its culture and values 1943 was a fertile year. The UGC invited the CVCP to explore the implications for the universities of post-war expansion and Mannheim articulated, to the benefit of many who were indebted to him, his belief in a 'militant democracy' which involved planning for freedom. F.R. Leavis, lecturer in English literature at the University of Cambridge, published *Education and the University*, and Brian Simon, who had been President of the National Union of Students in 1939–40, published *A Student's View of the Universities*.

Leavis entered the arena with a case for an 'English School' (the book's subtitle was '*A sketch for an "English school"* ') that would justify, in a way that the subject had so far failed to justify, 'its recognized position as chief of the humanities and its key responsibility for education'. He addressed the question: 'What, then, might be done towards making a School of English a real humane focus in a university, pre-eminently representative of the Idea, and capable of discharging the function of the university in the matter of liberal education?' He was not concerned with issues of university provision or access, war and reconstruction, social change and the social order, or any of the prominent themes that had been central to the relationship between the writers we have previously discussed and the transformations taking place around them. Instead, he used the teaching of English at Cambridge as a model for his concern to interpret 'the effort of a cultural tradition at main-taining continuity ... to restore in relation to the modern world the idea of liberal education'. His chapter on 'The idea of a university' was a credo that assumed problems wider than English and the university, but he scarcely made them explicit. Liberal education was to be regenerated in the ancient university, because that was where the tradition should be seen to live:

> The universities are recognized symbols of cultural tradition – of cultural tradition still conceived as a directing force, representing a wisdom older than modern civilization and having an authority that should check and control the blind drive onward of material and mechanical development, with its human consequences. The ancient universities are more than symbols; they, at any rate, may fairly be called foci of such a force.

Although much had been compromised there, 'they are still in more than form representatives of humane tradition'. It would be possible, therefore, to attempt 'at an ancient university an experiment in liberal education'. Leavis was not concerned about who the students were or what kind of an institution it was that they entered.

Despite his advocacy of a future based on his view of a School of English, Leavis's argument about the university was conservative. His 'idea of a university' was one that did not accept the transformations that had taken place, or look into any future other than the refurbishment of a tradition. He judged that 'a not altogether inconsiderable, if very small, minority do contrive to get something of an education (in the relevant sense of the word) at Oxford and Cambridge, as things are', because these universities 'are so much more than educational institutions'. The kernel of his argument therefore rested on successfully humane educational outcomes for a small minority. The rest were victims of an age of specialization and technical complexity, which had produced 'social and cultural disintegration', and the task was to bring specialist knowledge and training 'into effective relation with informed general intelligence, humane culture, social conscience and political will'. Here was the function that was 'pre-eminently the university's; if the work is not done there it will not be done anywhere'. Educating liberally meant creating a university centre, in a school of the humanities, in order to produce 'the man of humane culture who is equipped to be intelligent and responsible about the problems of contemporary civilization'. Hence the School of English, and hence Cambridge as the model. Unlike Löwe and the members of the Moot, Leavis was concerned with principles targeted in part on the university, but primarily aimed at stiffening the academic resolve of a specific group of teachers.[30].

Leavis's 'idea of a university' did not make explicit any targets beyond the humanities, and specifically English, and their ripples in the two ancient universities and his vision of a liberal education did not aim at spreading ripples very far. English was to be firmly in the centre of the diagram of a particular kind of university. Brian Simon's 'student's view' was aimed at positioning the university as a leader in social reconstruction, and his approach to the cultural changes necessary to achieve this placed the university on a broad, radical, international canvas – as broad as Leavis's was narrow. Simon emphasized how 'extraordinarily little thinking and discussion of the problems of the universities' had taken place in the past 30 or 40 years, and the universities themselves had 'certainly not been to the fore in self-examination and self-criticism'. In the present crisis and the opportunities for the future, he argued, 'it is a vital national duty of every social institution to re-examine in the light of modern values and modern needs its contribution to social development'. Things would not be allowed to go on 'in the old way' and there must be no return to the position of 1914–18 or September 1939. Technical and industrial development had been unco-ordinated and unplanned, thereby preventing people from fully enjoying 'the potentialities of modern scientific advance'. He consistently bracketed 'science and culture'. Society at large and the universities in particular needed to take part in the planned harnessing of science and its technological and industrial implications for the benefit of social advance:

> The dependence of social life in general, and of the cultural prospects of the people, on the technical and industrial level is quite clear. In particular, the last twenty years have seen tremendous advances which open up quite new prospects ... It is with these conditions clear in our minds, therefore, that we should consider the role of education, and especially of the universities, for the universities are key-points not only in the educational system but also in our social structure.

It should be the function of the universities to find ways in which science and technology could be devoted to social needs, and therefore to help their students to understand the prospects facing modern society and how modern knowledge, in technology, health, education and in science generally, could be used in the interests of the people. These were the political and social start-ing points for the questions universities were going to have to answer. Simon's vision encompassed the university and the educational system, the community and the nation and the international war effort. He saw the universities as becoming centres of 'a vital and creative culture, shedding their light over thousands and millions of people in their locality, closely linked with daily activities and problems, and essentially, therefore, at the disposal of the people'. The universities would attain this position by allying themselves 'with the forces of progress all over the world to overthrow the enemies of culture and science'.[31]

With one degree of rhetoric or another those who came out of a subject identity, Marxist politics or Christian faith, saw some imperative for change, whether this meant innovative reform or the revival of a tradition. With the exception of Leavis's approach there is a kind of continuum across these years of the war, a sense of the need not only to enter a new post-war world, but to plan for it. For example, early in the war, Sir Charles Trevelyan, who shared some of Brian Simon's radical political sympathies, wrote in an article on 'The equalization of education', that 'if there is a more democratic frame to the new international world it must have its counterpart in a more democratic society at home'. Only a few workers' children were able to enter 'the promised land' of the universities.[32] The writers of the early decades of the century were advocating new universities and colleges to provide such a promised land, but during the war demands were also being formulated for reform of the new, and 'reform' was as protean as 'culture'. Both, as we have seen, were interpreted in the vocabularies of justice and democracy, Christian faith and socialist ideals, and both were to be reinterpreted at and after the end of the war in terms of the demands of science and technology, and the manpower needs of industry and the schools.

When the UGC reported in 1948 on *University Development from 1935 to 1947* much of its commentary related to the period covered by this chapter, and particularly wartime experience. It drew attention to the 'debit side' of the impact of the war, including the emphasis on 'disciplines with direct utilitarian value', expedients justifiable only by 'the pressing needs of the moment'. By the end of the war these issues had further strengthened for the system as a whole the relationship between what the UGC described as the contrast between 'the cultural and the vocational aspects of university education'. There is a passage in the report that paints on a broad canvas the questions that surfaced in all these various ways before and during the war, and translates them into its own vision. It is as penetrating a passage as probably ever came from the UGC:

> The traditional form of cultural education at the older universities during the eighteenth and nineteenth centuries was conceived primarily for the benefit of a leisured and privileged section of society and concerned itself but little with the specific educational requirements of professional life. Those specialised forms of training were left to other agencies. The newer universities, on the other hand, have tended on the whole to emphasise the vocational function of training, though this generalisation is subject in many instances to important qualification. It is evident that, in the age which we are now entering, some effective synthesis of the two educational aims must be achieved. No university of the future can escape the duty of furnishing the majority of its

students with a type of training to some extent specifically related to their future careers. At the same time a university would in our view fail of its essential purpose if it did not, by some means or other, contrive to combine its vocational functions with the provision of a broad humanistic culture and a suitably tough intellectual discipline.[33]

This comprehensive passage (no doubt expressing, or at least echoing, the views of Moberly, still UGC chairman, but about retire and publish *The Crisis in the University*) captured fundamentals of the views that had been made prominent in the 1930s and 1940s. It pointed to unresolved questions that were to be crucial to debate and development in the decades following the war.

The UGC was well aware by the end of the war of factors that militated against success and high standards in a system that embarked on a sharp expansion of student numbers against a backdrop of a shortage of resources. As we shall see in the next chapter these and other difficulties had been made explicit during the war, notably – again in 1943 – when the pseudonymous 'Bruce Truscot' published *Redbrick University*. The UGC recognized that the maintenance of standards depended on the quality of students and on the quality of life and education provided by the universities. The maintenance of standards therefore depended on factors that included the quality of teaching staff, the staff:student ratio, and the adequacy of buildings for teaching, library, students unions, staff rooms and other purposes. Although these problems were exacerbated by post-war conditions, Truscot had in 1943 drawn attention to the relative poverty of the new universities, and the UGC commented that during the war 'there spread through the university world a healthy spirit of criticism and reflection which found provocative expression in such publications as those of "Bruce Truscot" '. Another element in this 'healthy spirit' was concern about the relative positions of teaching and research in the universities. Löwe had set research aside in his discussion as an area that did not require urgent attention. Truscot took the opposite view. The UGC acknowledged that there was a tendency to place undue emphasis on research and research outputs. It saw the post-war tendency as to some extent rooted in the demands of war for 'a sustained effort of concentration' on research that would help the war effort. However, it also acknowledged that:

the notion of research, both for its own sake, and for the results that may follow from it, has acquired in some minds a disproportionate value. 'Bruce Truscot', for example, chides us for remarking in our Report of 1936 that a University is *not less essentially* concerned to increase than to impart knowledge.[34]

The war, and particularly the period 1940–3, saw the development of a momentum of publications about the universities, but none of these had the same impact, within the universities but also much more widely, as did *Redbrick University.*

NOTES AND REFERENCES

1. V. 't Hooft, in International Institute of Intellectual Co-operation, *Students in Search of their University* (Paris: IIIC, 1938), p. 8.
2. Mountford, J., *Keele: An Historical Critique* (London: Routledge & Kegan Paul, 1972), p. 123.
3. IIIC, *Students in Search of their University*, p. 43.
4. UGC, *University Development from 1935 to 1947* (London: HMSO, 1948), pp. 14–18.
5. MRO, CVCP, MSS.399/3/UNI/1, University Development, parliamentary grant to the universities and university colleges 1936–37. Memorandum to the Chancellor of the Exchequer, pp. 2–10.
6. MRO, CVCP, MSS.399/3/UNI/1, Meeting between representatives of the University Grants Committee and the Committee of Vice-Chancellors and Principals ... 8th May 1944.
7. Berdahl, R.O., *British Universities and the State* (Berkeley, CA: University of California Press, 1959), p. 68.
8. Dent, H.C., *Education in Transition: A Sociological Study of the Impact of War on English Education 1939–1943*, (London: Kegan Paul, Trench, Trubner, 1944), p. vii.
9. Livingstone, R., *Education for a World Adrift* (Cambridge: Cambridge University Press, 1943), p. ix.
10. Conant, J.B., 'Introduction', in Harvard Committee, *General Education in a Free Society* (Cambridge, MA: Harvard University Press, 1945), p. v.
11. Simon, E.D., 'A citizen challenges the universities', *Universities Review*, November 1936, pp. 5–18.
12. For Simon's range of activities cf. *80th Birthday Book for Ernest Darwin Simon, Lord Simon of Wythenshawe*, privately printed 1959. A brief forward is by his wife, Shena D. Simon, and contributors include Kingsley Martin, Leonard Woolf, Charles Morris and Bertrand Russell.
13. Quoted in Mitchell, F.W., *Sir Fred Clarke: Master-Teacher, 1880–1952* (London: Longmans, 1967), p. 45.
14. Clarke, F., *Education and Social Change: An English Interpretation* (London: Sheldon Press, 1940), p. 1. Cf., Nash, A.S., *The University and the Modern World: An Essay in the Social Philosophy of University Education* (New York: Macmillan, 1943, 1943 edn, London: SCM Press), p. 162.
15. Scott, D., *A.D. Lindsay: A Biography* (Oxford: Blackwell, 1971), pp. 266–7, 344.
16. Dent, *Education in Transition*, p. 185.
17. Clarke, *Education and Social Change*, 6–9, 31, 43–9, 66.
18. Mitchell, *Sir Fred Clarke*, p. 106.
19. Clarke, *Education and Social Change*, pp. 1–5, 22, 26–7, 42, 69.
20. The collection of Moot papers at the University of London Institute of Education belonged to Clarke.
21. Kojecky, R., 'Appendix', *T.S. Eliot's Social Thought* (London: Faber & Faber, 1971).
22. FCMA, Clarke, 'Some notes on English educational institutions in the light of the

necessities of "planning for freedom" in the coming collectivized regime', XVI:II Ed and Misc 7, 21 May 1939.

23. Löwe, A., *The Universities in Transformation* (London: Sheldon Press, 1940), pp. 1–14 The Moot paper was entitled 'Some notes on university education', FCMA III:15:3, meeting of 9–12 February 1940. (Page references are to the book, not the typescript in the Moot papers.)

24. Ibid., pp. 21–6, 36, 49–62.

25. FCMA III:15, 9–12.February.1940, pp. 1–5.

26. Paton, D.M., *Blind Guides? A Student Looks at the University* (London: Student Christian Movement Press, 1939), pp. 7–9, 17, 70–3, 102.

27. A.S. Nash called it 'a penetrating, impressionistic study of life in one of "the modern" universities', *The University and the Modern World*, p. 20.

28. UGC, *University Development from 1935 to 1947*, p. 26.

29. Ibid., p. 76.

30. Leavis, F.R., *Education and the University: A Sketch for an 'English School'* (London: Chatto & Windus, 1979, orig. pub. 1943), pp. 15–32.

31. Simon, B., *A Student's View of the Universities* (London: Longmans, Green, 1943), pp. 11–14, 142.

32. Trevelyan, C. 'The equalization of education', *The Fortnightly*, March 1940, pp. 267–8.

33. UGC, *University Development from 1935 to 1947*, p. 60.

34. Ibid., pp. 16, 35, 58–60.

PART II
VALUES

4

'TRUSCOT':
'THE UNIVERSITIES'
SPEAKING CONSCIENCE'

Redbrick University[1] was published in 1943 under a pseudonym. It was the century's first book about English higher education to have a popular appeal, except, as Margaret Cole suggested in a review, 'for a few murder stories'.[2] Although the writers we have discussed reached out to some audiences, nothing had prepared the world of and beyond higher education for Truscot's outspoken, sometimes idiosyncratic but always vivid presentation of some of its innermost secrets. It was a profile and an exposé, a portrait and a programme. It was unprecedented, and wartime debate, in the view of Moberly writing only six years later, had been 'vigorously stimulated' by Bruce Truscot.[3] H.C. Dent talked of Truscot having 'dropped the equivalent of a high-explosive bomb into the academic world (and its blast stunned many outside it)'.[4] Truscot's *Redbrick and These Vital Days* followed in 1945, and *First Year at the University* in 1946. *Redbrick University* in 1943 had a dramatic appeal that the later books did not have, though the 1945 volume also won a response beyond the universities themselves. The derivation of the ideas and the reception of *Redbrick* suggest a relationship of writer and audiences, against a background of university history, experience and advocacy of change, different from any that we have previously discussed. Although its focus was on the inner life of these universities it shared the prevailing mood of addressing reforms needed for the post-war world.

The owner of the 'Bruce Truscot' pseudonym was E. Allison Peers, Gilmour Professor of Spanish at the University of Liverpool, who died in 1952 aged 61. The mystery of the pseudonym was not revealed until his death, the secret having been well kept by the half dozen people who had been party to it. It had been the subject of enormous, fruitless speculation. Reviews and correspondence sent to the author via the publishers testify to the considerable interest aroused by the book and by the mystery of its authorship. An academic reviewer of the sequel, *Redbrick and These Vital Days*, in the *Manchester Evening News* described how 'two years ago there was a man-hunt, sedate, unadvertised, since it occurred in the British universities. In every common-room, people asked "Who is Bruce Truscot, author of 'Redbrick University'?" '[5] Even in 1951 George Kneller, visiting from Yale, commented that 'everywhere I go up and down the country I am asked if I know Bruce Truscot'.[6] Peers had achieved for his creation what Eric Ashby called an 'Olympian anonymity'.[7] Truscot described his background as being in the arts but concealed his identity by a variety of stratagems. For example, in *First Year at the University* he asked his readers to forgive him 'if many of my illustrations are taken from English literature, as that happens to be my chief interest'.[8]

It is unlikely that guesses about *Redbrick* authorship were directed towards Peers, and if challenged he would have denied it. After Peers died and the secret was out, Sir James Mountford, his Vice-Chancellor, thought Peers might just have been mentioned among others who knew the University of Liverpool – which seemed a possible location of the author of the Truscot books. Mountford thought, however, that such a guess would never have been taken seriously:

> We knew Peers as an unusually productive and industrious scholar, as an outstanding teacher, as an apostle of his own subject, as a superb organizer of his own department. He attended meetings of Faculty and Senate with regularity, though if talk became diffuse he did not always stay to the end. He never shirked such share of committee work as fell to him ... His contributions to discussion and debate were infrequent and generally unobtrusive ... Always polite, and always a little reserved, he seemed almost to shun the gossip of academic politics ... It appeared incredible that such a man should have the inclination or the time to familiarize himself not only with the Charters, Statutes and Ordinances of many Universities but also with the less enduring effusions of the A.U.T. or the N.U.S. There are some of his colleagues perhaps who do not yet understand how it could all have happened.[9]

As an undergraduate at Cambridge Peers had not been able, since there was no lecturer in the subject, to take Spanish alongside French, and he opted for French and English. He was later to become an internationally eminent Spanish scholar[10] and holder of the chair at Liverpool. With a considerable scholarly reputation he would have spoken with some authority, not on 'the gossip of academic politics', but on the realities behind the outer profile of university education. There is no secret, however, about his reasons for choosing to launch *Redbrick* pseudonymously. He set out the three main reasons in *Vital Days* and repeated them in the 1951 Penguin Preface: he wanted his 'view of the modern university' to be judged on its merits, and not in relation to his established position; he wanted 'Truscot' to be able to say things 'in a challenging and provocative form' in order to stimulate discussion; and he wanted to 'speak out' while protecting colleagues whom he was criticizing from being identified. He drew a clear distinction between the balanced arguments and judgments of the scholar and the need, as he saw it in the early 1940s, for a voice which would startle 'the already over-complacent Redbrickian into serious thought, and perhaps even into some form of action'.[11] Champion of research though he was, there were limits to the research he could do for *Redbrick* under his self-imposed cloak of public silence. He could use a mixture of personal experience, acute informal observation, and what public data and records were readily accessible. No research activity that would have identified him as the author was open to him, but in many respects it was not necessary, given the kind of book he wished to shape. He had no access to the views exchanged amongst vice-chancellors, none of the kind of working party debates that later fed into Moberly's reflections, no interviews. *Redbrick* was a sustained meditation on what stemmed from a battle of the 'ancients' and the 'moderns' in the university arena. Unlike the public career of Peers himself, he wished Truscot to be seen not only as knowing the universities, but also as willing to argue a strong and controversial case for reform. If there were limitations to his 'research' they were not apparent, and he had found a framework in which to emphasize his convictions and commitments.

There is one important clue to a background on which Peers could possibly have drawn. In 1932, in the *Universities Review*, he published with a co-author an abridged version of an article on Spanish universities originally published in the *Bulletin of Spanish Studies*. The same volume also contained two articles following up on a previous article on 'What is wrong with the modern university?' and an article by McLean on 'University uniformity'.[12] Peers would no doubt have taken exception to the last of these (in the same issue as his own article), as misrepresenting the diversity of the new universities. Apart from the issue in which his article appeared it is possible that he saw the journal regularly. The *Universities Review* was published by the AUT, and Peers was certainly a member in 1927–28, but the AUT's records do not show whether his membership continued into the 1930s. If in 1927–28 he had read the *University Bulletin* (before it became the *Review*), he would have seen reports on AUT meetings, conferences on the universities, and articles on the University of Reading, Hull University College, 'The proper size of universities', 'The universities and industry', staff representation on governing bodies of Manchester University, and so on. In 1928–29 he could have read a review of Herklots and the obituary of Haldane highlighting his importance to Bristol and the new universities generally. In 1929–30 he would have seen articles on regionalism and research in the universities. If he did remain a member, he would have seen a review of Flexner in 1931, reviews of other books and in other years other relevant articles. Although of all of these only Herklots is mentioned in *Redbrick*, it is possible that Peers drew from them, if not inspiration, at least confirmation that he had something valuable to contribute to the popular understanding of the newer generations of English universities.

The basic reasons for this impelling need to 'speak out' lay both in the position of the late-nineteenth- and early twentieth-century university colleges that had become universities, and in their lack of a serious public 'voice'. The centres of cities like Liverpool had acquired their 'redbrick' buildings and embarked on building their identities on the basis of such local interests as metallurgy and medicine, textiles and the fine arts. By comparison with Oxbridge and to some extent London, however, the redbrick universities had made a different entry into the university landscape. The starting point for the emergence of Truscot was what Peers saw as the low status, poorer students (in both senses), mean facilities and lack of institutional purpose and attainment by the redbricks he knew. He recognized strengths in their urban roles – accessibility, cheapness and close teacher–student contact – but the deficiencies were all too clear, intensified by the impacts of war. This was the position of which Peers was aware, but the lack of a public 'voice' was equally clear. The universities had, as we have seen, their celebratory, anniversary, biographical or ephemeral historical literature. Liverpool, for example, had published a brief account of its 1882–1907 period in the latter year, and a twenty-fifth anniversary account of the period 1903–28. Birmingham had a 1911 collection of lectures on its early history, and a 1930 souvenir history of its foundation and development. Similar celebratory accounts existed at Manchester and other institutions. They were concerned with such matters as the foundation and founders, personalities and subjects, professorial appointments and examinations, finance and student numbers. Peers would have had little general literature on which to draw, and he showed no signs of being aware of the earlier literature we have discussed.

BREAKING AN AWFUL SILENCE

The combination of a flair for presenting the picture, the issues and a commitment to certain kinds of change won Truscot much support and applause, and forgiveness by most critics for weaknesses in the case he was presenting.

A reviewer in the *Universities Review* thought, as did other reviewers, that *Redbrick* was 'all the better for the provocative nature of some of his proposals', and a review in the *New Statesman* thought the book 'none the less valuable because his definitions as well as his conclusions are sometimes highly controversial'.[13] A professor of education at King's College, London, made an extended and extremely welcoming analysis of the book, which was 'the most important book in its field since Flexner's appeared in 1930, and it treats English Universities far more adequately, and with more understanding, than did that eminent American critic'. The book dealt with universities that did not exist when the nineteenth-century critics were writing:

> Although the author describes and criticizes at some length life at 'Oxbridge' and makes a few remarks about Durham and London, his book consists mainly of a searching and courageous examination of the remaining seven – which are often loosely called 'provincial', but which Mr. Truscot neatly labels 'Redbrick' ... his book indeed shows ... a wide and intimate knowledge of both Oxbridge and Redbrick, of their constitution, organization, and aims, and of the daily life of their staff and students, and is moreover ... admirably written ... he has certainly given us an informative, a sympathetic, and above all a challenging book. It appears most fortunately at a time when the whole of English education is under review; for this is the moment when we should clear our minds about the purpose of universities and their relation to the community.

The review makes the interesting point that although Truscot did not use 'such fashionable phrases as "equality of opportunity" and "the pupil as centre", his ideal is in line with current educational thought; it will be disputed only (to use another cliché) by vested interests'.[14]

H.C. Dent, editor of the *Times Educational Supplement*, one of the few people to whom Peers confided the secret, wrote a memorable obituary, in which he followed Peers's reasoning in inventing 'the lambasting controversialist who can see only one side of the case' (though Dent thought that the device was only partially successful because 'the scholarly Allison Peers will keep coming in').[15] The *Times Educational Supplement* itself (the author was presumably Dent) enthusiastically welcomed the book in 1943, and commented that 'it should also stimulate a great deal of the best kind of thought, and thus may become a prime mover of reform'.[16] An eagerness for reform in the ways universities, particularly the 'modern' universities, saw themselves and were treated runs through the whole of *Redbrick* and its sequel, and surfaces in all kinds of ways in *First Year at University* (where he draws the attention of his intended student-readers to his criticisms of universities in *Redbrick*).

There were reviews critical of particular aspects of the book, including its emphasis on research, or of what it omitted or neglected – for example, its focus on arts faculties, its lack of any treatment of economic or social science issues or the lack of comment on the position of women in the universities (which he tried to rectify in *Vital Days*). Max Beloff considered the weakness of the book to lie in its being 'an anatomy but not an ecology of our universities. Only rarely ... does the author look outside the universities themselves, to the society and institutions they serve.'[17] The fact was, however, that *Redbrick* proved extremely attractive to a very varied audience. It was reviewed extremely widely in the academic and other specialist journals, but equally so in the national press and local newspapers. Peers's collection of cuttings[18] includes supportive, even enthusiastic, reviews from local papers in Aberdeen and Liverpool, Manchester and Newcastle, Sheffield and Hampstead, and elsewhere. A review in the *Birmingham Post* thought it 'a unique contribution to the study of the British university problem', and one in *The Listener* considered that 'when all the books on modern educational problems are sorted out, this one will be found in the front rank'.[19] It was described repeatedly as 'persuasive', 'authoritative', 'important' and 'stimulating'. Academic reviewers, in spite of reservations, were generally supportive. H.H. Bellot, historian of University College, London, and Reader in Modern History at Manchester, wrote to Truscot via his publisher to express 'the delight with which I read your <u>Red Brick University</u> ... you seemed to me to have "spoken a mouthful", as the cousinhood would put it, and to have done so at a most opportune moment'. The Principal of the University of Glasgow wrote to say: 'I don't agree with all of it, but I thought it one of the most valuable contributions to the discussion of a vitally important University problem which have yet appeared.'[20]

The Vice-Chancellor of the University of Birmingham wrote in the *Manchester Guardian* that the book ought to sell 'not in hundreds but thousands of copies' especially in Oxford and Cambridge, and should be 'a bedside book for the Chancellor and mandarins in Treasury Chambers, Whitehall'.[21] Moberly, introducing his own book in 1949, singled out Truscot as having 'vigorously stimulated thought by his lively *Redbrick University* and its sequel', and in 1945 the *Manchester Guardian*, reviewing the sequel, described Truscot as having 'preached and disputed little ... but he turned up the light'. Warm commendations came from very varied directions.[22] Novelist Angela Thirkell, in *Books of the Month*, thought it deserved 'more space and more educated and thoughtful consideration than these columns can afford or this pen provide'.[23] A review in the science journal *Nature* commented on the 'charm and vivacity' of both books, and one in *The Times* thought the first of them contributed 'a fresh and vigorous appraisal of some of the problems involved in the rehabilitation and reform of our universities', and the second was 'as lively, close-reasoned and oracular in tone' (if less forceful than its predecessor).[24] Beloff, although with a range of criticisms of the book, described *Redbrick* as having been read 'by members of Redbrick common rooms as widely as any book of recent years ... not only read, but as the author would wish, discussed and argued about ... on the whole it was admitted to have provided an excellent basis for current discussions of its theme'.[25] 'For the moment', said the *Universities Review:*

> Mr Truscot has become the universities' speaking conscience. He has broken an awful silence; he has said, if nothing more, that there is a lot to say. For in a world where everyone was talking about education, there was a charmed circle of silence on the subject of the universities ... now we can all break silence if only to give him the cheers he deserves.[26]

The Times also referred to this silence, commenting on Truscot's treatment of a vital topic 'to which singularly little attention has yet been paid in public or on public platforms'.[27] This public silence, we have suggested, is one important context for the origin of the book. Peers was not party to the kinds of private discussions taking place in the Moot or the Christian Frontier Council, though, as we have suggested, he may possibly have encountered some of the limited public expressions of the views there debated. Discussion about the post-war future of the universities that took place in the UGC and the government developed most rapidly only after 1943, and then mainly in terms of predicting student numbers and manpower needs, notably in science and technology and school teaching, and also finance and the role of the UGC.[28] Some discussion of these and related themes did take place in the early years of the war in the AUT, the British Association and elsewhere, but when *Redbrick* appeared 'attention in public' had still been minimal.

One book that preceded *Redbrick* may have interested Peers. Löwe's *The Universities in Transformation* was different from Peers's view of the universities in most respects, and if he had read the book Peers could only have seen it as confirming his own intention to go provocatively in other directions. He gave no hint that he knew of Löwe's book, but it is likely that it was somewhere in the background. In February 1940 the Guild of Undergraduates at Liverpool held a conference on 'Universities and war' and its paper announced Löwe as the speaker – 'noted expert on university and students' problems'. His address was summarized in the *Guild Gazette* the following month and he clearly covered many of the themes of his book. The concerns of university education were being confined:

almost entirely ... to vocational specialization, little attention being paid the cultural and moral background ... The Universities should place more emphasis on the new humanities – political science, psychology, economics, etc. ... The Universities should endeavour to make clear the chaos of values that exists today.[29]

It is not inconceivable that Peers attended the conference, but more likely that he saw the report and knew the book. Löwe, however, considered the issue of research to have no urgency, and *Redbrick* gave it priority in the regeneration of the university spirit. Unlike Löwe, Truscot was concerned overwhelmingly with the inner working of the universities.

Brian Simon's *A Student's View of the Universities* was sometimes bracketed with *Redbrick* for review, though clearly its focus and messages were very different from Truscot's. Neither Simon nor Leavis elicited the same kind of public interest. The main wave of public discussion on platform and in print took place after the war, including the reports of the Percy committee on higher technological education in 1945 and the Barlow committee on scientific manpower in 1946, the creation of *Universities Quarterly* in 1946 and Moberly's *The Crisis in the University*. The commentators correctly emphasized that *Redbrick* had appeared at an opportune time and described Truscot as a pioneer. The book appeared half way between Beveridge's 1942 *Report on Social Insurance and Allied Services* and his 1944 report on *Full Employment in a Free Society*. Discussions of *Redbrick* were taking place at the same time as the consultations leading up to the 1944 Education Act. Peers did not draw explicitly on this wartime movement, but he shared some of its dynamic.

THE UNIVERSITIES

When Peers was writing *Redbrick* he was a senior member of what would now be considered a small university. In the academic year before the outbreak of war there were 50,000 students in British universities. Liverpool's share was just under 2,500, Leeds had just over 2,500, and Sheffield had 767. The only university with more than 10,000 students was the federal University of London, with 13,340. Focusing on England, Peers portrayed a dichotomy between Oxbridge and the nineteenth- and twentieth-century foundations. He left London out of his picture as a special case, because of its size and characteristics – its internal students totalled more than those of Oxford and Cambridge combined, and it had a large number of students taking external degrees – a system of which *Redbrick* strongly approved. He also omitted the University of Durham, seeing it as a shadowy replica of

Oxford and Cambridge: parents used to know of these latter two universities, heard rumours of a university in London, and 'there was also believed to be a university at Durham – wherever that was'.[30]

In 1956 the *Twentieth Century* had a special issue on the 'Redbrick universities' but contributors disagreed about the title, some preferring 'provincial' or 'modern' or 'civic'.[31] Beloff referred to them (in terms not unfamiliar when new generations of universities were under discussion in the next half century) as 'what the polite call the "newer" and the rude. the "provincial" universities'.[32] When Peers was writing, in addition to Oxford, Cambridge, London and Durham there were seven other universities. Of the university colleges still aspiring to university status the longest established was Nottingham, which obtained its charter in 1948. Leicester, Southampton and Hull struggled until different points in the 1950s to obtain theirs (in 1938–39, for example, Hull, established in 1927, had 162 students). The redbrick universities had been created to provide opportunities in their cities for middle- and upper-working-class families, and to further the industrial and commercial interests of their communities. Although Truscot referred occasionally to the ancient universities of Scotland, he said little of their character or their influence on English developments, and he did not include the colleges of the University of Wales, itself created in 1893, in his analysis. Peers, at the time of writing *Redbrick*, had been at Liverpool more than 20 years, he was aware of the common aspirations of the universities and their differences, their rivalries, purposes, strengths and weaknesses. He felt it was time to take stock and to argue for radical reforms.

Central to *Redbrick* was the critique of a university 'system' which gave Oxbridge all the advantages, including those of resources, residence and the networks that led to the most influential jobs and to privilege. Truscot traced with acerbic clarity the routes from Drabtown Municipal Secondary School for Boys to Redbrick University, and from public school to Oxbridge. He pointed to what later became known as 'meritocratic' education by indicating the adaptations Oxbridge was prepared to make in order to deprive Redbrick of its potentially most able candidates. Others were to echo Truscot's critique, particularly of an unfair and unjust distribution of resources. Commenting on *Redbrick*, Sir Ernest Simon reaffirmed Truscot's complaint about injustice in the allocation of resources: 'more and more facilities are being given to Oxford and Cambridge as against the other universities'.[33] Truscot's essential theme was that Oxbridge must not be allowed after the war to 'strangle' the redbricks. There should not be two large residential universities and ten others, but 12, each with its own distinctiveness, and with equal facilities, especially residential ones.

REDBRICK

Truscot's main comments on the redbrick universities fell roughly into four categories. First, their resource base and public funding had left them with drab and unsuitable conditions. Their buildings had to be within reach of staff and students living in city suburbs, were built in poor areas of the city, were not 'imaginative or appealing', and proved ultimately to be too small and inappropriate for their purposes: 'the grinning red brick, the dirty grey stone and the unspeakable blue and yellow tiles still remain'. Some impressive buildings had been added, but there was a common meanness about the sites and the buildings. Their resourcing had improved, but the national distribution of resources was still inequitable. If there was to be a 'Battle of the Ancients and the Moderns', the latter lacked 'only the munitions of war with which to do battle'. There is an outstanding passage in the 1951 Preface reprinted from *Vital Days* (a passage Dent rightly thought to be Truscot at his best) in which he apportioned blame: the Treasury for starving Redbrick of money; the schools for starving it of talent by sending their best pupils to Oxbridge; the professor and lecturer for doing too little research and teaching; laymen for the harm done on university councils; undergraduates for pursuing narrow courses of study – 'and these are only a few items of the diagnosis'.[34] It was a stern indictment of policy failures towards and weaknesses in the institutions that Truscot saw as inevitably dominating the future, if only they were free of domination by Oxford and Cambridge. The image of the redbrick universities was crucial and Truscot argued for them to be treated in ways that would secure their reputation and future. They suffered from what one reviewer described as 'a sneaking suspicion ... sometimes even among their staff and their students, that these are not *real* universities',[35] a suspicion encountered in later decades by those who experienced the acquisition of the university title by the Open University, the colleges of advanced technology or the polytechnics.

Second, the contrast of Redbrick's conditions with the advantages of Oxbridge generated other, specific criticisms. In 1943, when student residence was not yet broadly acceptable national policy, Truscot was strongly putting forward the case for an opportunity for all the universities to be able to develop residential facilities: 'it should be an axiom that every university must have sufficient hostels to accommodate a very large proportion of its undergraduates'. By 1945 he was surprised to detect an already widespread acceptance of his ideal and of the urgent need for action.[36] He wished to develop the strengths of the new universities, at the same time as wishing them to share in the advantages of the old. He undoubtedly played an important part in the movement towards acceptance of the need for redbrick student residence. His motives for advocating student residence stemmed from his awareness of the limited backgrounds and horizons of students from Drabtown Municipal Secondary School, and his eagerness for them to be able to share in the advantages of residential university communities.

Third, the weaknesses of the redbrick universities, in Truscot's eyes, were not just in the poverty of their externalities. His most caustic comments were reserved for the conduct of their academic staff, the nature of their organization, the quality of the educational experience. The most striking features of *Redbrick* and *Vital Days* relate to Truscot's probing of the inner life of the universities. Although he had a deal to say about organization and administration and student life, his main concerns were with the roles of academic staff. His most controversial message reached out into all aspects of the roles of universities – concerning research and teaching.

On the central issue of the importance of research there are two tactical mistakes in *Redbrick*. By locating research and teaching in separate chapters, in spite of disclaimers, Truscot made research *appear* to be divorced from teaching. He was tempted also to overstate a case, suggesting that it was research and not teaching, researchers and not students, that were vital to the existence of universities – a position which he explained and defended in *Redbrick* and elsewhere in various ways. In *First Year*, for example, he told the students – no doubt to their surprise, that since universities were founded for discovery, teaching was only 'incidental to their real work. You couldn't have a school without pupils ... But you could perfectly well have a university without undergraduates.'[37] Truscot's commitment to the purpose of universities as a search after knowledge led him to his most coruscating attack – on the failure of the professoriate to understand the need for research. Many commentators, sympathetic though they were, felt – like Peers's own Vice-Chancellor – that 'current opinion would not in general I think be prepared to go all the way with Truscot'.[38] His logic on research began with his assumption about the central purpose of advancing knowledge, and continued through a series of arguments and detours and critiques to emphasize the 'centrality of research and teaching – a single and indissoluble aim'. He went further and talked of the need to encourage vocational aspirations as part of the ideal of service for which universities stand: 'In the ideal of service all three functions – research, teaching and vocational training – have their natural meeting-place.' The final step in the argument was the sustained attack on the paucity of research conducted by academics – though critics were quick to indicate that this attack related only to Arts Faculties. In his chapter on 'The leisured professor at bay' he agreed with one reviewer that what he had previously done was break 'the conspiracy of academic silence' relating to Arts Faculty research. His attack was on two fronts. Academics put in too few teaching hours and badly managed their time – including that of committees. While they had a right to free time and vacations, these were used unproductively. Truscot's attack was on the professors (not just in Arts Faculties and not just at Redbrick) who, once appointed, 'produce practically nothing'. From that kind of analysis in *Redbrick* he moved on to lambaste the Professor Deadwood kind of figure in *Vital Days*, those who publish nothing for 20 years because they have nothing to publish: 'a *large number* of idle professors are ruining the traditions of their calling'. In *First Year* he explained to his readers that there are 'workers and drones in academic hives', and if only the entire university community, 'professors and lecturers as well as undergraduates', understood what a university was 'and lived up to it, university life would be transformed'.[39] Truscot's proposed solutions included: a research requirement for academic staff; a sabbatical entitlement accompanied by a clear statement of the purposes to which it was to be put; the abolition of tenure, to be replaced by short-term appointments with annual reporting, and more care in making appointments. He talked of lecturers' 'laxity' and incompetence and advocated a course of training of at least three months. In an article in the *Times Educational Supplement* in 1946 he added:

> More should be required of the successful candidate for a junior lectureship than to have graduated with first-class honours and published an article or two in a learned journal. Until a training college is established in the technique of lecturing, graduation from which should normally be obligatory, he should be expected, before appointment, to deliver a trial lecture. He should further be asked to submit a general plan of the research which he proposes to pursue over a period of (say) ten years.

He also saw benefits in universities being subject to inspection.[40]

He vigorously attacked Professor Deadwood ('that sprawling figure in the horsehair arm-chair by the fire', asleep) in a visit to 'A Redbrick Tea-Party' which he wrote for the *Universities Review.* Young Professor Jim Livewire declares his agreement with Truscot in an argument with Professors Dusty and Deadwood, the former of whom protests:

> 'Researches, indeed! Now, let me tell you once and for all, for the ordinary university teacher I don't believe in research. Let him keep abreast of his subject, and put in his six or eight hours' honest teaching, and look after his students, and do his share of committees … do all that conscientiously and there won't be much change out of a week. And you'll need your Saturdays for rest.'
>
> 'But I get my rest on Sundays,' interjected Livewire meekly. 'Do we really work so hard that we need two-sevenths of term and the whole of the vacations to rest in?'

THE UNIVERSITIES REVIEW

A Redbrick Tea-Party

OH, yes, you can get afternoon tea at Redbrick University—if you know how. Not that, even in peace-time, you were ever encouraged to. Viewing the matter objectively you might suppose that the University authorities would do their utmost to stimulate the social life of the place and combat the impression prevailing in the city that Redbrick is just a superior kind of municipal day school. But not they! All the administrative staff, of course, are refreshed daily at half-past four with buns and tea; but they, poor things, have to work on till half-past five, or sometimes even later. The teaching staff is different. As the last lectures of the day end at 3.45, there is no earthly reason why any of them should be about the premises after that hour—and most of them have left by three. So if any professor or lecturer is eccentric enough to want to attend the meeting of a students' society, or to put in an hour or two of overtime at the University Library, he must either go tea-less, or he must address a request for refreshment (in writing) to the Junior Bursar, who hands it to the Lady Housekeeper, who in turn transmits its contents to the cook. Then, at the hour specified (which may not be earlier than four nor later than half-past) there enters the Common Room one of the University Charladies about to start her evening's cleaning, bearing a pot of tea and a slice of well-worn cake and oozing a nicely compounded blend of superiority and disapproval. As a sequel, on the first of the next month, the delinquent receives an account from the Junior Bursar for the sum of sevenpence, which, until paid, reappears on the first of each subsequent month under the disguise of "Account Rendered."

Oh, yes, you can get afternoon tea at Redbrick University. But——

At exactly twenty minutes past four on that Wednesday afternoon in February, three things happened. First, the ancient clock on the dilapidated mantelpiece of the Staff Common Room struck a tinny half hour: the Staff always kept it ten minutes fast to minimize the risk of losing their homeward buses. Secondly, the door opened and the charlady barged down a tray containing tea for three with a "Your tea, sir" of super-disapproval. Thirdly, Professor Deadwood—that sprawling figure in the horsehair arm-chair by the fire—woke up.

He woke up with a start. Where was he? Removing *The Times*, which was covering his face, he surveyed the high-ceilinged room with the large round table, the dirty distempered walls and the framed prints dating from the middle years of Queen Victoria, and realized that he was in the Redbrick Common Room. But why? The fire was out—it was timed to expire between three and four. He ought to have been home long ago. His daily lecture was at two: he hadn't lectured after two (or before eleven) since the term he came to Redbrick from Oxbridge nearly twenty years ago. And what was that ridiculous tray of tea-for-three doing on the table?

Professor Deadwood stood up and stretched his long limbs. Not so young as one used to be .... Going to sleep in the afternoon and all that ....!

"What, you here after closing-time!" exclaimed Dusty, the Professor of Latin, flinging the door open with most unseemly energy. (Dusty, the Latinist, and Crusty, the Professor of Anglo-Saxon, were the two Senior men on the Arts side, and Deadwood, who detested them both, was counting the terms to their compulsory retirement: they had such a disconcerting habit of blunt and tactless speech, of which the latest remark was only one more example.)

As he spoke, Dusty held open the door for a stranger, whom Deadwood peeringly recognized as a well-known Classical Don from Oxbridge. Bringing up the rear was the Professor of English Literature, Jim Livewire.

Then Professor Deadwood understood. At five, there was to be a local meeting of the Classical Ass. Dusty was the President. The Oxbridge Don must be the speaker. As for Livewire—well,

5. 'A Redbrick Tea-Party', by 'Bruce Truscot', *Universities Review*.

'*I* do,' said Professor Deadwood. 'I only have five lectures a week and yet, I can assure you, I never have a spare moment. There is always something to be done: testimonials, don't you know, or notes from the Registrar, or set books to prescribe, or committees to attend, or students to interview. I'm always in my room by half-past ten – except of course for week-ends: I don't come in on Fridays.'

Deadwood protests that his whole life is devoted to research, but it can't be served up for inspection: 'it's so *intangible*. Somehow you can't put it down on paper.'[41]

Truscot's fourth theme was that in these and other respects Redbrick lacked a clear understanding of the nature of a university. The emphasis on research was one point of entry into this debate, but there were others. Universities did not, for example, do enough to establish for students how a university differs from a school, and what it meant for a university to be a 'community'. He was very much aware of the difficulty of establishing the difference when many students lived at home, travelled long distances, and did not share in the advantages of residence of Oxbridge students. In *First Year* he explained to students that 'the university is a kind of half-way house between school and the world'.[42] Another point of entry was his dismissal of external membership of university courts as unhelpful and intrusive in the academic autonomy of institutions, which he was anxious to strengthen. He also frequently criticized, as did many others in the 1940s and after, the trend towards specialization in the school and university curriculum, as well as attempts to overcome it by a misguided search for a 'general culture' through the accumulation of subjects. It was, he believed, by broadening the approach adopted within subjects and within the honours degree that the problem had to be tackled.[43]

Another point of entry into the debate was the subject of a paper that was read for him at an international conference on 'Some comparisons between universities'. Truscot's topic was 'Contact with the student mind', deploring the gap between the professor or lecturer and the students. Coincidentally the paper was published in the proceedings, edited by Ernest Barker, and next to a paper by Fred Clarke on the universities and teacher education. By the latter part of an honours course, affirmed Truscot, undergraduates should be seeing the professor as a 'fellow-worker, a fellow-seeker'. He repeated his *Redbrick* call for more seminar teaching, which required appropriate teachers. It was 'all-important' to establish closer contact between the universities and the schools, and professors could spend a term teaching in schools, not that 'Professor Inaccessible should descend to the Lower Third'. A term spent with a sixth-form class 'would bring him nearer to the minds of his own freshman than anything else' – while the class teacher could be lecturing on his special subject to first and second year university students. University staff could visit schools for discussions, and universities could (in peace-time) arrange lectures for the schools. School students were often working as a team with their sixth-form teacher, and ways should be found to enable new undergraduates to find 'as skilled a teacher and as understanding a friend' in the university.[44]

In all of these connections Truscot described, criticized and attempted to redefine and look ahead. His most conservative predictions related to student numbers and their relation to other aspects of the future of the university. He rejected proposals radically to increase student numbers after the war and opted for a limited increase of no more than 30–40 per cent, which was later roughly the view of Moberly as chairman of the UGC, in opposition to the more radical projections of the Barlow committee.[45] Given efficient entrance tests, Truscot even suggested, numbers might not increase at all. Some commentators, like one in *Nature*, thought he tended 'to under-estimate the post-war demand for science graduates', and although Truscot was making cautious predictions the real crisis about student numbers had still not taken shape. *Universities Quarterly* in 1949 thought that 'the most striking thing about the "crisis" in the universities is that it has blown up so suddenly', and contributors to a symposium on Moberly's *Crisis in the University*, like the Principal of Ruskin College, Oxford, considered that 'never before has change been so rapid'.[46] The post-war debate about numbers was partly about the total size of the university system and partly about the scale and nature of individual institutions, and Truscot's predictions were rapidly overtaken by pressures he had not anticipated. The debate that began in the 1940s was about how large a university dare become. Anxious cries of overcrowding were heard. In 1946, for the Treasurer of the University of Liverpool it was 'well recognised that changes in size beyond a certain degree involve a change of kind', and the Vice-Chancellor felt that 'we are indeed facing the greatest crisis since our foundation'.[47]

Redbrick had been concerned, however, not just with numbers, but also with the nature of a university community, and Truscot's argument for residence was another factor in his willingness to countenance a reduction in student numbers. Like many others from the 1940s he worried that increased size would mean a weakening of the student–staff relationship and the worsening of amenities, to the detriment of the kind of students that attended Redbrick University. This possible loss of contact was to be a constant theme in the following decades. For Truscot and for many after him it was residential accommodation that was the crucial element in a university community, and it was an important part in the way he defined the purpose of a university, the role of its teachers and the necessary vitality of the student experience. A.H. Halsey has argued that this advocacy and other elements in Truscot's commitment to an old ideal meant 'an abasement before Oxford and Cambridge traditions and an abandonment of the modern urban conception of the university' that had motivated its founders and promoters. A.J.P. Taylor asserted, probably on similar grounds, that Truscot was simply wrong to want Redbrick to be residential.[48] The point for Truscot, however, was that given what he saw as limited post-war expansion it should be possible, by providing residential opportunities, to extend an equality of advantage. He may have been abandoning a nineteenth-century conception of the urban university, but he had judged that conception to be short-changing the kinds of students he witnessed struggling to have something resembling a university education. He was not alone. The only point at which Brian Simon's *Student's View* coincided with Truscot's was Simon's advocacy of student hostels as a means of combating the weariness of the student, mentally 'jaded, bruised, and battered' by the travel and the intensive pressures of the day. He, like Truscot, wanted for these students an 'opportunity of leisure' that was too often lacking in the university environment.[49]

A commitment to the future of Redbrick was for Truscot a commitment to the provision of adequate state aid 'to an extent undreamed of. For where else is the money to come from?' The state, in providing public money, had the right 'to exert an appropriate degree of public control'. Nevertheless, with state control of the universities threatening autonomy and its benefits, 'to-day, as thirty years ago, some of us are regarding such a possibility with trepidation'.[50] Adequate and equitable state funding, academic autonomy, a degree of accountability, residence, scale ... these were some of the inter-related issues that Truscot addressed. They also related to other important decisions universities needed to make. Without going too far, for example, in attempting to be a 'service' to its city and region, the university could, in Truscot's view become a regional 'power-house', share in a widened extramural activity (at the time the prerogative of Oxford and Cambridge), become 'a centre of knowledge and thought', develop its library and publishing activities, and in general become 'a university with its doors flung open, its lights blazing and its great halls filled on wellnigh every night of the week'. All of this depended, however, on his vision of the professor oriented towards research and scholarship – 'no cloistered academic' but a pivotal figure in this dissemination of knowledge and culture, the means of filling the university's lecture halls in response to some scientific discovery, some little-known country in the limelight, some book or theory that had become the subject of public discussion. This 'power-house' role of the university also depended on the proper functioning and accelerated procedures of university government, though Truscot only cautiously supported the extension of the membership of senates and other committees to non-professorial members. He also rejected the notion put forward by 'some ultra-democratic persons' of student representation on senates, and the view of the NUS in 1940 that students had a right 'to a share in the government and administration of the universities'. This, he held, 'shows an entire misconception of the nature of a university', which, as he continued to hold throughout, was essentially 'a body of mature seekers after knowledge' and excluded the immature from the governing process.[51] Although the NUS and others continued to press for student representation, it was not until the 1960s that it came – in Britain as in other countries – to the forefront of higher education politics.

'WHERE YOU TURNED'

Tracing the course of Truscot's reputation is to plot the trajectory of his certainties and ambivalences in rapidly and profoundly changing conditions, often losing sight of his role as advocate, protagonist and pioneer. In the post-war situation those who saw *Redbrick* as overtaken by the speed, scale and nature of events, criticized with sympathy. Moberly, in 1949, praised Truscot for having 'vigorously stimulated thought' and for reminding universities of the tradition of scholarly investigation. In what Moberly saw as 'the twilight of liberalism' in the twentieth century, Truscot was one of those sounding 'a spirited note of recall to its ideals', although in Moberly's view this kind of liberal humanism could no longer serve as a university model.[52] Dent, in 1953, had reservations about aspects of *Redbrick* but it was, 'when all criticism of it has been made, one of the most notable books on an educational topic written during the present century'.[53] Mountford considered it one of the chief books of the period, and Armytage, in a history of the *Civic Universities* in 1955 estimated that 'of all the books and pamphlets published on university affairs during the war, none had such an immediate and widespread appeal as Bruce Truscot's *Red Brick University*, which went through two impressions in 1943'.[54] Simmons, writing a history of the University of Leicester in 1959, considered that *Redbrick*, 'for all its crudities and imperfect balance, did what no other had ever succeeded in doing: it made the modern universities interesting to a wide circle of readers'.[55]

A historical exchange from 1983 helps towards a perspective. At a symposium on the 400th anniversary of the University of Edinburgh F.S.L. Lyons located the beginnings of post-war debate about the idea of a university in *Redbrick*, which he saw partly as an acute and sometimes mordant account of the anatomy of a civic university, and partly as an attempt to redress the balance between the ancient and the modern universities. But he also saw it as a traditional view of the university, failing to anticipate the great expansion after the war, and offering a 'novel, if also naïve' attempt to fuse the traditions of research and teaching. In the event, however, 'the opening of the floodgates after the war made Bruce Truscot's reflections almost irrelevant'. Robert Anderson, however, commenting on the idealism and university foundations of the post-war years, disagreed with Lyons's emphasis:

> Perhaps we should also take into account those two classics of the 1940s, *Red brick university*, by the pseudonymous Bruce Truscot, and Sir Walter Moberly's *The crisis in the university*. In his lecture Professor Lyons rather depreciated the influence of these books, but for a long time they were where you turned if you were looking for ideas about university education.

Research was now taken for granted in a way that 'does not seem have been the case when Truscot was writing'.[56] It is important to remember that *Redbrick* was for a long time one of the places 'where you turned' for ideas.

It is difficult but valuable to situate *Redbrick* and its intentions in the university circumstances of the 1930s and early 1940s, and to listen to its passions. Truscot's most critical judgments were reserved for those features of university reality that he considered in need of urgent change, but he did not share 'ultra-democratic' views which could not be squared with his picture of priorities for the future health of Redbrick. There are difficulties in making judgments knowing that the numbers of higher education students was to reach not tens but hundreds of thousands, that Redbricks and other 'modern' or 'new' universities were to make the seemingly large institutions of the 1940s and 1950s look very small, and that some of the debates about public funding, accountability, representation or administration were to be transformed from the parameters within which *Redbrick* knew them. It is surprising, given the massive changes of scale and procedures, and the myriad specific changes in external and internal pressures and scrutinies, that so much of *Redbrick* remained intact, or re-emerged in new but recognizable forms.

In a broadcast script he wrote in 1943 for the BBC African service Truscot said that he envied the universities that would be born into the post-war world, and that would 'become the heirs to all the resolution and practical idealism which are emerging from our past sufferings'.[57] 'Resolution and practical idealism' do not simply emerge, they are made, and Peers, writing as Truscot, was one of the makers. It is possible to define his work as representing an imaginative flourish at the end of an old order, although not far-sighted enough. Judgments about his analysis and proposed reforms, in this as in other connections, need to be made in relation to a variety of contexts, and reasons for his judgments and priorities. This applies, for example, to his reservations about student or outside membership of university councils, to his lack of discussion in *Redbrick* of the position of women, but also to his attack in its sequel on salary discrimination against women, and on their lack of promotion.[58] Peers fashioned *Redbrick* in that period of the war when it was necessary and possible to look ahead to the reconstruction of what had been disrupted and shattered, and what had been unacceptable in pre-war Britain. The values to be addressed were social values, the obstacles to social justice investigated by Beveridge, the forecasts of the needs of education – schools, adult education and higher education. For Peers the immediate context of his argument was the inequities in the shape of higher education, but he then turned attention to the issues which, though they were internal to the university, were also the key to making the redbrick universities the significant presence that he wished for them. It was not the terrible events and threats of the world outside but the unacceptable and the desirable within the universities that drove his analysis. The one brief chapter on the purpose of a university was a defence of what he considered it most important to defend, a critique and a programme, almost a manifesto. It was an insider's proclamation of what was or needed to be right, unlike Moberly's later protracted cry of universities and a world without direction amidst irresistible external pressures.

The mission of 'Bruce Truscot' was to break a silence at an important moment. It is a pity that in the 1951 volume, after incorporating the chapters from *Vital Days*, Peers did not return to a reflective discussion of the system and its purposes, statuses and possibilities. He did, however, end his first volume with an appeal to shape the future in the spirit of the founders of the redbrick universities:

> Not all the plans of the great founders of the newer universities proved successful. But when their plans failed, they thought out new ones. They kept on thinking. They kept on experimenting. They kept on believing.

In something of the language of future space odysseys he hoped that the universities would 'venture boldly, risk failure and win the satisfaction and happiness of the pioneer'. The final chapter in the combined 1951 volume ends with the words: 'The first thing is always the vision.'[59] Peers was appealing to a university audience, especially to those who could help to reform the roles and emphasize the responsibilities of the academics. He was also addressing the active populace outside who needed to know what was fundamentally right about the redbrick universities, but also what kind of help was essential to enable them to live up to their mission, open the doors and keep the universities' 'lights blazing'. *Redbrick* was not in the mould of the writings of the sociologists, but it took a stronger public social and political stance than they did in opposition to the injustice of Oxbridge privilege. It was a profoundly committed case for the equalization of resources that would allow the redbrick universities to serve the communities that had created them. It spoke to audiences that knew and should remember, or should learn, the importance of the local universities that had emerged out of the efforts of the nineteenth and early twentieth centuries.

NOTES AND REFERENCES

N.B. Many of the reviews of Truscot quoted are from cuttings preserved in the E. Allison Peers archive at the University of Liverpool, and it has therefore not always been possible to provide full publication details, for example, of page numbers.

1. The author used *Red Brick* for the 1943 title, *Redbrick* for the 1945 sequel *Redbrick and These Vital Days*, and *Red Brick* for the 1951 Penguin edition, which brought together the original book and five of the nine chapters of the second book. From 1943 he used '*redbrick*' adjectivally and substantively, and regretted his title use of *Red Brick*. *Redbrick* is used here throughout, and quotations are from the 1951 edition.
2. Cole, M., review of *Redbrick*, *Tribune*, 15 October 1943.
3. Moberly, W., *The Crisis in the University* (London: SCM Press, 1949), p. 7.
4. Dent, H.C., *Universities in Transition* (London: Cohen & West, 1961), p. 112.
5. Pear, T.H., 'Cap, gown, and the future' (review of *Redbrick and These Vital Days*), *Manchester Evening News*, 17 August 1945.
6. Kneller, G., letter to Faber & Faber, 1 December 1952, PP D265, box 1, envelope 37.
7. Ashby, E., 'A note on an alternative to halls of residence', *Universities Quarterly*, vol. 5, 1951, p. 150.
8. Truscot, B., *First Year at the University: A Freshman's Guide* (London: Faber & Faber, 1946), p. 74.
9. Mountford, J., 'Bruce Truscot', *Bulletin of Hispanic Studies*, vol. 30, 1953, pp. 10–11.
10. Cf. 'Introduction' to Mackenzie, A.L. and Allan, A.R. (eds), *E.A. Peers, Redbrick University Revisited: The Autobiography of 'Bruce Truscot'* (Liverpool: Liverpool University Press, 1996).
11. Truscot, B., *Redbrick University* (Harmondsworth: Penguin, 1951), pp. 14–15.
12. Cavenagh, F.A., 'What is wrong with the modern universities', *Universities Review*, April 1932; McLean, R.C., 'University uniformity', in ibid.; Jones, P.M., 'Where modern universities are wrong', in ibid., October 1932.
13. Carré, M.H., review of *Redbrick*, *Universities Review*, vol. 16, 1943/44, pp. 34–6; Mackenzie, N., 'The universities and the future' (review of *Redbrick* and Simon, *A Student's View of the Universities*), 30 October 1943.
14. Cavenagh, F.A., 'The modern university' (review of *Redbrick*), *Journal of Education*, 1943, p. 482.
15. Dent, H.C., 'Bruce Truscot', *Universities Quarterly*, vol. 7, 1953, p. 330.
16. *Times Educational Supplement*, 'Universities of the future: "Oxbridge" and "Redbrick" ', 28 August 1943, p. 373
17. Beloff, M., 'Outside Oxbridge', 11 September 1943, p. 745 (journal not identified, PP).
18. In the Archives of the University Liverpool, assembled by Peers via the publisher, Faber & Faber.
19. Priestley, R.E., review of *Redbrick*, *Birmingham Post*, 27 July 1943; *The Listener*, review of *Redbrick*, 2 September 1943.

20. Bellot, W.H., letter to Truscot, 27 December 1943, PP envelope 39 (2); Hetherington, H.J.W., letter to Truscot, 15 September 1944, PP envelope 39 (2).
21. Robertson, C.J., review of *Redbrick*, *Manchester Guardian*, 13 August 1943.
22. Moberly, *The Crisis in the University*, p. 7; *Manchester Guardian* comments on *Vital Days*, 27 June 1945.
23. Thirkell, A., review of *Redbrick*, *Books of the Month*, September 1943.
24. Brightman, R., *Nature*, review of *Vital Days*, 13 October 1945; *The Times*, comments on *Redbrick* and on *Vital Days*, 18 August 1945.
25. Beloff, review of *Vital Days*, *Time and Tide*, 7 July 1945.
26. *Universities Review*, 1943, PP D265, box 1, envelope 38.
27. *The Times*, 7 August 1943.
28. Gosden, P.H.J.H., *Education in the Second World War* (London: Methuen, 1976), pp. 422–30.
29. *Guild Gazette*, 27 February 1940, p. 1; 12 March 1940, p. 3.
30. Truscot, *Redbrick*, pp. 45–50.
31. *Twentieth Century*, 'To our readers', vol. 159, p. 98.
32. Beloff, 'Outside Oxbridge'.
33. Simon, E., 'The future of Manchester University', *Manchester Evening Chronicle*, 17 November 1943.
34. Truscot, *Redbrick*, pp. 26–8, 64, 15.
35. Mackenzie, 'The universities and the future'.
36. Truscot, *Redbrick*, pp. 56–8, 281–2.
37. Truscot, *First Year at the University*, p. 9.
38. Mountford, JM D498/1/210.
39. Truscot, *Redbrick*, pp. 158, 328, 337, 352; Truscot, *First Year at the University*, pp. 8, 13.
40. Ibid., pp. 112–15, 300–2, 345–6, 349; Truscot, 'The ideal university', *Times Educational Supplement* [1946].
41. Truscot, 'A redbrick tea-party', *Universities Review* [1944–45], pp. 39–40.
42. Truscot, *First Year at the University*, p. 18.
43. Truscot, *Redbrick*, pp. 73–4, 174–6, 181–4, 286–94; *First Year*, p. 84; Mountford, *Keele: A Historical Critique* (London: Routledge & Kegan Paul, 1972), p. 125n (referring to Truscot's approach to a 'breadth of outlook' in the Honours system).
44. Truscot, 'Contact with the student mind', in Association of University Professors and Lecturers of the Allied Countries in Great Britain, *Some Comparisons Between Universities* (London: The Association, 1944), pp. 17–20.
45. Price, G.L., 'The expansion of British universities and their struggle to maintain autonomy', *Minerva*, vol. 16, 1978, pp. 368–71.
46. 'The mission of a university – a discussion. Introduction', *Universities Quarterly*, vol. 4, 1949, p. 15; Elvin, L., 'The universities and social change', in ibid., p. 24.
47. Sir John Hobouse, speech at meeting of University Court, 27 November 1946 (printed record), PP D265, box 1, envelope 38; MS of article for *Liverpool Daily Post* (1946), JM, D498/1/2/5.
48. Halsey, A.H., 'The idea of a university: the Charles Carter lecture, 1984', *Oxford Review of Education*, vol. 11, 1985, p. 127; Taylor, A.J.P., *Oxford Magazine*, 10 February 1944.
49. Simon, B., *A Student's View of the Universities* (London: Longmans, Green, 1943), p. 96.
50. Truscot, *Redbrick*, pp. 297–8.
51. Ibid., pp. 88–9, 221, 240–54, 353–70.
52. Moberly, *The Crisis in the University*, pp. 4, 43, 49.
53. Dent, 'Bruce Truscot', p. 33.

54. Mountford, 'Bruce Truscot', p. 11; Mountford, *Keele*, p. 123; Armytage, W.H.G., *The Civic Universities: Aspects of a British Tradition* (London: Benn, 1955), p. 278.
55. Simmons, J., *New University* (Leicester: Leicester University Press, 1959, orig. pub. 1958), p. 129.
56. Lyons, F.S.L., 'The idea of a university: Newman to Robbins', in Phillipson, N. (ed.), *Universities, Society and the Future* (Edinburgh: Edinburgh University Press, 1983), pp. 130–1; Anderson, R., 'Comment', in ibid., p. 164.
57. Truscot, 'Responsibility of the university towards the public', Appendix 2 in *Redbrick and These Vital Days* (London: Faber & Faber, 1945), p. 211.
58. Truscot, *Redbrick*, pp. 320–7; Dyhouse, C., *No Distinction of Sex? Women in British Universities, 1870–1939* (London: UCL Press, 1995), pp. 244–5 (for an approving glance at Truscot, accompanied by some critical hindsight).
59. Truscot, *Redbrick*, pp. 254, 374.

5

POSTWAR:
'A FERMENT OF THOUGHT'

The experience of Nazism, Fascism and war inevitably raised issues for education in general and the universities in particular about their possible future roles in defending and strengthening democracy. With increasing clarity from 1943 writers brought the universities into the centre of discussion about the future, as in their different ways Mannheim and the Moot, the Christian Frontier Council, Clarke, Löwe and Peers had done. Bonamy Dobrée, professor of English at Sheffield (and someone who had been suspected of being 'Bruce Truscot') firmly argued in 1944 that there was only one point of agreement among those who thought about universities, 'namely that such institutions exist to benefit civilization' and uphold broad cultural values. For him a traditional elite, 'those who form the enlightened public opinion of the day', no longer existed in the shape of an old governing class or dominant Christian values, but an elite of some sort was necessary and it would have to be created consciously. Universities were not the only ones who could do it, they were not the only path to leadership, but was it not for them to produce men and women 'who share a sense of civilized values'? Arts faculties, about which he was writing, had the duty not of sterile scholarship but of 'making contact with the vital problems of the day'. Not until these faculties understood that their problem was one of 'deep understanding ... will they regain their proud place, now lost, as the real centre of the University idea'.[1] Sir Walter Moberly later described this article as having 'rightly attracted a good deal of attention'.[2] Dobrée's 'elite', very different from what Leavis had proposed through a reformed 'English school', was not unlike the active, influential minority advocated by Löwe and others in Christian terms. Translated into cultural terms, the view of Professor John Macmurray (writing in the same issue of the *Political Quarterly* as Dobrée) was that universities were 'primarily a centre of cultural life and cultural progress'. They should be giving 'cultural leadership' but were failing to do so at a time of the disintegration of national culture. It should be a place where knowledge was unified, but instead it had become a 'common house of disjointed specialisms'. It was necessary to replan and rethink the university system, 'if indeed it can be called a system'.[3] This notion of the universities at the centre of cultural life, civilized values and the formation of a cultural elite was an increasingly powerful one as the war drew to a close and in the years that followed. Sir Richard Livingstone built his 1948 lecture and short book *Some Thoughts on University Education* on the notion that: 'if you wished to destroy modern civilization, the most effective way to do it would be to abolish universities'. Not that they were playing their 'immense part' in modern civilization effectively. They were not playing a 'directing part' but were serving aims set by others, and this meant a defect in the education they provided.[4]

The concepts were not identical, but representing, defending and further-ing civilization, culture and democracy served as similar bases on which to construct views about the desirable or necessary roles of the university. A book which explored much of this conceptual territory was *The University and the Modern World* by Arnold S. Nash, first published in the United States in 1943, and then in England by the SCM Press in 1945. Nash, who had left England for the United States in 1939, admitted to being much influenced by Mannheim's sociology, by Clarke's application of sociology to education (he described Clarke as 'the most creative figure engaged professionally in British education to-day'), and by the work of Adolf Löwe. In the book Nash quoted a letter from Löwe emphasizing his conception of the importance of preparing 'a creative minority' for the future political task: 'to overlook ... the restricted power of any educational effort which is not fostered by political and social reality, would be a hopeless idealism'. Nash discussed 'the plight of the liberal democratic university' in sociological terms: 'the real crisis in the universities of to-day has its origin in the crisis in liberal capitalist democracy, for a university, like any other social institution, expresses both the vices and virtues of the social order in which it exists'. In those countries that still proclaimed allegiance to liberal democratic forms of government:

> the cardinal problem of the place of the university in a democratic society cries to the heavens for a solution ... in order to stand against the totalitarian challenge the contemporary university in the liberal democratic world can no longer be content to regard itself simply as a centre for the efficient distribution of factual knowledge ... A planned economy is inescapable ... hence a planned university. The real question becomes, therefore not, 'Shall we or shall we not have a planned university?' – that is not a live option – but rather, 'On what basis shall it be planned, and to what purpose?'

He approached the issues that this raised from a starting point in a version of the sociology of knowledge, what he termed a 'relationist' position between that of outright relativism and the absoluteness of truth, emphasizing the importance of understanding the social origins of fashions of thought. Nash agreed with those who shied away from university 'neutrality' and he sought, not a new dogma or orthodoxy, but a way for the Christian teacher 'to share in a task of supreme moment. It is to help create a *Weltanschauung* which steers a middle path between the Charybdis of liberal atomism and the Scylla of totalitarian dogmatism'.[5] Following the publication of the book in the United States he contributed an article to a symposium on 'the future of the liberal arts college in a democratic society' (to which John Dewey also contributed). Nash's argument was directed against the view that liberal education was a 'real education' and separated by an abyss from professional education, which was not a 'real education' but 'merely vocational'. Courses in the liberal arts were also, he insisted, 'in a disguised form, vocational education of a pronounced and undeniable type'. Given the impact of modern science and related technical developments, it was useless to try to justify liberal education 'in its traditional sense, unrelated to vocational training, as adequate for the demands of the modern scientific and democratic world'. Students entering university-level education were already engaged in training for a future profession, and 'vocational education *with a difference*' (his italics) was what was necessary, taking note of the values of the Renaissance tradition, and helping students to see their future profession 'as it has evolved in man's long struggle with himself, with nature, and with society' and in the context of contemporary society.[6] As a professor of Christian ethics in California, addressing an American college issue, Nash was articulating an issue that was also to be central to considerations of British higher education development in future decades.

Livingstone's *Some Thoughts on University Education*, delivered as a lecture to the National Book League in 1947 and published the following year, contained aims not unlike those of Nash, but involved propositions of a different kind. Livingstone gave the lecture in the year he retired as Vice-Chancellor of the University of Oxford. In the 1920s he had also been Vice-Chancellor of Queen's University, Belfast, where he had focused attention on the training of teachers and on the creation of a faculty of theology. The historians of Queen's in this period describe him as 'deeply concerned ... about the nature and function of academic education'. As a classicist he was 'intent upon convincing his colleagues, as well as the world at large, of the unique value of humane, and especially of classical, studies' – drawing in part on his experience as a student of the classical humanism of Oxford – but not easily transplanted, the historians suggest, to Belfast.[7] During and after the war Livingstone expressed his concerns in a sequence of books dealing mainly with classical and humanistic views of school education. *Education for a World Adrift*, in 1943, focusing on education for character and for citizenship, was one place where he made clear his view that *more* education and access to *knowledge* were not enough. In the great interest being shown in education, something more was needed: 'knowledge is important, still more so is the power to use it; but most important of all is what a man believes, what he thinks good and bad, whether he has clear values and standards and is prepared to live by them'.[8] *The Future in Education* had earlier in the war focused on adult education and the book was reprinted eight times between its publication in 1941 and 1945. He saw adult study as a new function for the university, and he saw adult education as furthering the important growth of sociological studies.[9] This book became what Dent described as a bestseller in the field, reviewed in almost every newspaper and periodical of standing: though it had 'a profound and far-reaching effect', the field of adult education did not in fact become a priority for immediate post-war reconstruction.[10]

Some Thoughts on University Education was where Livingstone most directly voiced his concerns about education at this level. It was undergraduate education that needed reform and most revealed the weakness of the universities. In the development of specialisms, undergraduate education as a whole had never been thought out. At Queen's University, Belfast, a quarter of a century or so earlier 'the departmentalism apparently inevitable in modern academic life (and not only in modern universities) was abhorrent to him'.[11] Like some other writers in this period he had reservations about science and its lack of concern for human values. In the humanities it was literature, history, philosophy and religion that most fully kept 'the human problem continually before the mind'. The most important task was 'to bring home to the student the greatest of all problems – the problem of living', and to give guidance in it. There were therefore two main components to the solution needed for the university – philosophy and religion. It was disastrous for the student to be left 'without a philosophy of life, however provisional, a definite view of the ends to which it should be directed and of the principles by which it should be ruled, a clear idea of good and bad in conduct'. He advocated approaching the problem directly and 'to make a study of religion or of philosophy an essential element in every university course'. The purpose was not to indoctrinate but to ensure that 'no one should pass through the highest stages of education without considering the greatest problems of all'.[12] In stronger language, in an article in *Universities Quarterly*, Livingstone looked for 'decisive measures', making the study of the major problems of philosophy a condition of obtaining a degree.[13] Livingstone was stirred by the times to question the whole basis of university education.

It is clear from the nature of this argument, even at a National Book League lecture, as it was equally clear in the comments of Dobrée and others, that the messages were being directed overwhelmingly towards an academic audience. The contexts, first of the late period of the war and then of the election of a Labour government and a commitment to 'planned democracy', presented these writers with acute definitional problems regarding the university. While the CVCP, with its degree of new-found strength, could focus on expansion, funding and the implications for university independence, these writers looked for more fundamental solutions, ones that could give the university a new, reinvigorated centrality. Changing the university in this sense meant changing the outlook and mission of the university teacher, pointing students towards the difficult issues that lay beyond the immediate curriculum, reinterpreting Christian or other values in terms of a vastly changed society and world order and ways out of the uncertainties that had resulted. For some of those who, like Clarke, had taken part in the Moot and engaged with Mannheim, as well as others attracted by the new ideas, the 'relative novelty' of the sociological approach, and its relationship to the search for a 'social revolution'[14] was one important element. For such people this merged with the issue of imbuing the university with a search not just for 'truth' and the presentation of knowledge, but also with a sense of purpose, of more fundamental understanding. In 1948, addressing the needs of a democratic society in *Freedom in the Educative Society* (which he dedicated to the memory of Karl Mannheim), Clarke reaffirmed his long-held views in a new framework. The idea of an 'educative society' had been won, it was in place and the danger lay both in the loss of individual freedom and in social or cultural disharmony – it was not the business of the national educational system to determine what the 'common body' of knowledge, beliefs and values should be. Although he was not here directly considering the role of the university, his reaffirmation of the relevance of Christian belief was one that had implications throughout education. The structure of education could not be built 'on moral and intellectual confusion, even though we call the confusion democracy'. There were, he concluded, 'some healthy signs that thought about education is beginning to take the measure of its contemporary problem. It will need to do so, and that quickly, lest the educational effort should lose all sense of its ultimate purpose in a maze of organised "busyness".'[15]

As with Nash's transatlantic analysis, equally transatlantic was the sense that a way had to be found through the diversities of democracy without the benefit of a traditional, unifying set of values. The Harvard Committee's approach to *General Education in a Free Society* had encountered and explained the same problem, proclaiming that 'a supreme need of American education is for a unifying purpose and idea. As recently as a century ago, no doubt existed about such a purpose: it was to train the Christian citizen.' Such certainty had disappeared, and 'we are faced with a diversity of education which, if it has many virtues, nevertheless works against the good of society by helping to destroy the common ground of training and outlook on which any society depends'.[16] Coming from different directions, analysts and advocates could interpret civilized values as religious or humane, and both pointed also to the nature of culture and cultural leadership. Ortega y Gasset's *Mission of the University* became important in the search. This was an address he had given in Spain in 1930, a translation of which appeared in the United States in 1944 and after the war became more widely known in Britain. Clarke reviewed it in *Universities Quarterly* in 1947. Culture was for Ortega the prime concern of the university. It was:

> the system of vital ideas which each age possesses ... the system of ideas by which the age lives ... any age presents very disparate systems of convictions. Some are a drossy reminder of other times. But there is always a system of live ideas which represents the superior level of the age ... this system is the culture of the age ... In our age, the content of culture comes largely from science. But ... culture is not science ... Culture does with science ... the same thing the profession does. It borrows from science what is vitally necessary for the interpretation of our existence.

The university had become disastrously dominated by 'inquiry' – a confusion between research and teaching functions, which had meant an undermining of the cultural unity of the university, hence 'the historic importance of restoring to the university its cardinal function of enlightenment'. His argument led to the proposal that a 'Faculty of Culture' should become the nucleus of the university, but the crucial message was the need for the university to be concerned with revealing to students 'the paths of life in a clear light'.[17]

Ortega's became one more voice amongst those speaking within the university to those who might hear the call for an urgent review of the nature of the institution and its purposes. The creation of *Universities Quarterly* in 1946 confirmed the nature of the primary audience being addressed by the galaxy of writers contributing to it. That the message was also being transmitted within religious or political or professional forums did nothing to weaken the sense that this was now an acute internal issue for the universities themselves, hopefully amenable to pressure from other directions. The *Quarterly* reflected such pressures, by reporting on conferences where these issues were raised, publishing articles that probed not only the detail of university curricula and planning but also the universities' mission and their relationship to the state.

It responded warmly to the issues raised by the CVCP in its 1946 policy document, and to the open agenda for discussion the *Quarterly* had itself defined when it was launched. In 1948 it reaffirmed that the problems listed in the original prospectus remained 'the crucial problems of to-day'. These continued to include issues of research and teaching, student numbers, staff recruitment, administration and specialization, but also the mission of a university: 'Are the lines of demarcation between a university and a technological college valid to-day? Do university students receive a balanced general education which gives them an understanding both of the arts and of the sciences and of the problems of modern society …?' The problem that had attracted most attention in the journal had been that of 'the number of students and the demand for entry'.[18]

In 1946 the SCM Press published a series of pamphlets by Christians exploring university issues. A reviewer in the *Universities Review* saw these pamphlets in the context of 'increased recognition of the place of the university in society' – to which the pamphlets would make an important contribution. They had probably not been published as a book in order 'to suit the small literary appetite and perhaps still smaller purse of the under-graduate'.[19] A general preface to the series was written by R.H. Preston, Study Secretary of the SCM, 'a pupil of Robbins and a convinced democratic socialist', and co-author of a book on *Christians and Society*.[20] Preston underlined the fact that many of the problems addressed in the series had been discussed 'in the last year or two, largely owing to the work of the pseudonymous Bruce Truscot, who has written the first British book on the university to be widely read since Cardinal Newman's *Idea of a University* in the nineteenth century'. The pamphlets resulted from the work of a commission of senior members of universities in 1944 and 1945, and the target audience was clearly defined: some were addressed to 'junior members of the university; but it is hoped that most of them will be of interest to a wide range of both senior and junior members'.[21]

CLIMACTERIC

The wartime concerns, ideas and plans for reform were not superseded by the realities of the world after the war. The shape and horizons of the universities continued to be the subject of debate, but influenced by new pressures. The universities, in one description, 'quite suddenly in 1946 … passed through a climacteric. For the first time in their history more than 50 per cent of their income came from Parliamentary grants. The Government … had become a majority shareholder in the academic industry.'[22] Anxieties about dependence on government funding, and therefore about intrusion into university independence, had a more serious basis than in the earlier decades of the century or than even Truscot had feared. Reporting on the post-war period, the UGC described the impact on its work as continuing to grow 'in volume and in complexity', because of the 'very large' increase in the total budget for distribution, the earmarking of parts of recurrent grants, the large scale of grants for capital purposes and the limited grants for university buildings. The 'burden of work' reflected the increased number of university institutions and of students.[23] Between Truscot's analysis and predictions of 1943, and the appearance of Moberly's *The Crisis in the University* in 1949, the university system passed through more than one form of climacteric. The roles of government, the UGC, the CVCP and the universities themselves changed in response to the anticipated end of the war, and then in the difficult and demanding, but also idealistic, years of post-war planning and reconstruction. The concerns of the period of Nazism and the advent of war, debated in ways we have suggested, were thrust into enhanced prominence. Not only social conditions surviving from the pre-war years and fears about the economy, but also the defence of democracy, the renewal of its institutions, and the nature of the university's aims and values, were serious concerns for many for whom the failures of the past included the failures of the universities. The increased tensions of the emergence of the Cold War had repercussions within the universities. Discussion of size, numbers, funding and associated issues and problems was rarely far from questions of the purposes of the universities in an age of transformations that were greatly different from those of the previous half-century. Built into the concerns were also the elements of optimism associated with the implementation of the post-war Welfare State. In particular the planning of the education system in general, following the 1944 Education Act, had immediate and longer-term implications for the universities. Most immediate was the demand for teachers, scientists and technologists.

At the beginning of the war there had been 50,000 students in the whole of the United Kingdom. The number fell to about 37,000 throughout the war, and by 1949–50 this had risen to over 85,000. The number of universities remained unchanged until charters were granted to Nottingham and Southampton in the early 1950s. The UGC divided the English universities into categories: Oxford and Cambridge; London and Durham (both founded in the early nineteenth century); the nine 'civic' universities plus Nottingham and Southampton; three university colleges that had not yet obtained charters, but which 'resemble the English civic universities' – Exeter, Leicester and Hull; the new University College of North Staffordshire (later Keele University), which received its charter in 1949 and admitted students for the first time the following year. The Manchester College of Technology taught technological subjects that led to degrees of the University of

Manchester.[24] This is the brief statistical background to the 'climacteric' of the immediate post-war period. The universities were aware of the variety of pressures that these statistics represented – including the specific need for categories of professionals for collaboration with medical and other health services.

In July 1946 the CVCP published a 16-page statement entitled *A Note on University Policy and Finance in the Decennium 1947–56,* prepared for the UGC but clearly intended also to address the universities at large. This was widely perceived as a radical document, one that moved the CVCP and the universities more firmly to the centre stage of policy making than ever before. The CVCP was interpreting the 'climacteric' in financial terms, but with a strong sense of purpose and policy. It had been considering 'several problems of the first magnitude, namely the relationship between the demands made upon the Universities of this country for the immediate future and the means that can be relied upon to meet those demands'. The statement responded to the flurry of reports produced towards the end of the war and afterwards on a wide range of national needs, including the 1944 reports of the McNair committee on the supply of teachers, the Goodenough committee on medical education and the Barlow committee's 1946 report on scientific manpower. The CVCP affirmed a position more strongly than had been the case with its previous dealings with the UGC and government. Maintaining standards required appropriate conditions 'as never before, a more realistic regard for a more intimate perception of needs which in the national interest are over-whelmingly pressing ... *the improvement of the Universities' resources is seen to require a first place in the programme of educational expansion*' (italics in the original). Development needed to be balanced within institutions, and the demand for more scientists and technologists should be matched in other faculties: 'if the University population must be doubled in science [as Barlow recommended], it should be approximately doubled all round'. New buildings were needed for teaching and research, and for student accommodation. The requirement was not, it argued, any new universities, but the 'expansion of existing institutions properly'. Underlying all of this the CVCP presented a summary of the situation and enunciated a principle:

> During the last few months the Committee of Vice-Chancellors and Principals has been earnestly concerned with a general problem of the first magnitude, namely, the relationships between the demands made upon the Universities of this country for the immediate future and the means that can be relied upon to meet those demands ... the aftermath of war presents a field in which the old methods, the methods of gradual, piecemeal and laboured development are no longer enough.[25]

The final section of this report began with an implication for this coming ten-year period. The proportion of university income from government sources would be increased from roughly one-third to three-quarters, and 'the financial dependence of the Universities on Government grants will be correspondingly increased. It is sometimes presumed that an increase in Government finance may require a corresponding increase in direct Government control'. Some government guidance was indeed necessary, since only the government had certain kinds of relevant information and it had to satisfy itself that the universities were teaching 'every field of study that in the national interest ought to be cultivated', and that resources were being used efficiently and economically. The universities individually and collectively could be expected to adopt policies that would 'serve the national interest', and there would therefore be more government guidance than before. Although it was right that the universities should be accountable, they should nevertheless 'continue to be in the fullest sense self-governing societies ... properly subject to criticism, and affected in their fortunes by the public judgment of their policies'. Governments had in the past responded correctly to university weaknesses in discharging their responsibilities, and as a result 'the national service of the Universities has been of higher order than would otherwise have been attained'. The UGC, which had not prescribed but advised and guided, was crucial to this process. The statement ended with an emphasis on the universities, as well as the UGC, needing to play their part in 'the co-operative planning of the whole University system'. Much discussion had recently taken place in 'wider university circles', and the CVCP itself had brought in experts on two specialist committees to report on matters of general importance to the universities. More such specialist advice would follow, and closer co-operation would take place among the vice-chancellors and with the UGC 'to ensure the complete fulfilment of their common task'.[26]

The new *Universities Quarterly* published extracts from the document, particularly this final section. Sir Ernest Simon, its founder and chairman, described the document as 'of outstanding importance' and an 'almost revolutionary memorandum'. He pointed out how much the government had consulted the CVCP during the war, and although it was only a consultative body, a national negotiating body was needed for the universities, and 'there can be no doubt that the universities are unanimous that the Committee of Vice-Chancellors and Principals must fulfil this function'. This was the first time that the CVCP had ever issued such a public report.[27] Sir Lawrence Bragg, of the Cavendish Laboratory, Cambridge, wrote in with a reservation about the co-ordination of university policy: nothing must be done to under-mine 'the right kind of university independence'.[28] In the *Universities Review*, Roy Pascal, Professor of German at the University of Birmingham, warmly welcomed the report for its 'refreshing imaginativeness and energy', and urged all members of the universities to study it. The vice-chancellors' attitude 'betokens what might almost be called a revolutionary change in university policy, for they accept far-reaching obligations to the country and a collective will to meet them'. He questioned the wisdom of requiring a balanced development of faculties, since in different universities there were already different balances: 'we do not want our universities to become one-faculty institutions, but we are a long way from this, and need not shy from an alteration of the existing balance as from a scarecrow'. He thought the final section of the CVCP report somewhat conservative, because it failed to show how university staffs generally could be employed in 'ensuring a satisfactory and steady improvement of the universities', and because it did not address the issue of financial awards to students. However, he did not wish to end on a critical note, as 'the Vice-Chancellors' statement is an exhilarating document. It affirms the universities' dignity and responsibility with a clarity rarely reached before, and can properly claim the warm appreciation and support of university staffs and of the general public.'[29] In more ways than one the universities were passing through a climacteric.

An insight into the new self-consciousness in the universities is provided by the launch of *Universities Quarterly* in November 1946. A detailed prospectus for the new journal had been issued, on the basis that 'the need for a journal wholly devoted to University Education and the vital problems affecting university development has grown in urgency during recent years'. The journal would encompass reports on universities in other countries and it was not intended only for university staff, given that the war years had brought industry and university research into a closer relationship, one that the journal hoped to strengthen. It was hoped that the journal would also interest 'those taking part in public life, the Civil Service, local government, and the secondary schools and technical colleges'. The prospectus contained an impressive list of people who had promised to contribute, and it set out a long list of issues for discussion in this 'period of almost revolutionary change and development' for the universities.[30]

The decision to launch the new journal was taken at a meeting of the Executive Committee of the Association for Education in Citizenship at its meeting on 28 February 1946. The resolution passed at that meeting was: 'That the Association approves of the proposal made by Sir Ernest Simon to found a "Universities Quarterly" on the lines of his letter' (of the previous month). Simon had founded the Association in 1934 and was its chairman from then until 1947. He had written on the subject of citizenship, and had co-authored, for example, a small book on *Training for Citizenship*.[31] The Association would not at first sight seem the most likely midwife for the birth of the journal, but the explanation lies in Simon's mounting interest in the universities since his close association with the University of Manchester

Introducing

Universities
Quarterly

FIRST NUMBER NOVEMBER 1946

Editorial Board

Aims and Scope

Page Three

6. 'Introducing Universities Quarterly', 1946.

began during the First World War and especially in the years preceding his 1946 initiative. In 1943, for example, he had written a paper on the American universities, had sent a copy to Abraham Flexner and been in correspondence with him.[32] He had written to Cyril Burt for advice on the subject of intelligence quotients (IQ), as part of Simon's drive to use the position at the University of Manchester for a broader national argument.[33] He funded a research study at the University, which shows that half the students had an IQ of 127 or over (equivalent to a fairly good honours degree). Nationally, however, only one-sixth of young people with an IQ at that level ('highly intelligent young persons') were attending a university. It should therefore be possible to double the number of university students capable of such a 'fairly good honours standard'.[34] The researcher at the University was Grace Leybourne-White, who published on the topic and whose work was the basis of the similar argument of the Barlow Committee on *Scientific Man-power* on the reservoir of able potential students who would make it possible to double the number in the universities.[35] Among his many activities, therefore, Simon had become a campaigner for university education, willing to explore and to fund developments – and he was to provide important resources for *Universities Quarterly* including in the early years to employ its own research assistant.

As Chairman of the University of Manchester's council he gave an annual speech from 1941 that also showed his alertness to the public position of the universities. He reviewed Truscot's *Redbrick*, as we have seen, and in 1943 he repeated to council that 'in particular, he [Truscot] points out the way in which more and more facilities are being given to Oxford and Cambridge as against the other universities'. The following year he underlined that 'one of the most important and encouraging movements at the present time is the great and rather sudden development of public interest in the universities, or at least in certain aspects of university education, during the last 12 months'.[36] In a speech to the AUT in 1945 he talked of big developments for the universities, and the fact that there was 'for the first time for a long period a ferment of thought on fundamental university problems'.[37] Even apart from his initiative on the new journal he was particularly involved in 1946. He attended a vice-chancellors' conference, where the discussion, he noted, had been 'futile', simply suggesting that people might do what they were already doing. The conference programme 'totally ignored the Barlow report', and he wrote a note (including to P.M.S. Blackett, Professor of Physics at Manchester) asking whether the AUT and the Association of Scientific Workers should move an emergency resolution, or whether he should do so himself.[38] He wrote an article for *The Times* on 'National need for students', commenting on 'report after report' in the previous two years, demanding 'more scientific research and the production of more high-grade scientists', as well as more students in general.[39] He wrote the piece for *Universities Quarterly* applaud-ing the CVCP's *A Note on University Policy and Finance in the Decennium 1947–56.*

This was the frame of mind in which Simon decided to create the journal. There were doubtless two main reasons why he took the proposal to the Association for Education in Citizenship. The Association had not been particularly concerned with university education, though he had himself included it in his contribution to the 1935 *Training for Citizenship*, which was published with the approval of the Association, and which reflected 'brief surveys ... with regard to the problem in universities and training colleges, and in continued and adult education'. Even university graduates, he com-mented, 'have by no means always the qualities of citizenship'. Specialist university training should in theory be followed by self-education and participation in public affairs, but in the competitive modern world this rarely happens: 'irrelevant learning, of however high a type, does not in itself make a competent citizen', whether the competence be on 'the use of the Greek particle, or in the latest theories of physical science ... great classical students or great scientists are quite capable of combining the best thinking on their own subject with violent prejudice and complete muddle-headedness on public affairs'.[40] In its publicity the Association described its aim as being 'to advance the study of and training in citizenship, by which is meant training in the moral qualities necessary for the citizens of a democracy', including clear thinking in everyday affairs and knowledge of the modern world. It collected information on what was happening in this regard in schools 'and in other educational institutions', and it aimed to co-operate with other bodies (for example, the Historical Association) and to suggest courses and promote discussion at all levels of the educational system in defence of democracy and freedom.[41] Simon would have felt that his new initiative fitted in with the overall aims of the Association. A second reason why Simon chose the Association would have been the composition of its Council. The minutes do not indicate which members were present on the day the proposal for a *Universities Quarterly* was presented, but Simon would have been confident of sufficient support. The President of the Assocation was Sir Henry Hadow, author of a book on *Citizenship* in 1923 and Vice-Chancellor of the University of Sheffield. H.A.L. Fisher and Lord Passfield (Sidney Webb) were among the Vice-Presidents. The 65 Council members included a considerable array of academics, such as Sir Walter Moberly, Harold Laski, G.D.H. Cole, Sir William Beveridge and Barbara Wootton.[42] Another member was Kingsley Martin of the Turnstile Press, publisher of the *New Statesman*, whom Simon approached early in 1946 about the publication of the new journal. Although there was some turbulence in the publishing relationship Turnstile continued to publish *Universities Quarterly*. The journal was owned by the Association until 1950, when it was handed over to the Press (and in the same year a letter from the editor, Charles Morris, mentions Simon's 'further £100 for three years for someone to help with the editorial work')[43]. Simon chaired the editorial board from its inception until 1959.

On several occasions Simon had talks with representatives of the *Universities Review* with a view to a possible amalgamation, but there was agreement on there being room for both. The editorial board of *Universities Quarterly* and early contributors were widely representative of academic life, and many others were involved in discussions with the board or with Simon himself, who kept notes of his discussions with an enormous range of academics and public figures. The journal itself, within the post-war restrictions on paper, managed to produce 2,000 copies of its first issue and to attract 1,700 subscribers. The editorial board minutes, however, indicate how difficult it was from 1948 to maintain the subscription level (in 1952 the minutes record that 'We are still puzzled ... by the indifference of Oxford and Cambridge Colleges, despite publicity').[44] Although the board minutes reflected the difficulty of obtaining articles, in fact the journal contained an impressive range of material. In the first three issues Livingstone published his address on the humanities and sciences, and J.D. Bernal wrote on science and humanism. There were articles on general education (including developments in this field at Harvard and Columbia), universities in the British colonies, the universities and industrial research, and the arts graduate and business. Lord Beveridge wrote on science and the social sciences, and R.A Butler, at the time Minister of Labour, on the study of technology. From the outset the *Quarterly* contained symposia. In addition to general education, the first three volumes contained such groups of articles on university philosophy, engineering, modern languages, the arts, mathematics and statistics, medical education, general science and the social sciences, the tutorial system, 'entry and career' and higher education in the United States. Books on higher education were reviewed. The subjects of articles included the UGC, the University of London, halls of residence, European studies, departments of education and other aspects of the curricula, life and work of the universities, and to some extent also the sixth forms of schools and other related topics. Geoffrey Templeman, medieval historian at Birmingham, wrote on 'The modern universities', mainly about teaching methods, the difficulty of providing tutorial support, the narrowness of departments and studies and the competing demands on lecturers.[45] G.M. Trevelyan, historian and master of Trinity College, Cambridge, wrote on 'The mission of the universities', believing that the universities were 'more important to the nation than ever before', and their scope and area of influence had been extended by the rise of the new universities. Although the university population had increased, it was still too small, and it was essential that professors and lecturers should be able to teach and to be 'scholars and men of learning and research'. For all these reasons, he was:

> extremely anxious that more money should be provided for university expansion. And in my opinion much the greater part of it ought to go to the newer universities which lack the liberal endowments with which private benefactors of old enriched the Oxford and Cambridge Colleges ... London may be big enough in numbers, but it would benefit greatly by residential and social accommodation for its vast army of students. But the other universities and university colleges are, I apprehend, too small even in numbers ... But the large expansion which I should like to see in the newer universities and university colleges must be an expansion of the whole university, especially of its staff, and not merely an expansion of the number of students which by itself would do more harm than good.

Although Trevelyan saw no danger of any government making the universities agents of party propaganda, there were dangers of government interference in the management, student intake and curriculum of the universities. Government subsidy was essential, but so was respect for their independence.[46] This remained an inescapable theme.

POINTERS

The universities were going to change, and so was the conception of a system of higher education. Expansion was inevitable, but there were profound problems of a different kind from those that tormented writers like Nash and Livingstone. The mounting impact of technology and the industrial demand for graduates were to highlight difficulties even more acute than those Ortega and these two writers identified with regard to science in the interpretation of culture. The nature of technology and controversies over its place in higher education were to emerge rapidly as key questions in higher education. They had surfaced in the late nineteenth century as Britain's industrial supremacy began to wane, and as the new redbrick universities shaped their curricula. Technology was on the national agenda as a result of wartime experience and expectations of national needs. The Percy committee, which reported on *Higher Technological Education* in 1945, was clear about the problem:

> The evidence submitted to us concurs in the general view: first, that the position of Great Britain as a leading industrial nation is being

endangered by a failure to secure the fullest possible application of science to industry; and second, that this failure is partly due to deficiencies in education.

The committee explored the types and levels of provision in universities and technical colleges, and suggested ways of organizing 'higher technological education which will be more responsive and adaptable to the needs of industry'. It recommended the inclusion in technological courses of management studies (although the current state of the literature in the component subjects of management was thought by the committee to be poor). It recommended the establishment of a National Council of Technology to represent the colleges of technology, and a new, appropriate qualification, on the title of which the committee failed to degree. Percy himself thought the colleges of technology should be treated as a group, some of which could become university institutions or faculties of technology of a neighbouring university, and graduates of the colleges could become associates or fellows of Royal Colleges of Technology. He thought this would be better than 'premature imitation of University degrees'.[47] There is a continuity in Percy's views from his advocacy of local colleges in his 1930 *Education at the Crossroads*. A National Advisory Council for Education in Industry and Commerce (NACEIC) was established in 1947–48, but it was not until 1955 that the National Council for Technological Awards (NCTA) was created to award 'degree equivalent' qualifications. It was a further decade before these Diploma in Technology qualifications were superseded by those of the Council for National Academic Awards – degrees it awarded to students on the courses it 'validated' in its associated colleges and polytechnics. The controversy continued to focus on whether higher technological studies could be accommodated in universities, should be separated off to the advanced technical colleges, or both. The controversy extended beyond the engineering subjects to all 'vocational' studies – and there were those who believed that vocational subjects generally should be situated in new higher technical education institutions.[48] Those on the other side of the argument pointed to the anomalous positions of medicine and law as vocational subjects in the universities.

The Barlow committee on *Scientific Man-Power* (with a remit that also included technology) reported a year later, proposing that the output of scientific graduates be doubled, with all that this implied for funding, staff recruitment and possible infringement of university independence – and the committee did strongly oppose any such infringement. It did not, however, believe 'that the maintenance of the Universities' independence is in any way incompatible with the extension and improvement of the machinery for adjusting their policy to the needs of the country'.[49] The range of issues therefore firmly under discussion from this point concerned not only the nature and location of higher technological studies, but also the implications of the responses of universities or other higher education to industrial or national needs. Controversy was not absent from discussion amongst scientists and technologists. At the Home Universities Conference in 1949, the opening speaker on 'The place of technological education in university studies' was Sir Lawrence Bragg, who had been a member of the Percy Committee. His view was that 'our higher technological education is on the whole deplorably low in standard'. He thought the future lay in building up 'new centres of higher technical education of University rank, which are masters in their own house', though some branches of technological education could still stay in the universities. The higher technological institutions were needed 'desperately for our country's well-being', and they should have prior claim on whatever the country could afford. Some speakers in the discussion that followed thought that progress had in fact been made since the Percy report, that Bragg was too pessimistic about the standard of higher techno- logical education, that there were strengths – for example in aviation – that rested on a group of modern technologies, that technological education required the scientific training only available in the university, and that the universities (for example Cambridge engineering) were perfectly capable of developing the qualities desirable in a technologist.[50]

Another pointer to prominent future concerns was continued uncertainty about university funding in changing economic circumstances, and the protection of university autonomy. *Universities Quarterly* pointed out that in the couple of years since its foundation in 1946 'interest in the problems of university education has become more widespread, and, if anything, a solution of some of the problems has become more complicated because of the economic situation'.[51] Almost any development that depended on government funding could be seen to be a two-edged sword. The final section of the CVCP's 1946 statement was devoted to examining the proposition that an increase in government funding could mean increased government control, and the prominence given to the topic indicated how profound the concern had become in the universities.[52] To the Barlow committee university independence was 'cherished',[53] and for the moment there were only minor distinctions amongst the expressions of commitment to this independence. A Fabian Society pamphlet on the universities urged not central diktat but sensible planning. This did not mean that universities 'should surrender their independence', or that there was demand from any quarter that they should do so: 'but it would be no surrender of independence if the universities were so to adjust the conduct of their affairs as to meet the requirements of the present situation'.[54] The direction in which higher education might go was, however, uncertain. The limited available funding meant controversy about its distribution. Should priority go to new institutions or to the expansion of existing ones? What was the appropriate size for a university? What priority should be given to student halls of residence? Two views of this period from within universities suggest how far into them the analyses and controversies had reached. In 1947 the head of the drama department at the University of Bristol began an article by mentioning various contributions to these discussions – including Truscot, the AUT and Ortega – and commented that 'already the discussion of the purpose and future of universities begins to have a history'.[55] Two years later the Warden of Crewe Hall, University of Sheffield, began a contribution to a symposium on Moberly's *The Crisis in the University* with a reflection on the main issues – whether the university was primarily concerned with 'teaching and the transmission of culture, or with the advancement of knowledge, or with both'; whether it should devote itself to general education or specialization; and what stand to take on 'moral, religious, and ideological issues'. Ortega was again mentioned, as was 'the controversy about the nature, functions, and duties of the universities, which has been intensified in the last few years'.[56] The discussion was beginning not only to 'have a history', but also to resonate at different levels within the universities.

One war was over, but a different kind of war was a daily threat and cause for protest as well as alarm, in a world – in Livingstone's word – that was 'adrift'. Counting the costs of the recent battlefields, concentration camps and destroyed cities could not be detached easily from the effort of reconstruction. How had it all happened, and why? And where was it leading now? Rebuilding civilization did not mean rebuilding the same one – society and its institutions and services, including education, had to change, but there were new anxieties, uncertainties and enmities. The targets of discussion before, during and after the war were neither obsolete nor irrelevant. Many of the issues concerning administration or other 'domestic' issues of the universities readily crossed over into those about university purposes and values, amid these wider considerations. The world 'adrift' was to become translated by Sir Walter Moberly into *Crisis in the University* in 1949 and the extensive debates it aroused, and also by Eric Ashby's, with a somewhat different message, into *Technology and the Academics* a decade later. From the late 1940s the purpose and future of the universities continued to 'have a history', one of rapidly changing emphases in their dialogue with rapidly changing environments. The bases and importance of this dialogue were most vividly illustrated by Sir Walter Moberly.

NOTES AND REFERENCES

N.B. References in this chapter are also sometimes to archive items from which it has not been possible to establish all details, such as page numbers.

1. Dobrée, B., ' "Arts" faculties in modern universities', *Political Quarterly*, vol. 15, 1944, pp. 341–5, 352).

2. Moberly, W., Address to Home University Conference, London, Association of Commonwealth Universities, 1949, p. 10.

3. Macmurray, J., 'The functions of a university', *Political Quarterly*, vol. 15, 1944, pp. 277–9.

4. Livingstone, R., *Some Thoughts on University Education* (London: Cambridge University Press, 1948), pp. 7, 19.

5. Nash, A.S., *The University and the Modern World: An Essay in the Social Philosophy of University Education* (New York: Macmillan, orig. pub. 1943; 1945 SCM Press edn, London), pp. 14–16, 22–5, 162–74, 184.

6. Nash, A.S., 'The liberal arts college and professional education', *American Scholar Forum*, vol. 13, 1944, pp. 398–400.

7. Moody, T.W. and Beckett, J.C., *Queen's, Belfast 1845–1949* (London: Faber & Faber, 1959), pp. 502, 508.

8. Livingstone, R., *Education for a World Adrift* (Cambridge: Cambridge University Press, 1943), pp. ix–xi.

9. Livingstone, R., *The Future in Education* (London: Cambridge University Press, 1941), pp. 105–6.

10. Dent, H.C., *Education in Transition: A Sociological Study of the Impact of War on English Education 1939–1943* (London: Kegan Paul, Trench, Trubner, 1944), pp. 177–8.

11. Moody and Beckett, *Queen's, Belfast*, p. 502.

12. Livingstone, *Some Thoughts on University Education*, pp. 7, 12–15, 21–3, 28.

13. Livingstone, R., 'A wider outlook', *Universities Quarterly*, vol. 1, 1946–47, p. 248.

14. Simon, J., 'Promoting educational reform on the home front: the *TES* and *The Times* 1940–1944', *History of Education*, vol. 18, p. 202.

15. Clarke, F., *Freedom in the Educative Society* (London: University of London Press, 1948), pp. 16, 44–5, 95–6).

16. Harvard Committee, *General Education in a Free Society* (Cambridge, MA: Harvard University Press, 1945), p. 43.

17. Ortega y Gasset, J., *Mission of the University* (orig. pub. Princeton University Press, 1944; 1992 edn, New Brunswick, NJ: Transaction Publishers), pp. 49–54, 60–70.

18. *Universities Quarterly*, 'The Universities Quarterly and university problems', vol. 3, 1948–49, p. 427–8.

19. R.L.B., 'University pamphlets', *Universities Review*, vol. 19, 1947, p. 121.

20. Nash, *The University and the Modern World*, p. 185.

21. Preston, R.H. General preface, for example. in Baillie, J., *The Mind of the Modern University* (London: SCM Press, 1946), pp. 5–7.

22. Ashby, E., 'A voluntary club', *Times Higher Education Supplement*, 20 October 1989, p. 17.

23. UGC, *University Development. Report on the Years 1947 to 1952* (London: HMSO, 1953), pp. 5–11.

24. Ibid., pp. 7–11.

25. CVCP, 'A Note on University Policy and Finance in the Decennium 1947–56', London, 1946, pp. 1–7, (in MRO, CVCP, UGC box no. 1).

26. Ibid., pp. 14–16.

27. Simon, E., 'Comment', *Universities Quarterly*, vol. 1, 1946–47, pp. 191–2.

28. Bragg, W.L. 'Correspondence', *Universities Quarterly*, vol. 1, 1946–47, p. 308.
29. Pascal, R., 'The vice-chancellors speak up', *Universities Review*, vol. 19, 1947, pp. 123–4.
30. *Introducing Universities Quarterly,* pp. 1–3, SP M11/5/1.
31. Simon, E. and Hubback, E.M., *Training for Citizenship* (London: Oxford University Press, 1935).
32. Letter from Flexner to Simon, 1 September 1943, SP M11/10/4.
33. Letter from Simon, 24 September 1943, and two replies from Burt, in SP M11/1/15. Simon had read an article by Burt in *British Journal of Educational Psychology*, in June 1943.
34. Note by Simon, 26 March 1946, SP M/11/16.
35. A suggested editorial note by Simon for *Universities Quarterly*, 3 December 1946, SP M11/15. Leybourne-White's article, 'The intelligence of university students', reprinted from *Pilot Papers*, March 1947, is in this file.
36. Copies of speeches as Chairman, 17 November 1943, p. 6, and 22 November 1944, p. 1, SP 11/4/46.
37. Notes for speech to AUT on 'The government of Manchester University', 12 March 1945, SP M11/4/5.
38. Copy of note written at universities' conference, and a note on the conference afterwards, September 1946. The only positive thing he heard at the conference was an address by Livingstone on 'The humanities and science', which he thought should be published in *Universities Quarterly*.
39. Simon, E., 'National need for students. Formidable tasks confronting the universities. Responsibility of Grants Committee', *The Times*, 1 August 1946. Cutting in SP 11/4/2.
40. Simon and Hubback, *Training for Citizenship*, 'Preface', and pp. 12–13.
41. Association for Education in Citizenship, leaflet including application form and statement of its 'object' and 'methods'.
42. Ibid., where the list is given in full.
43. Simon to editorial board members, 14 November 1950; Charles Morris to Simon, 17 November 1950, SP M11/5/4.
44. Editorial board minutes, 31 August 1952. The board minutes are in SP M11/5/1.
45. Templeman, G., 'The modern universities', *Universities Quarterly*, vol. 2, pp. 41–7.
46. Trevelyan, G.M., 'The mission of the universities', *Universities Quarterly*, vol. 3, pp. 480–5.
47. Special Committee on Higher Technological Education (Percy Committee), *Report* (London: HMSO, 1945), pp. 5–6, 19–27.
48. See for example, James, E., *An Essay on the Content of Education* (London: Harrap, 1949).
49. Committee appointed by the Lord President of the Council (Barlow Committee), *Scientific Man-Power* (London: HMSO, 1946), pp. 20–1.
50. Bragg, L. 'The place of technological education in university studies', followed by report of discussion, in Home Universities Conference, *Report of Proceedings 1949* (London: Association of Commonwealth Universities) pp. 72–97.
51. *Universities Quarterly*, vol. 3, 1948–49, p. 427.
52. MRO, CVCP, UGC box no. 1, pp. 14–16.
53. Barlow Committee, p. 21.
54. 'Quintus', *Universities and the Future. A Report Prepared for the Education Committee of the Fabian Society* (London: Fabian Society, 1947), pp. 7, 21–3.
55. Taig, T., 'One-Year Plan', *Universities Review*, September 1947, p. 34.
56. Adams, J., 'Aims and methods', *Universities Quarterly*, vol. 4, 1949, p. 59.

6

MOBERLY: 'THE *STATUS QUO* AND ITS DEFECTS'

Bruce Truscot's had been a sharp, unexpected wartime voice. Sir Walter Moberly's, only six years after *Redbrick*, was of a very different kind, speaking from a quarter of a century of public visibility, heading two institutions and the UGC. Truscot, in the war, was highly focused on the university. Moberly – critics suggested – confused the crisis of the university with the world crisis. What he undoubtedly did was bring the range of earlier experience and extensive discussion into the landscape of *The Crisis in the University*. He published the book in 1949, the year he left the UGC. Although it incorporated ideas that he had elaborated before, it went a great deal further and amounted to a full-scale account of the ideas that underpinned the history and present dilemmas of the universities. It was the first important twentieth-century philosophy of university education, embodying his advocacy of the university and of its transformation to respond to the values and needs resulting from the dangers and dilemmas of the times. Before contemplating the causes of present discontents he elaborated a three-phased history of the universities:

> We had the Classical-Christian university, which was later displaced by the Liberal university. This in turn has been undermined but not as yet superseded, by the combined influence of democratisation and technical achievement. What we have, in fact to-day is the chaotic university.[1]

'The chaotic university' is at least as expressive of Moberly's intentions as 'crisis'. In relation to the latter he had to determine with some difficulty the relationship between crisis inside the university and other kinds of crisis – including world crisis, the crisis of democracy, intellectual crisis and the crisis of belief and faith. All were related, but ultimately what he was compiling was a set of arguments with which to begin resolving the deficiencies of the universities, overcoming 'chaos' through the agency of 'a community of Christians'. Moberly was well aware, as a former Oxford student, lecturer in philosophy at Aberdeen and Oxford, Professor at Birmingham, Principal of the College of the South West, Exeter, Vice-Chancellor of the University of Manchester and from 1935 chairman of the University Grants Committee, of the strengths and weaknesses of the university. As a founder and core member of the Christian Frontier Council and the Moot he sharpened his views in association with groups of academics and others who shared his concerns about the university, education and society – including Clarke and Mannheim, T.S. Eliot and the Christian authors of the 12 'University reports' published by the SCM.

Moberly attended a conference convened by the Christian Frontier Council and the SCM in September 1946, and he gave the opening address on 'From Newman to the pamphlets!' The SCM had two years earlier set up a commission to explore is future role, and the Christian Frontier Council had been engaged in discussions that addressed university issues. The 1946 conference was seen as continuing this engagement with the future of the university, and it agreed that a book embodying the kinds of ideas discussed there was needed. It was to deal, for example, with the university's function as a cultural agent, its failures, its anti-Christian (not its neutral) structures, and it would be for staff, students and the public 'on the function, the aims and the defects of the contemporary University'. One person should write it, but the way forward was left to a group of six people, including Moberly and Professor Roy Niblett, of the University of London Institute of Education.[2] Moberly acknowledged discussion of the pamphlets by the conference, which agreed in general the diagnosis and policies. It was felt that

> owing to the confusion of purpose which they share with the modern world, universities are at present crippled in performing their most important function; that Christians have a vital contribution to make, though much work remains to be done by them before that can be clearly formulated or become effective.

The writing of the book was deputed to him, and 'the committee approved my synopsis, saw the book in draft, and made useful criticisms and suggestions'.[3]

His 'rehearsals' for the task date back to his time as student and teacher of philosophy – with a focus on the philosophy of religion – and as Vice-Chancellor of the University of Manchester, where many of the threads of the arguments he was to weave into the book were first made public. His period at Manchester began in 1926 and he spoke frequently in the University and in the city. An early engagement was to address a Classical Association meeting in the city on 'The ideals of citizenship'. He was reported as saying that 'thinking about civic ideals without reference to the experience and literature of Greece was like trying to think about religious problems without reference to the experience and literature of the Hebrews'.[4] In 1929 he addressed a conference on 'The present position of adult education', complaining that, although there were some 100,000 students engaged in adult education in some form, only 1 per cent of education budgets went to adult education.[5] In 1930–31 he had an exchange of correspondence with Abraham Flexner, whose analysis of the English universities Moberly read and commented on: 'it is proving a most valuable and exciting stimulus of thought'.[6]

Throughout his eight years at Manchester he was actively and publicly promoting the University and higher education. The historian of his period at the University explained that for anyone who had worked there when Moberly was Vice-Chancellor 'it is impossible not to realize to what a wide extent his influence here was incontestably of high, and indeed of unique, value', but it was also impossible not to criticize 'some implications of his academic ideals'. He had come to the University with 'a passionate conviction that a university's function is to render its unique service to the highest interests of humanity'. His ideals and those of the University were formulated differently: it was when 'the spirit seeks to formulate itself in creed that the dissidence appears'.[7] Moberly had clear and public views regarding the ways in which the spirit of a university should enter into practice. When he wrote to his colleagues in August 1934 announcing that he would be leaving at the end of the calendar year, he explained that the offer of the Chairmanship of the UGC had come as a surprise, but that he had decided it was 'a call I cannot rightly refuse'. He had not intended to leave Manchester but 'I have had a growing conviction through these last weeks that there is a work to be done at the Grant Committee of great importance to the British Universities generally and that it is my business to try to do it'. Not to accept would mean 'neglecting a public duty'.[8]

The views Moberly held by this time were expressed forthrightly in a speech he gave at a farewell dinner in December 1934. He pointed to the virtues and dangers of a 'provincial' university like Manchester, but was more critical of academic coteries which had their 'esoteric standards' and were ignorant and contemptuous of all that lay outside – theirs was a greater 'provincialism'. He approved the mixed form of university governance, part of its strength deriving from the useful contacts through the Court with the life of the area. Oxford and Cambridge were 'practically self-governing guilds of teachers, but I am not a Guild Socialist'. The heavy demands of committee work on the time of professors were becoming intolerable, and 'incompatible with any considerable research work, at least during term time'. The solution lay in a greater willingness to devolve responsibilities. Having selected some of these key points in his experience of the operation of the University, he went on, unusually in the circumstances of a farewell dinner, to spell out his 'academic ideals' – presaging the views he was to develop in the 1940s. He began with a criticism:

> ... the principal test of any University is the effect it has on the mass of the students who pass through it. And here, I think, none of us are quite satisfied. Most of our graduates go out into the world well qualified technically in the particular subject in which they have taken their degrees. But when we ask 'are they, as a result of their university life, specially qualified for posts of responsibility or for intelligent citizenship'? we cannot feel so confident. Here the University's educational success is less assured.

Part of the problem lay, in a university like Manchester, with such difficulties as the lack of personal contact amongst students and between them and staff, and student union 'aloofness' towards the University authorities. But he then broached the topic that was to dominate his future statements about higher education. What he called 'the most dangerous ground of all' was his experience of modern universities where he had been 'painfully conscious of a hiatus'. The older universities had developed when there were 'common convictions about the nature of man and the universe', reflected in their faculty of theology and the ceremonies that testified to their religious basis. The modern universities, however, reflected

> the uncertainty and the disunity of the modern world as a whole in regard to ultimate convictions. They were often founded in conscious reaction against the narrowness and exclusiveness, the jealously maintained sectarian privilege, the dogmatically closed mind, which the older universities maintained through so much of the nineteenth century. They have rightly insisted that creed should be no barrier either to student or to teacher ... But as a result they have largely declined to treat all of those themes about which men care most passionately.

The conclusions that followed were to remain central to his future view of the university:

> [A] man's basic philosophy of life is the most important thing about him ... students are in fact much occupied in the effort to find one. They are

canvassing the social, moral and religious traditions in which they have
been brought up ... if all we have to oppose to them is the shirking of
all questions of ultimate belief as difficult and dangerous, the future
will be with them and not with us ... in any university, a student might
reasonably hope to be able to hear a considerable number of teachers
thinking aloud on such topics and giving to them the same sort of
quantity and quality of attention that they give to other subjects ... In
all controversial subjects students will listen with respect, and will
derive benefit from listening, to reasoned discussion by mature and
trained minds.

Moberly apologized to his audience for 'intruding' his personal views on
them, but he felt obliged to 'tell you without reserve what I really think' in
saying farewell to 'a great university in the making'.[9]

He had found a confident, personal voice in which to propound a philosophy
of higher education. In 1940 he presented his paper to the Moot and in 1944
he gave a presidential address to the Classical Association on 'Plato's conception of education and its meaning for to-day'. In the latter he discussed the
importance of having a philosophy of life, the universities' abdication of their
responsibility for introducing students to issues of values, the qualities of
leadership and the Christian tradition[10] – all of which hark back to his
Manchester farewell speech. In 1948, probably at the same time as finalizing
The Crisis, he gave an address to a Congress of the Universities of the British
Commonwealth on 'Relations of the state and the universities', and the views
he expressed there on university autonomy and the implications of increasing
state support, as well as keeping alive moral and spiritual values ('one of the
vital functions of Universities') resurfaced in his book.[11] Moberly's Moot
paper, 'The universities', began historically, considering 'the traditional
humanist ideal', focusing on Newman and Oxford and Cambridge, with their
residential communities and 'liberal' studies, though even in the nineteenth
century their religion was 'much diluted'. The Scottish universities were 'less
unlike those of the Continent than are Oxford and Cambridge', and the modern
universities were a 'conscious revulsion' against Oxford and Cambridge 'as
the homes at once of religious tests, of fleshpots and sinecures, of dead
languages and lost causes'. At the modern universities, urban and local, non-
residential and concentrating on lectures, students tended to see the degree as
the route to a job, and their attitude to work was 'illiberal', with 'only time
for a breathless scamper over the recognised course'. Traditional classical
humanism did not seem to link with or illuminate 'the actual industrial world'.
The modern universities had other weaknesses. Their corporate life was weak,
and they had failed to answer such fundamental questions as 'What is Man?
What is the nature of the Universe? How is life to be lived?' The universities

7. Sir Walter Moberly speaking on the television programme 'Viewpoint' about changes in the Church in his lifetime. (Courtesy of Sir John Moberly.)

in general had an aversion to religious or political controversy and many teachers denied that it was part of their duty to touch on such themes. Students saw their teachers as living in a 'vanished world'. The university 'confesses itself unable to contribute anything to the acquisition by its students of a philosophy of life or to the formation in them of an ethos or way of living'. Moberly's examples in this critique were ones that he was later to use in other places:

If you want a bomb the chemistry department will teach you how to make it, if you want a cathedral the department of architecture will teach you how to build it, if you want to keep your body in health the physiological and medical departments will teach you how to do so. But if you ask whether and why you should want bombs or cathedrals or healthy bodies the university is content to be dumb and impotent.[12]

One of his themes in criticizing the university in this respect surfaced when he introduced his own and Löwe's papers at the meeting of the Moot, when he again rejected the idea of the .'neutrality' of modern universities as 'really an abdication' in trying to 'protect' students against dangerous views. At a later meeting he suggested that going from school to university meant being transformed from adolescent to adult status, and 'he did not want anything that would keep people in a younger or more juvenile status',[13] a view that also re-emerged in *The Crisis*. Moberly was expressing his view of students' adult status more than a quarter of a century before the age of majority was lowered to 18. In his paper, turning to religion, he further castigated the supposed 'neutrality' of the modern university. It was not neutral: 'if you omit religion and ethics from your educational system, you do not teach nothing concerning them, you teach that they are to be omitted'. Such an abdication may have been relatively harmless in a more stable age, but in this end of an era 'such complacency is ungrounded'. From this beginning he developed an argument for the universities to lead the community in promoting a movement towards a 'Christian Britain' (his quotation marks), but he did not address the detail as he was to do later. He saw the advantages to the modern universities of their urban community setting, but they were still 'poor relations' and needed to find ways of developing their corporate life. He was not convinced there was a case for any considerable increase in student numbers, as the road to the secondary school would first need to be widened. The pressing demands for vocational studies and specialists raised the question of whether it was for the universities to provide them – though they had always provided vocational training for parsons, lawyers and doctors, and in the nineteenth century men of affairs, civil servants and others. Was not the humanist ideal 'essentially based on privilege'? The solution. in seeking a 'new humanism', lay in a strategy that we have already seen to be central to the thinking of Moberly and his colleagues concerned with the position of Christianity in the university. The strategy did not involve government pressure or (mainly) public agitation but 'the conversion, in the first instance, of small groups of the abler teachers in the various universities. They have to be convinced of the reality and nature of the crisis and of the role which the universities might play.'[14] Moberly had here mapped out the essentials of the book that was to point towards the kind of leadership in the academic community that he advocated.

MANY HANDS

Moberly missed few meetings of the Moot, and from February 1942 he was also actively engaged in the Christian Frontier Council, which was created as a result of discussions in the Moot, and which was directed 'towards Christian ends by means outside ecclesiastical organization'.[15] The Moot was less completely targeted on Christian ends, although in its discussions of values, purposes and policies non-Christians could take very similar standpoints: it was 'predominantly but not exclusively Christian'.[16] The voices heard at the Moot spoke with varying degrees of radicalism. One of the most controversial contributions on education was a paper by H.C. Dent, discussed at a meeting in 1942, where his 'Reform in education' paper began:

> This an age of revolution. Only revolutionary conceptions translated into revolutionary methods can meet its challenge … Our present systems of education (there are at least two …) are highly undemocratic … their basic philosophy is that not of a democratic, but of an acquisitive and competitive society, in which the prizes are privilege, power, and the well-filled purse … We must entirely rethink our conception of the educational process in terms of the needs of a democratic society.

He proposed that university education and higher technological training should be transferred to adult education.[17] Moberly did not agree that the acquisitive spirit was 'embodied in the whole system', and was opposed to the proposal 'to scrap the system and start afresh'. Fred Clarke's response was similar: you could not 'recreate education from top to bottom as a step to making a new society … history did not work like that'.[18] In the discussion on adult education Moberly felt that the 'spiritual impetus' of the earlier adult education movement had been lost, and the Workers Educational Association and the university tutorial system had become 'conservative institutions'.[19] He obviously attached much importance to his participation in such discussions, and not even his duties as Chairman of the UGC kept him away from them, or from following his convictions elsewhere. At the joint Commission of the SCM and the Christian Frontier Council that began to meet in 1944 he heard papers on the future tasks of the universities. He will therefore have been aware of the active part being played by the SCM, which discussed 'The philosophy of the university' at a meeting in 1944, on the basis of a paper which saw university life as fundamentally sound, but 'our interest however is the spirit of University education'.[20] The SCM had a series of regional secretaries whose reports reflected both attitudes amongst university students and the concerns of the SCM itself. The Midlands area report for 1945, for example, explained that 'the modern universities in the Midlands reflect very clearly the prevailing materialism of the age and the absence of any universally accepted beliefs about the purpose of life'.[21]

The SCM was also closely in touch with the trends of Christian and other opinion on the universities represented by the writers we have discussed. In 1944, the letter convening the commission of which Moberly was a member explained that 'the whole question of the future of the University is to the fore at the moment', and referred to the books by Truscot, Brian Simon, Löwe, Clarke, Paton and Nash (the last of which was shortly to be published by the SCM Press), as well as articles by Nash and Niblett. Various university bodies, including the AUT and the NUS were 'considering the post-war situation'. Reflecting views contained in much of this work, and the series of pamphlets published by the SCM, the letter indicated that:

> We in the S.C.M. have been feeling for some time that it is necessary to re-think the basis of the liberal university and the place of the S.C.M. in it ... In short, we feel that the S.C.M. has tended to be a movement at work in the university because it finds there a number of people to whom the Gospel ought to be preached, but that it has not done much towards understanding the purpose of God for the university as such, or what it means to be a <u>Christian</u> student.[22]

After the war the SCM published a *Memorandum on the Student Christian Movement and Education*, reviewing university and college education. It suggested that 'perhaps an ideal university ... should have a threefold function – to educate – to search for truth – to be a centre of "light and learning" to the community in which it stands'. It saw a role for the university in the service of democracy, including through adult education. It quoted a passage from A.E. Zimmern, wondering whether the universities had understood their task of 'interpretation' and 'mediation' and whether that was possible 'until their personnel has been largely humanised and enriched, and their range of interest and study extended and broadened? ... Will war ... send a refreshing breeze through the cloisters and council-rooms of our academies?'[23]

When the joint commission had done its work and the joint conference with the CFC had been held in 1946, the SCM also held a study conference that looked at the issues concerning the Christian in the university, as a preliminary to a larger conference the following year. A study syllabus was drawn up 'by many hands', containing a series of study themes, each with a bibliography containing the kinds of works we have considered (from Newman in the nineteenth century to Herklots and Flexner onwards in the twentieth), as well as a wider literature covering questions of values, science and society. The themes covered the contemporary university: 'the modern university has disintegrated ... there is no community of knowledge'; its history: 'a materialistic philosophy based on scientific achievement has taken the place of a philosophy of life based on religion'; the 'idea of a university man':

> the university has always tended to reflect the society and culture in which it exists ... the chief difference about our present situation is that the University does not reflect any one society or any one culture. What it reflects is rather the disintegration of both society and culture ... The University man should ... be a leader as well as a servant of society.

The next steps would include locating staff and students who would 'act as a leaven in the University lump'.[24] The 'many hands' were also aware of many voices, and the formulations of Löwe and Nash, Moberly and Ortega and the University Pamphlet writers echo around these passages.

PLATO AND PUBLIC OPINION

Moberly gave his presidential address on 'Plato's conception of education and its meaning for to-day' to the Classical Association in 1944, the year that Livingstone gave a Rede Lecture at Cambridge on 'Plato and modern education'. There is no obvious direct connection between the two, though from before the war there had been some controversy about Plato as liberal or as autocrat, even neo-Nazi. R.H.S. Crossman had triggered some of the discussion in 1937 with *Plato To-day*, which underlined Plato's adherence to a caste system and the training of a reactionary elite. Livingstone, relating Plato to the needs of 'modern education', and Moberly considering those of 'to-day', both appealed to and defended Plato's approach to education – in troubled times that matched those of wartime Europe. The deductions, even for two Christians, were not entirely the same, but both found in Plato a summons to tackle a fundamental human problem.

Livingstone's formulation of the Platonic question was: 'What should men believe about life, how should they live it, in what state of society can the good life be best lived, how can we create such a state?' The system was stagnating, 'indispensable' applied science was needed in education, and the main danger lay in the absence of values, belief and philosophy. The universities were failing to provide a very adequate aim and to equip their students for life: 'everyone needs a philosophy of life, a sense of values by which to judge and use the gifts of material civilization ... a hierarchy of values'. Universities made no provision for training not just the chemist, engineer or economist, but also the human being. The 'Idea of Physics, or the Idea of Economics, or the Idea of Exact Scholarship' were the crown of university education, and though they were important 'they do not exhaust human excellence'. Progress could be made in steps: achieving a clear view of 'what human beings should be', providing some study of religion or moral philosophy, and ensuring that all teaching paid 'as much attention to values as to facts'. Plato, a master of diagnosis, could not cure: 'if he did not solve a problem, he always knew what it was'. In education, 'most of his suggestions are perfectly practical'. His doctrine of 'training to goodness' was the means of answering such questions as 'what should men believe about life?' and 'how should they live it?'[25]

In his discussion of Plato Moberly's Christianity was more explicit. He ended his address in fact by affirming that Platonist and Christian could unite on one fundamental principle: 'Without vision there can be no sound educational policy', but his steps to this finale were unlike Livingstone's. Moberly's argument began with an outline of 'the articles of Plato's educational creed' – including education as the most fundamental of activities and a general education as its most important feature. A 'true' philosophy of life was a gap education needed to fill. All of this fed into Moberly's scheme of things: 'an educational system which is not based on some philosophy of life, held with clarity and conviction, is a contradiction in terms ... Have we nothing to offer beyond a vague hodgepodge of conventional morality, slightly tinged with religious sentiment?' He illustrated his view with the argument he had used in 1940: a university trained a student to be a chemist or a linguist, but not to judge good from bad; to make a bomb or a cathedral but staying 'dumb and impotent' on why you should want such a thing. This was 'abdication'. Plato's elements of 'the good life', a hierarchy of values, contrasted with the reality of life in Plato's day and in Moberly's:

> To-day the cinema, the street, the Sunday newspaper, the cheap novelette, sometimes the home, are, tacitly but effectively, spreading the cult of the trivial, shoddy and second-rate. Against them the schools fight an unequal battle until the children reach the age of fourteen. After that, during the most formative years, they have till now been in no position to fight any battle at all.

Moberly found most of the criticisms of Plato as 'the first Fascist' misleading. This was the Moberly of the Moot and the Christian Frontier Council, having accepted the argument of planning for freedom. Any critic of Plato and a planned educational system, deprecating its interference with individual liberty, had to answer the question: 'What is the alternative?' Children did not have liberty, being 'shaped all the time by outside influences'. The real choice was 'not between interference and non-interference but between responsible and irresponsible interference'. From such starting points Moberly made explicit the Christian implications of his interpretation of Plato. He was consistently to maintain, as did others in the forums in which he worked, that 'there will always be need for a leaven; that is, for a group of persons within the educational system with a clearer philosophy and a stronger conviction than the average'. In their role of permeation Christians and Platonists would also be united by a common principle: 'Without vision there can be no sound educational policy.'[26]

At the Classical Association, as earlier, Moberly was speaking as to colleagues in a fraternity, clarifying, appealing for the formation of the 'leaven' that he saw as the most vital and credible way forward in difficult times. He was still choosing the audiences he wished to influence on this journey, with a message and a search he had begun seriously to define long before the war.

THE STATE AND THE UNIVERSITIES

Not surprisingly, given his career, Moberly saw increasing state involvement with the universities as an important component of the domestic and inter-national crisis he perceived. In 1948 he made other contributions to the debate about the universities and the state. He gave a Rede lecture at Cambridge, which served as a public dress rehearsal for the book that he had probably already finalized, and the lecture in fact reappeared centrally in one of its chapters. He gave an introductory address to a Commonwealth Universities conference. His years at the UGC had familiarized him with the growing relationship, especially after the war, between the universities and national policy formulation, including the reliance of government and its agencies on data from investigations by commissions and the UGC's own resources. The year 1948 also saw the publication by the UGC of *University Development from 1935 to 1947*, which reflected, among other things, the calculations underpinning arguments about university expansion. The report quoted the Barlow committee's conclusion, based 'largely on the evidence of certain intelligence in the country to allow university numbers to be doubled and standards to be raised concurrently'. The UGC pointed out, however, that the vice-chancellors, taking 'a more cautious view of the possibilities, considered that more investigation was needed before any firm conclusion could be reached'.[27] Moberly inclined to the vice-chancellors' view, fearing that too rapid an expansion would mean a serious lowering of quality.[28]

It is difficult to see in general terms to what extent Moberly influenced the UGC or was influenced by it. He held firm views in his UGC role on specific issues, such as student numbers. He supported A.D. Lindsay in his proposal to establish the University College of North Staffordshire, and he was engaged for two years at the UGC in the consideration of its application for acceptance. The UGC's 1948 report, the last under Moberly's chairmanship, welcomed the University College as an experiment. His views about the relationship between state needs and university autonomy helped to guide the UGC in its dealings with the institutions collectively and individually – Dent speaks of Moberly's 'wise and kindly leadership'[29] and the UGC, four years after Moberly had left, reflected on 'the wisdom and insight which he displayed in the conduct of our business during that critical period'.[30] Roy Niblett, who was a member of the UGC, described Moberly as 'one of the most influential figures of his time', and under his chairmanship the monthly meetings of the UGC 'could spend the whole of the morning session discussing broad issues of purpose and policy, leaving mere money matters to the afternoon!'[31] Many of the judgments and formulations of the UGC were at least guided by him, including those on student accommodation and research. The 1948 UGC report, as we have seen, echoed analyses he had made and was to repeat in his book: the report contrasted, for example, the 'traditional form of cultural education at the older universities' with the 'vocational function' of the newer universities, and argued for some form of synthesis of the two.[32] Perhaps Moberly's presence is most felt in this report, in the breadth of the issues it was prepared to discuss.

In relation to the role of the state, Moberly was committed to inevitably growing state funding, the important role of the UGC and the invaluable autonomy of the universities. In his 1949 address on 'Relations of the state and the universities' he emphasized that in no country could 'the supreme political authority be completely disinterested in the affairs of the Universities', given that they were powerful and publicly important bodies. A limited measure of supervision was necessary: although autonomy could not be 'absolute or unconditional' a high degree of autonomy was vital. Anything that threatened the autonomy of universities had to be resisted – whether it be political interference, 'tidy-minded administration' or demands for standardization or for 'some quick and tangible returns'. The greatest danger was possible state interference through 'conditions connected with State subsidies'. State support for the universities had risen to about one-third of their income between the wars, and had risen further since. By 1952 state grants would total about six times what they were in 1938. It was the role of the UGC to ensure that funds were 'wisely and effectively' used, but also that the 'responsible independence of the Universities' was not sacrificed.[33] Responding to the discussion that followed this address, he agreed that the universities needed to help the world to understand the transformations taking place. There was a relationship between universities' difficulties and public perception and opinion: 'in democratic countries we cannot work except in touch with public opinion, and, if University autonomy is to be respected, public opinion must come to value it'.[34] In this presentation Moberly did not go much beyond assertions about the status quo, but in the late 1940s there were no other analysts who saw any further through the mists surrounding the universities.

Opinion about the universities was changing, as educational opportunity in general was becoming a stronger focus of post-war public attention. Moberly began his 1948 Rede lecture on 'Universities and the state' (reported fully in the *Times Educational Supplement*) by pointing out that public interest in the universities had increased: 'public opinion was inclined to do more for them and to expect more from them than it used to do'. He repeated the arguments for autonomy and academic freedom ('if you were engaging Toscanini and his orchestra you would do well to leave to him the major voice in deciding the programme'). There were aspects of academic life best left to the universities: regimentation had an unfavourable impact on creative thinking – 'the highest task of the university'. Society needed the university not only as 'agent' but also as 'mentor', a role that required a certain independence and the absence of political interference. In this lecture as elsewhere Moberly presented a case against 'complete autonomy', more precisely than in his conference address:

> [T]he British universities were not State universities; but the nation could not regard them simply as private and voluntary societies, free without question to make their own rules, to go their own way ... In certain, highly important, respects at least they were national institutions; they powerfully affected national life at a hundred points and were vital to its well-being. They depended increasingly on the financial support of the Treasury, and they recognized obligations not only to this or that section but to the whole community. Hence the State as 'the operative criticism of institutions' had a certain responsibility for keeping universities up to the mark.

There had to be an important degree of acceptance by each side of the other, with statesmen and higher civil servants 'warmly sharing in that "scrupulous respect and fond and fervid affection" for the universities which Gladstone ascribed to the whole community. On their side the university authorities in recent years had had a keen sense of duty to the nation.' They had even invited government and its representatives to give them guidance on public needs, notably specialized manpower. This relationship was particularly important since it was necessary to extend 'the tacit understanding that had hitherto existed between the universities and the governing class ... to a much wider public', given the process of widening access to the universities. Moberly could not miss this opportunity to define again the overwhelming challenge that faced university and society alike: unless civilization was to collapse amidst the uncertainties, 'some new integration of effective belief must soon be achieved which could issue in a new community of purpose. To-day that was the problem which dwarfed all others.' Would the universities be able to act as 'pioneers in this most vital of reconstructions', or would they simply reflect the confusion and convulsions of the world at large?[35]

THE CRISIS

The Crisis in the Universities contained four main categories of argument: the nature of the universities' crisis; particular problems of the work of the universities; external relationships; remedies to the problems. The first of these, the crisis, was historical and contemporary. The 'Christian–Hellenic' university and the 'Liberal' university that had replaced it in the nineteenth century were now under pressure from the 'technological–democratic' or 'scientific– utilitarian'. The rise and dominance of applied science and the emergence of an ever-growing constituency of students had brought powerful elements of a new culture to the universities. The universities reflected the world crisis, the result of two world wars and the threat of the atomic bomb. Whatever was planned or done in the years ahead would be done 'in the imminent peril of world-wide disaster ... this physical insecurity is matched by a moral and spiritual insecurity ... the generation which has acquired these stupendous powers of destruction is full of fear and suspicion'. The world had witnessed 'bestial cruelty, lust and lawlessness, not only as an occasional morbid aberration, but rampant and in power. The veneer of civilization has proved to be amazingly thin.' Over large parts of the world binding convictions had been lost and 'there is confusion, bewilderment and discord ... the cake of custom is broken, the old gods are dethroned and none have taken their places'.[36] The war had also 'produced in the public mind a more lively and sympathetic interest in the universities', and in the universities themselves there was 'a new sense of expectancy'. However, the university was 'a Babel'. There is no common means of intercourse because the different sections dwell in different intellectual worlds. On the main questions ('What are universities for? What effect should they have on their alumni? What are their responsibilities to the outside world?') some university teachers gave 'discordant answers', some none at all. The universities' realities did not match up to their professed ideals, and there was a disastrous taboo on dealing with contentious political and religious questions. Moberly devoted some of his strongest passages to the universities' fragmentation and their abandonment of their students. Their traditional role had been to train students for leadership in a stratified society. This was no longer believed in, but no other accepted ideal had taken its place.[37]

Second, Moberly related the work of the universities to these broad failures and silences. Would they be able to adapt to the insecurities? This question became translated into ones that included leadership and community identity. The universities needed to address these questions in broad and detailed terms. The implications of specialization had to be confronted. Oxford and Cambridge were producing First Class graduates who went for employment, say to the Ministry of Agriculture or the Board of Trade, with neither practical experience nor theoretical training in farming or commerce. The redbrick universities trained the student for competence in particular employments, but with little education that had looked 'to his life as a responsible human being and a citizen'. Arts and science lived in their own separate intellectual worlds. The focus was examinations and curricula were overloaded. The redbrick universities already contained more than half of the British student population, but these universities were still often looked upon as poor relations, and were in fact poor, though opportunities probably lay ahead. Improvements in corporate life were possible, but they would not slavishly follow the 'aristocratic traditions' of the old universities.[38]

Third, as in his Rede lecture and elsewhere, Moberly articulated the possible implications of increased state financial support. The universities needed guidance, accountability and freedom from government control. He rejected the arguments for and against 'complete' autonomy as a false antithesis. As Nash and others had done he accepted the case for university planning, and a quicker response to urgent social needs. All the partners involved had to be increasingly aware of the true purpose of universities and of the conditions in which they could do their best work. To be useful to the local community the universities needed a large measure of autonomy, and the universities had to help the community to understand the reasons. As in his farewell speech at Manchester, Moberly admitted that the university's position in the local community could mean parochialism and other dangers – including insufficient variety in the student body and the 'uninspiring physical setting' of an industrial city. But there were important compensations, including the development of appropriate curricula and the availability of the resources of the city, including relations with the schools and the development of adult education.[39]

Finally, having set out his historical typology of universities, he also set out what he called a series of 'spurious remedies'. 'Scientific humanism' was one such remedy, which he could respect but which he firmly rejected. A return to 'classical humanism' he also rejected as discredited, too identified with a society based on privilege, from an era before people had 'awoken to the unsatisfied demands of social justice'. In that era the university had been too exclusively 'engaged in producing cultivated gentlemen'. Although invaluable lessons could be learned 'from the classical strain in our cultural tradition, as a complete philosophy of life on which to base university education it was 'too rarefied, too naïve, too static and, in a sense, too parasitic'. Was a third remedy to urge universities to return to the 'explicitly Christian basis' of the older European universities? Appealing though this might be, it was impracticable, inequitable, destined to be a sham and for a variety of reasons 'defective'. Moberly therefore knew that there were no easy solutions. The universities could at least adopt a form of 'positive neutrality', actively promoting discussion of the burning questions, and the authorities could monitor the extent to which their institutions were promoting 'a convincing philosophy of life'. This was more a question of different parts of the university engaging in a common task and developing a sense of fellowship than one of formulating 'a theoretical common minimum'. Within the nation and internationally there were already common principles, containing a significant Christian element, shared by the universities and on which they could build, particularly through what he and others had called the 'leaven', a creative minority who could turn a neutral society into a Christian one. The thoughtful Christians in the universities needed to identify one another, come together, undertake common action and enter into dialogue with other groups with different philosophies of life, and persuade universities that 'all inhibition of discussion of the burning questions of the day must be removed, for any attitude towards them is preferable to apathy and drift'.[40] *The Crisis* was an extended, affirmative expression of all the issues, directions and dangers that Moberly had considered in all the contexts in which he had been engaged.

'THE KEENEST ATTENTION'

The impact of Moberly's book was different from that of *Redbrick University*. The universities, unlike in 1943, were engaged in the turmoil of actual and projected expansion, the present and expected cross-currents of post-war uncertainties and aspirations. The universities had to confront the changes and policies directed at social renewal, and vocal constituencies were emerging to advocate the new or defend the old. The *Universities Quarterly*, introducing a series of articles on Moberly's book, explained that the 'deep interest' in the book showed that 'in university circles at least, the storm, if storm it is, did not come altogether out of a clear sky. If there had been any complacency, it was clearly only superficial. Underneath there was much debate – and much difference of opinion'.[41] Academic reviewers broadly welcomed the book enthusiastically, though with varying degrees of scepticism about some aspects of its underlying thesis. Inevitably it was the Christian message that caused most hesitation, but even those who disagreed with it mainly treated the direction of the argument with respect. From Moberly's involvement with the Christian organizations that had given rise to the book, wrote a Professor of Classics at University College, Swansea, Moberly had 'emerged with a clear and matured opinion', and he had as a result written 'a frank, even a hard-hitting, but sensitive and scrupulously fair book. It will be carefully read and will do much good.' Senate and faculty members would recognize Moberly's 'chaotic university' in their experience and their deliberations would be 'deepened and helped' by his discussion. Despite the weakness of his Christian case 'he is both uncompromising and reasonable'.[42] Another reviewer thought that of the large number of recent books and reports Moberly's analysis went 'deeper than most of them', providing no solutions but his argument could not be ignored or 'lightly rejected – or lightly accepted'. At least he had shown what the problems involved. 'This is, in all senses, a big book', wrote one reviewer, 'and the only way to arrive at a true impression of it is by careful reading and discussion'.[43]

The way *The Crisis* was received is clear from the group of articles published by the *Universities Quarterly*. The journal's first editorial response was to describe it as the first 'since Newman's to deal with the philosophy of university education'. There had been 'the widest publicity' for the Harvard report on *General Education in a Free Society*: the Americans were well ahead in the discussion of the vital problems and it was to be hoped that Moberly's book would lead to 'fresh and vigorous thinking on the fundamentals of university education'.[44] Introducing the discussion in the next issue it described the 'crisis' as having blown up suddenly, since they had seemed to be enjoying 'the sunshine of public favour ... yet now the "crisis" in the universities is given the keenest attention in the public press'.[45] Lord Simon, offering a 'consumer's view', welcomed the book as from 'probably the greatest living authority on the varied aspects of university work and life in this country', and raising problems of fundamental importance. Simon saw the crisis, however, as one of the Western democracies rather than of the universities. The minor post-war crises of the universities (staffing, accommodation ...) were being dealt with and overcome. The last five years had seen increased government grants, and the universities were carrying out the responsibilities that the country laid on them: 'it is nonsense to talk about a "crisis in the universities", at least in any ordinary meaning of the words'. He did not agree that the moral crisis of the democracies meant that more should be done to help students discover basic principles – the universities were already producing graduates 'who render great services to democracy in the field of public affairs' and whose abilities and integrity had never been equalled. From more than 30 years of involvement with the University of Manchester he based his argument substantially on his admiration for the University, its staff and its students.[46] Roy Pascal, Professor of German at

Birmingham, discussing 'The universities and social purpose' came from a starting point the opposite of Simon's, emphasizing as Moberly had done the relationship between the international dilemmas and those of the university:

> The ferment of thought about the universities, during and immediately after the war, was provoked by the threat to our national existence and institutions, and by our realization of the immense importance of the universities in the national life ... the underlying principle of all the reports, articles and books on the universities in this period was to formulate the universities' responsibilities to society ... As a result the tasks and problems of society are more directly mirrored in the universities than ever before.

Pascal thought Moberly had done a great service in posing the question in terms of the relationship between the international crisis and that of the university. Like Simon, however, Pascal thought that Moberly, particularly as recent Chairman of the UGC, had failed to take account of the changes taking place in the universities, and of 'the spiritual and practical forces which *are* responding to the "needs of the times" '. The modern universities were ready to fulfil the duties of 'a true university', overcoming their past financial deficiencies. Universities were conducting experiments in encouraging students to think, and the recent history of the university could be seen to have enriched university traditions. He did not accept Moberly's belief that religion was necessary to enable the universities to promote a sense of meaning and value – an important start would be by giving students the opportunity to examine 'the social and philosophical bases of their studies'.[47]

These and other contributions to the *Quarterly* discussion accepted the importance of the issues Moberly had raised, without necessarily identifying them with the dilemmas of the wider world or agreeing that the universities had abdicated their responsibilities. A Christian commentator stressed that many of the virtues Moberly highlighted were not solely Christian virtues, many of them being 'upheld and practised no less conscientiously by our colleagues who claim to be agnostics or humanists'.[48] Lionel Elvin, Principal of Ruskin College, Oxford, in the most substantial of the contributions, considered this a period of 'unusual difficulty' rather than crisis, and he did not think that the universities were failing to guide students on fundamental questions any more than they had done in the past. The challenges had changed, but students were responding as seriously as ever. Moberly had most crucially focused on democracy, 'the most important social idea, and the most important social change' of the time. There were changes needed, including increased resources for the redbrick universities and, as Truscot had argued, improved conditions for their students:

... a university day which consists of emergence from a home or lodgings in some industrial city, transport by way of a crowded 'bus, or tram or train to a lecture in a smoke-stained nineteenth century building, and then back by 'bus or tram or train again. Halls of residence would do a great deal.

Students at Redbrick 'deserve something very much better than they get now' if the universities were to match their position to an increasingly democratic society.[49]

Moberly delivered an opening address on *The Crisis* to a Home Universities Conference at the end of 1949. Reporting on the conference *Universities Quarterly* reflected that his book was 'still just as conducive of argument as it was when the book first appeared'. A respondent at the conference had criticized Moberly's wish to 'Christianize' the university, but the report thought that the conference as a whole 'clearly felt that Sir Walter had not wished to press upon the universities any specific solution', rightly pointing to a vacuum at the centre of university life.[50] At the conference he defended his use of 'crisis', not because the universities were faced with greater difficulties than at times in the past, but because they and their communities were faced with critical decisions that must be made: 'The worst danger is drift. If the Universities do not make a contribution to the re-examination of values comparable with that which they admittedly made on the scientific side to the war effort, we shall commit the treason of the intellectual.'[51] He took the opportunity to comment briefly on some of the criticisms in the *Universities Quarterly* and on Michael Oakeshott's article entitled 'The universities' in the *Cambridge Journal*, to which some of the *Quarterly* contributors had also responded.

Oakeshott, conceding that Moberly's book 'deserves to be studied', did not wish to be taken for 'an alien and unfriendly voice'. The remainder of the 30 pages of his article, however, were a kind of pained argument intermixed with outbursts of unrestrained anger. He described Moberly's concerns about 'crisis' in the university as based on 'what is trivial', the tone as being hysterical, incoherent and, paradoxically, 'faithless'. As far as university studies were concerned, what was new and 'in touch with the vital ideas of the age' had made literature, philosophy and history seem 'secondary, remote and ineffectual', and Moberly's ideal was therefore nothing better than 'an unconditional surrender to the absence of discrimination'. The world as Oakeshott knew it offered 'no desirable model for a university'. He belaboured Moberly's suggestion that the time was right for university reform because of the current wave of ' "social planning" for a new and better world', and he defended the recent history of Cambridge and Oxford against the charge of educating a leisured class. In contending that Christian–Classical culture conflicted with 'the unsatisfied demands of social justice' Moberly's book echoed 'the bogus boldness of those who say, "These things have come to stay; we must accept them", this book too often surrenders to all that is worst in the current disingenuous cant'. For Oakeshott the current interpretation of 'social needs' was narrower and less coherent than it had been for centuries: 'every crisis is hailed as a God-given opportunity to remodel society. And we are told here that the task of adjusting the universities to the world ... may most profitably be undertaken now because we have just emerged from a war.' None of this, in his view, was credible. The only real crisis of the universities was a result of the excessive number of undergraduates. It was clear to anyone who worked in the overcrowded university that it was an illusion that there was a 'large untapped reserve of men and women who could make use of this kind of university but who never had the opportunity of doing so'. Those in power (and he identified Moberly with them) who wanted to flood the universities with 'this sort of undergraduate' would cause the universities 'a destructive metamorphosis'.[52]

What was new in this controversy was that Moberly had transferred a long-standing discussion within a concerned minority into a serious debate about fundamentals in the wider university community. Basically the disagreement between Moberly and Oakeshott resided in two areas. First, the world and all its dangers and confusions were, in Moberly's view, reflected in the university in unprecedented ways, requiring and providing an opportunity for fundamental reforms. Oakeshott accepted none of this. Second, and related to the first, Moberly was sympathetically aware of and focused on the new shape of the university system, the poverty of Redbrick University and the experience of its students, the position of the universities in society and the economy, the implications for their curricula and procedures. Oakeshott was aware of and focused on the pressures on university traditions as represented by Cambridge and Oxford. Moberly replied in the *Cambridge Journal*, agreeing with little of Oakeshott's argument. He pointed to misinterpretations of basic theses of the book, including the accusation that he wished the university to copy the world, whereas he wished it to 'wrestle with the major *questions* which the world is asking, but it should not simply reflect the world's *answers* or failure to answer'. He defended Redbrick students, with their economic insecurity, as against those with privilege derived from public schools and the ancient universities. The 'traditional, carefree character of student life' as described by Oakeshott was based on a different level of financial security. Oakeshott had also described the university as bestowing the gift of the 'interim', an interval in which students had a period of withdrawal, but Moberly doubted whether this had ever been widespread in the Redbrick universities. It was important, Moberly underlined, for debate to take place, and Oakeshott had contributed, but since *The Crisis in the*

University was addressed to dons its thesis 'will stand or fall according as it does or does not carry conviction to those most intimately concerned'.[53]

The complex debate generated interest and was referred to in further commentaries on the book and its impact. Mansell Jones, Professor of French at the University of North Wales, Bangor, published an account of 'A debate on the "crisis" ' in 1951. This was mainly a critique of the positions taken by Oakeshott, whom he accused of complacently defending the 'ancien régime', in terms that did not square with Mansell Jones's own 'rumination over academic problems' over the past 40 years. These were indeed troublesome times, and the pressures and gravity of the problems had 'greatly increased, while the tempo of the discussion has quickened'. He agreed with Moberly's view of the urgency of the problems and rejected Oakeshott's opposing tenet that reforms should not be undertaken in troublesome times. It was precisely in such times, Mansell Jones suggested, that reforms were planned, and what Oakeshott was offering was a case for doing nothing, a 'typical academic apologia for procrastination'. Offering Cambridge and Oxford as *the* tradition was unacceptable, though it was true that the modern universities were building their own traditions too slowly and not distinctively enough: 'The title of Professor Oakeshott's article is "The Universities"; but his interest remains exclusive.' Perhaps the most considered commentary on Moberly's book came, in fact, in Mansell Jones's article:

> It is time that someone denounced the *status quo* and its defects and fully time that directives were suggested and objectives clarified. Many from their student days have waited for this to be done ... that the general problems should be disengaged and defined as clearly and critically as possible before being tackled by the practical administrators, and that this should be done by someone of authority and eminence whose word must be considered. *The Crisis in the University* goes far to realize such a hope.[54]

The ripples from the book continued long and wide. Four years after Moberly had left the UGC it commented on the book and the related discussion in its quinquennial report.[55] In 1954 Dent surveyed the years 1946–52 in education, outlined the issues facing the universities and commented that 'all the foregoing questions and others yet more profound were brilliantly analysed' in *The Crisis in the University* (though he thought this a 'perhaps somewhat too sensational title').[56] Berdahl in 1959 discussed many of the 1940s commentaries, but thought it had been left to Moberly 'to present the most searching of university critiques ... Sir Walter was able to integrate many of the various strands of concern about the universities.'[57] The book continued to be cited, quoted and discussed in ensuing decades, and as

Anderson commented in 1983 – as we have seen – on Truscot and Moberly, 'for a long time they were where you turned if you were looking for ideas about university education'. They represented a time when Christianity had been a 'live force in British intellectual life'.[58]

A historian of Protestantism and American higher education has also pointed out the extent of the impact Moberly's book had in the United States. As a 'learned and penetrating analysis of the crisis in the modern university as symptomatic of a larger crisis in modern Western culture', the book attracted immediate attention, with the American churches newly engaged with issues of higher education:

> On the American scene, his book fell into an excited discussion, which was already well under way ... Nevertheless, his articulation of the issues, bringing together, in considerable detail, the historical, theological, and educational considerations, was a fundamental influence in shaping the Americans' subsequent understanding of the university question ... *The Crisis in the University* can be seen as a kind of benchmark of the beginning in earnest of mainline American Protestantism's concerted postwar efforts to engage American higher education anew.

The effort was a serious and sustained one, but one that had more or less petered out by the end of the 1960s.[59] In England Moberly's impact, therefore, was different, being aimed at and reaching a largely university audience. The active movement that continued to promote his ideas was a limited one mainly of Christian academics. The groups concerned, culminating in the Higher Education Foundation, continued to discuss these kinds of issues relating to values and higher education.[60] Events and processes overtook *The Crisis in the University*, as they had done *Redbrick University* and the publications of the early twentieth century.

'THIS GRAND INQUEST'

Moberly himself continued to promote his ideas, in lectures, in print and from his position as the principal of Cumberland Lodge, a new foundation to promote 'the investigation and discussion of the nature of Man and Society; the exposition of the Christian interpretation of Life in relation to the various secular alternatives, and to stimulate research on these and similar matters'.[61] In 1950, for example, he published a lecture given at the University of Manchester on *Universities Ancient and Modern*, in which he was no less assertive about 'Oxbridge' and 'Redbrick' than he had been in *The Crisis in the University*. The chief aim of Oxbridge had been to produce 'an elite of educated gentlemen', and it exerted its influence indirectly, in collegiate surroundings transmitting a cultural inheritance 'generation by generation', an ethos absorbed 'not only through the ears but through the eyes'. Redbrick had grown differently by virtue of its 'indigence' and deliberate policies. It had not set out to educate an elite in the same way, and it was regional and 'provincial'. He reaffirmed the decay of old certainties: 'Our world is no longer "Christendom" ', and it was in need of some 'new integration of effective belief'. This had not been a particular concern of the modern universities, but he saw a hopeful sign in the attention now being given in many of them to 'serious discussion of ultimate questions and of their bearing on university life'.[62]

The following year Moberly reviewed a book on Newman in the *Universities Quarterly*, published a collection of three lectures on *Responsibility*, concerned with the conception (including the Christian conception) of justice after the Nüremberg Trials, the 1948 Criminal Justice Act and 'prolonged discussion of capital punishment', and delivered a lecture at the University of St Andrews, on *The Universities and Cultural Leadership*.[63] In the last of these he explored again the traditions of the universities, asking whether the benefits of a university education and their contribution to the nation could still be the universities' aim, as when Newman defined them. His answer was that these aims, though urgent, were far harder to achieve, the conditions of life and of the universities, student 'bias' and lack of financial security militated against leadership aims as traditionally understood. Education for social responsibility was 'still a legitimate and necessary task for universities'. His argument was a variation, in leadership and cultural terms, of his former advocacy of a Christian 'leaven' for the universities. Public opinion was 'produced by the few and solidified by the many', and therefore university teachers and alumni should be 'among the few who set the tone'. The corporate life of the university, the mix of backgrounds, opinions, nationality and race brought to it by its members were crucial. Students had to learn to engage with others who held different views, asking not only what those views were, but also why they had come to hold them. Developing these essential mental habits 'should be the university man's distinctive contribution to the forming of public opinion'. The strength of this affirmation lay in Moberly's sense of the nature of the university community within the national and international community:

Our age is notoriously an age of transition and the upshot is not yet clear. Behind our political struggles lie differences of fundamental doctrine, and there is need for strenuous thinking about the great issues of right and wrong, liberty and order, faith and scepticism. In particular we need to determine more clearly our attitude towards the spiritual heritage we derive from Hellenic and Hebrew sources. How much in it are we to reject? How much are we to accept and to make the foundation of our social order? It is only if the universities take a full part in this grand inquest, and if much of the creative thinking required emanates from them, that their students are likely to find inspiration for leadership in a changing world.[64]

NOTES AND REFERENCES

1. Moberly, W., *The Crisis in the University* (London: SCM Press, 1949), p. 50.
2. SCM 1944–46, University Conference minutes, 1946.
3. Moberly, *The Crisis*, pp. 9–10.
4. *Manchester Guardian*, 'Classical Association meets in Manchester. Dr Moberly on the Ideals of Citizenship', 8 October 1926.
5. *Manchester Guardian*, 25 March 1929.
6. UMJRL, V206, 6 June 1930, 3 February 1931.
7. Charlton, H.B., *Portrait of a University, 1851–1951* (Manchester: Manchester University Press, 1951), pp. 131–2.
8. UMJRL, Vice-Chancellor's Files, 146, typed letter to colleagues, 14 August 1934.
9. UMJRL, C Series, 90, typed report of a speech by Sir Walter H. Moberly on the occasion of a dinner to the Vice-Chancellor and Lady Moberly, 14 December 1934, passim.
10. Moberly, W., *Plato's Conception of Education and its Meaning for To-Day* (London: Oxford University Press, 1944), passim.
11. Moberly, W., 'Relations of the state and the universities', Association of Universities of the British Commonwealth, *Report of Proceedings*, 1948, (London: AUBC, 1951).
12. Moberly, W., 'The Universities', typescript, FCMA III: 15, 1940, pp. 1–13.
13. Report of meeting, 9 December 1940, FCMA III 15 p. 3; FCMA XIII 80 p. 9.
14. Moberly, 'The Universities', FCMA III:15, 1940, pp. 14–22.
15. Kojecky, R., *T.S. Eliot's Social Criticism* (London: Faber & Faber, 1971), Appendix and p. 162.
16. Taylor, W., 'Education and the Moot', in Aldrich, R. (ed.) *In History and in Education: Essays Presented to Peter Gordon* (London: Woburn Press, 1996), p. 162.
17. Dent, H.C., 'Reform in education', FCMA XIII 81, Education Group 16 May 1942, pp. 1, 4 (Dent himself does not seem to have been present).
18. Report of discussion on Dent's paper, FCMA XIII 80, p. 6.
19. Report of discussion on paper by Livingstone on adult education, ibid., p. 15.
20. SCM, box 243a, University Commission, meeting 4 August 1944.
21. SCM, box 243b, Staff reports 1944–46, file May 1945, Midlands Area General Report, by Winifred Jones.
22. SCM, box 243a, University Commission, file Hawarden 1944.
23. SCM, *Memorandum on the Student Christian Movement and Education,* n.d. [late 1940s], pp. 6–7, SCM box 247 Miscellaneous 1946–55.
24. SCM, box 248, 'A draft syllabus by many hands', in preparation for a conference at Westminster the following January.
25. Livingstone, R., 'Plato and modern education' (1944), in Livingstone, *The Rainbow Bridge and Other Essays on Education* (London: Pall Mall Press, 1959), passim.
26. Moberly, *Plato's Conception of Education and its Meanings for To-Day*, passim.
27. UGC, *University Development from 1935 to 1947* (London: HMSO, 1948), p. 32.

28. Price, G.L., 'The expansion of British universities and their struggle to maintain autonomy: 1943–46, *Minerva*, vol. 16, 1978, pp. 366–72.
29. Dent, H.C., *Growth in English Education 1946–1952* (London: Routledge & Kegan Paul, 1954), p. 175.
30. UGC, *University Development. Report on the Years 1947 to 1952* (London: HMSO, 1953), p. 6.
31. Niblett, W.R., 'An absence of outrage: cultural change and values in British higher education 1930–1990', *Reflections on Higher Education,* vol. 2, pp. 6–7. Cf. also Niblett, W.R., *Life, Education, Discovery* (Bristol: Pomegranate Books, 2001), p. 100 (the article is also reprinted here).
32. UGC, *University Development from 1935 to 1947*, p. 60.
33. Moberly, 'Relations of the state and the universities', pp. 11–17.
34. Ibid., pp. 44–5.
35. 'Universities and the state. Sir Walter Moberly at Cambridge', *Times Educational Supplement*, 20 November 1948.
36. Moberly, *The Crisis*, pp. 15, 30–48.
37. Ibid., pp. 21–4, 50–70, 295.
38. Ibid., pp. 146–7, 170–84, 195–200.
39. Ibid., pp. 225–60.
40. Ibid., pp. 71–3, 93–103, 106–7, 110–33, 261–8, 298–309.
41. *Universities Quarterly*, 'Notes', vol. 4, 1949, p. 11.
42. Farrington, B., 'The university in the modern world' (Review of *The Crisis*), *Journal of Education*, vol. 81, 1949, pp. 424–6.
43. A.B.R., review of *The Crisis, Universities Review*, vol. 21, 1949, pp. 193–4.
44. *Universities Quarterly*, vol. 3, 1948–49, p. 633.
45. *Universities Quarterly*, 'The mission of a university – a discussion', vol. 4, 1949, p. 15.
46. Simon, E., 'University crisis? A consumer's view', in ibid., pp. 73–9.
47. Pascal, R., 'The universities and social purpose', in ibid., pp. 37–43.
48. Adams, J., 'Aims and methods', in ibid., pp. 63–5.
49. Elvin, L., 'The universities and social change', in ibid., pp. 24–36.
50. *Universities Quarterly*, 'Notes', vol. 4, 1950, p. 119.
51. Moberly, W., opening the session on *The Crisis in the University* at Home Universities Conference 1949, *Proceedings*, Association of Universities of the British Commonwealth, 1952, pp. 14–15.
52. Oakeshott, M., 'The universities', *Cambridge Journal*, vol. 2, 1949, reprinted in Fuller, T. (ed.), *The Voice of Liberal Learning: Michael Oakeshott on Education* (New Haven, CT: Yale University Press, 1989), pp. 105–35, passim.
53. Moberly, W., 'The universities', *Cambridge Journal*, vol. 3, 1950, pp. 195–213, passim.
54. Mansell Jones, P., 'A debate on the "Crisis": Professor Oakeshott versus Sir Walter Moberly', *Universities Review*, vol. 23, 1951, pp. 117–21.
55. UGC, *University Development. Report on the Years 1947 to 1952*, pp. 12–13.
56. Dent, *Growth in English Education*, p. 194.
57. Berdahl, R.O., *British Universities and the State* (Berkeley, CA: University of California Press, 1959), p. 85.
58. Anderson, R., 'Comments' in Phillipson, N. (ed.) *Universities, Society and the Future* (Edinburgh: Edinburgh University Press, 1983), p. 164.
59. Sloan, D., *Faith and Knowledge: Mainline Protestantism and American Higher Education* (Louisville, KY: Westminster John Knox Press, 1994), pp. vii, 40–3.
60. Reeves, M., *The Crisis in Higher Education*, (Milton Keynes: Open University Press, 1988). The 'Acknowledgements' point to the creation of the Higher Education Group as a result of Moberly's book.

61. Judge, H., 'A forum for students: Cumberland Lodge, 1947–1960', in Reeves, M. (ed.) *Christian Thinking and Social Order: Conviction Politics from the 1930s to the Present Day* (London: Cassell, 1999), pp. 123–4.
62. Moberly, W., *Universities Ancient and Modern* (Manchester: Manchester University Press, 1950), passim.
63. Moberly, W., review of McGrath, 'Newman's University, Idea and Reality', *Universities Quarterly*, vol. 5, 1951, pp. 392–5; *Responsibility* (London: Oxford University Press, 1951); *The Universities and Cultural Leadership* (London: Oxford University Press, 1951).
64. Ibid., pp. 10–12, 21, 23–7.

7

1950s: 'MODERN NEEDS'

In 1950 the *Universities Review* began a defence of the redbrick universities:

> Judging by the spate of books, reports, pamphlets, articles and letters to the Press which have been published during the last few years on universities it would appear that this subject is no longer neglected as it once was by the people of this country.[1]

Public interest reflected the growth of the universities themselves, the concerns within them and those to which they were responding. At the beginning of the 1950s the UGC's typology of the UK institutions on its grant list was based on chronology. There were 23 institutions, of which 16 were universities, the others being university colleges (Southampton, Leicester, Exeter and Hull and the new university college of North Staffordshire) and two colleges of technology, the Manchester College of Technology and the Royal Technical College, Glasgow. The first group comprised the ancient universities of Oxford and Cambridge and their separately endowed colleges. The four Scottish universities of St Andrews, Glasgow, Aberdeen and Edinburgh were also ancient foundations, but bore 'little resemblance to the ancient English universities'. Next in 'seniority' came Durham and London, both founded early in the nineteenth century. A fourth group contained eight 'civic universities' – Manchester, Birmingham, Liverpool, Leeds, Sheffield, Bristol, Reading and Nottingham. Fifth was the University of Wales, which contained five constituent colleges and the Welsh National School of Medicine.[2] Southampton became a university in 1952, followed by Hull in 1954, Exeter in 1955 and Leicester in 1957. How slowly a half-century of advocacy of an extension of university education was being achieved was made editorially clear by *Universities Quarterly* when Southampton received its charter: 'The foundation of a new university is still a rare enough event to quicken the academic pulse.'[3] The pre-war total of 50,000 full-time university students peaked at

85,421 in 1949–50, declined to 80,602 in 1953–54 and was nearly 90,000 in 1956–57, by which time the UGC was arguing for further expansion only on strict conditions, including the availability of employment for students graduating from expanding faculties, and a guarantee that 'increase should not involve a decline in the standards reached by students'.[4] Established universities looked with anxiety at possible increases in student numbers beyond some figure around 3–5,000, a very distant target for some of the newer universities. In 1956 the Council of the University of Manchester thought it should not go beyond 4,500 full-time students 'in the foreseeable future', apart from any increase in the somewhat separate Faculty of Technology.[5] In 1953–54 Leeds had 3,270 students and Liverpool 2,920, Exeter had 932 and Southampton 963. At stake in considerations of size were issues of funding new buildings and finding student accommodation, staffing, standards and a sense of community or identity. For Southampton 'the omens are fair ... It is small enough to grow without losing its sense of community.'[6] The question of numbers was to become an acute one for a new generation of universities in the 1960s, and the conception of 'community' was to remain a difficult balance between the Oxford and Cambridge college and the needs of the 'Drabtown' student.

Purely in terms of student numbers Oxford and Cambridge were being left a long way behind. One account of the 1950s describes the civic universities by the close of the decade as being 'much larger and more confident and everyone was aware that the Oxbridge connection was no longer as powerful as it had been'.[7] The criterion of size does not, of course, supersede that of power. Certainly the civic universities were increasingly visible on the national and international stage. In 1953 Sir Sydney Caine, Vice-Chancellor of the University of Malaya (three years later to become Director of the London School of Economics), attended a Commonwealth Universities Congress in Cambridge, and tried to deduce from the congress the 'change in character of United Kingdom universities'. It was clear from the statistics 'that the old universities of Oxford and Cambridge have long ceased to hold the predominance which was traditionally theirs. In numbers they are far out-weighed by London alone or by the combined mass of the provincial or city universities.' Oxford and Cambridge had contributed little to general discussion at this congress, and though there was no doubt about their 'continued under-lying influence and pervasive tradition' he felt that 'the new ideas, the new developing forces, were to be found in the newest universities'.[8] This analysis underestimated the 'underlying influence' of the ancient universities. There were other ways of locating them in the university and national landscapes. In 1958 A.H. Halsey reflected on their continuing position, suggesting that there had been no change in their 'dominating position in the structure of British university life. Both in their self image and in the public mind they are clearly differentiated from all other institutions of higher learning.' He quoted an example used by an American sociology colleague, Edward Shils: 'If a young man talking to an educated stranger refers to his university studies, he is asked "Oxford or Cambridge?" And if he says Aberystwyth or Nottingham, there is disappointment on the one side and embarrassment on the other.' Halsey thought it unlikely that Redbrick was destined to be the university of the future: 'Oxbridge has never had a firmer grasp onto its position at the apex of British educational and intellectual life.' Despite their high standards of scholarship the Redbrick universities' 'challenge to the social dominance of the ancient foundations has so far been completely without success'.[9] This 'social dominance' was to continue through all the changes in higher education in the following decades.

As student numbers continued to increase at an unsteady pace there was little general literature about expansion until the late 1950s, when the UGC decided to create a wave of new universities. Who wanted what for the civic universities of the 1950s related primarily to the financial pressures of expansion and to the nature of curricula in expected expansionist conditions, a result of the increased numbers of school students staying on in the sixth forms and the prospective increase in numbers as a result of the 'bulge' – the post-war rise in the birth rate. From one of the newer universities, D.G. James, Vice-Chancellor of the University of Southampton, wrote in *Universities Quarterly* in 1956 that the journal's contents in recent years could be divided into two parts – the pedagogic and the administrative, neither of which seemed to make 'a startling or vivid appeal to the academic mind', and education 'as a subject of reflection and enquiry, occupies a not quite respectable academic limbo'. The *Quarterly*, he maintained, had not helped to unite the universities, even though they now held a place in the nation's intellectual life 'far more pre-eminent than ever before'. James described the position shrewdly:

> [W]ith some dozen new universities spread up and down the land in the great centres of population, what is the situation in English universities now? It is, I should say, one of peculiar *inarticulation* – in both senses of the word: universities are disjointed and apparently incapable of clear speech. As knowledge increases, and study becomes particularized, we seem to have lost (if we ever had them) our unity and our speech; we too rarely speak to one another ... about the subjects in which we are professionally immersed; we seem not to possess powers of exposition.

There were exceptions, but *Universities Quarterly* had not managed to become a centre for real discussion of what was going on and what was not going on in the universities. The implication was that the pedagogic and the administrative needed to be brought more than in the past into 'a firmer context of purpose and enlightenment ... bringing our silence into speech'.[10]

The basis of James's remonstrance can be seen clearly from the contents of the journal in the five years 1950–54. A prominent feature was the continuing series of symposia: in 1950 on the university teaching of psychology, the use of lectures and schools and universities; in 1951 the teaching of English studies and postgraduate studies, selection for the universities and university research; in 1952 religion and the university, the teaching of philosophy and of the history and philosophy of science; in 1953 Russian studies, the teaching of politics and of history (the latter in schools as well as universities); in 1954 health and the student, and the sixth form. In addition to the symposia there were contributions on television, radio and drama; residence, general education and the classics; and higher education in countries around the world. Book reviews and articles occasionally covered adult education and a range of academic topics, but there was little continuing or basic discussion in the journal of the kind that had been prompted by Moberly's book in 1949, little that could be classified as 'purpose and enlightenment' in James's conception. The growing attention to technology, to which we shall return below, was attracting some of the passion of debate. Sir Charles Morris published in 1954–55 a three-part discussion of 'The idea of university education', and from 1956 a small number of articles began to re-address the history and philosophy of ideas about university education, or to defend the university as 'a way of life'.[11]

At the heart of expansion, whether reflected in concerns or complacency, were still the issues of state intervention and university independence in relation to the government funding needed for expensive subjects and developments, though the issue remained relatively muted for most of the 1950s. A crucial reason was the degree of confidence in the role of the UGC, widely perceived as continuing to hold the state sufficiently at bay. The UGC itself was determined to maintain its 'buffer' role. At the end of its review of the period 1947–52 it commented:

> The prospect that the universities will continue to make an increasing call on the public purse and draw a rising proportion of their income from the state cannot but occasion a certain anxiety. That it increases our responsibilities is undeniable. We are regarded by the universities as the guardians of their liberties; by the Government as responsible for ensuring that the increasing sums placed at our disposal are spent to best advantage in the national interest.[12]

Five years later, referring back to this commentary on the 'mutual dependence' of the state and the universities, the UGC confirmed that hopes of this continuing partnership had been justified, 'the more so because the period has not been without its stresses'.[13] Not everyone, however, was sanguine on this score. At the 1953 Commonwealth Congress Sir Sydney Caine's impressions 'made immediately apparent the way in which the whole university body is more and more dependent on the State for finance'. This was particularly the view of the American university presidents who were present, and who were 'particularly concerned about the extent to which universities might be losing their independence as a result of that high dependence on State finance'. The British representatives had tried to respond reassuringly to these concerns, but the issue, Caine felt, had been addressed in insufficient depth: 'the real point which seemed to emerge was that the United Kingdom universities are actually very largely at the mercy of the State', and their academic independence had been preserved thus far only because the full power given to the State had simply not been used. What would happen 'if there should be a change in this attitude of mind on the part of those in control of the State machine is nothing like so clear'.[14]

'IN A MORE FUNDAMENTAL WAY'

At the beginning of the 1950s, as *Universities Quarterly* indicated, 'the universities are still in the news, and in the editorials. Everybody seems to be quite clear that universities matter enormously', but though they must 'measure up to the times ... they must see that they remain universities'.[15] The post-war expectations had not yet become 'inarticulate', and Moberly's *Crisis* was 'still just as conducive of argument as it was when the book first appeared'.[16] However, no one continued Oakeshott's attack, and the world view, the threat of international conflict and the crisis of values within the universities also became momentarily without a prominent, representative voice. A quarter of a century after Flexner's valiant intrusion into British higher education another American set out, in a book published in 1955, to relate the story of *Higher Learning in Britain* in recent years. George F. Kneller conducted what W.H.G. Armytage described as 'the anatomy of academics', and the result made 'strange, and often incredible, reading', as Kneller moved around the operating table.[17]

Kneller's account consisted of a reading of the system and some of its intricacies, linked to interpretations of Truscot and Barlow, Moberly and Nash, Livingstone and Leavis and others. The book was based in large part on discussions with many of the current protagonists, but it had little public repercussion. The insights into the system did not seem as fresh as those of Flexner in another situation had been, and the mirror to the authors was distorted by a sense of the weakness of British argument by comparison with that in the United States. Kneller detected a lack of purpose that a century before had been clear and unquestioned, and within the past generation 'a series of seismic shocks from the outside world has rocked the very foundations of university thought'. Some of the writers had struggled unsuccessfully or ambivalently to re-establish the underlying values of university education, unable to respond to the blandishments of science and restore a sense of the unity of knowledge. Whether discussing science or vocationalism or curricular issues generally he thought he heard confused answers to the questions. Thought about the purposes of university education was 'of infinite scope and variety, ranging from those who defend what they consider to be the university's essential isolation from social turmoil to others who champion its newly acquired place of leadership in national progress'. The crisis in British universities was being defined in different ways – as a moral crisis, a cultural or regional crisis, a social crisis, a cosmic crisis and a variety of others – including the absence of a crisis at all.[18] Sir Charles Morris pointed to Kneller's approval of much in the British system, but also his dismissal of every school of thought he had encountered: 'he thinks very little indeed of British thought in this field ... All is gloom, almost wilful gloom. I do not think Professor Kneller finds a single candle throwing its little beam from this naughty world. The fault is evidently a national one. Or perhaps it is old Europe.' Morris was disconcerted by Kneller's criticism of British inability fundamentally to address the need for change, and by his failure to reveal the 'educational secrets' of the best American universities.[19] Whether it was Kneller's gloom or British academics' conservatism and dislike of being anatomized, the book's insights were not widely seen as illuminating.

In the mid-1950s university aims and purposes were no longer the targets they had been. Livingstone did not continue into the 1950s the flurry of relevant publications he had produced in the 1940s. Nothing American in the 1950s had the same resonance as the Harvard Committee's *General Education in a Free Society* in 1945 – though in limited ways this did continue to be a point of reference in England in the 1950s. Within the university community the focus was relatively narrow. For the *Journal of Education* in 1956 the question for education as a whole was 'how radically we are prepared to transform our education system and to redeploy the country's intellectual resources' – but the objectives and the consequences of doing so were too vaguely understood to justify a launch into 'this particular educational space, if we knew how'.[20] The *Universities Review* looked back in 1960 on the prodigious expansion of the previous decade, a time of 'abounding vitality and soaring hopes ... never has the impact of the university upon society been so great'. For many university teachers, however, it had also been a time of disillusionment, frustration and widespread discontent, and by 1960 the journal was therefore arguing that the university system needed to be overhauled and modernized.[21] One occasional focus of discussion was, in fact, the universities' system of governance and administration, including the status and roles of non-professors – and the issue of internal democracy was to become a salient element in the conflicts of the 1960s.

The nature of general education and the curriculum was also a focus of discussion, one that frequently acted as proxy for former debates about aims and values. The nature of a 'liberal education', often used as a synonym for 'general education', had been debated since the days of ancient Greece, but its significance in the 1950s had to do with pressures towards and away from specialization, dilemmas about the structure of the curriculum in changing times, and the mounting demands from the 1940s for significant increases in the numbers of students in science and technology. One aspect of the dilemma was pointed up by John Macmurray, a philosopher speaking at the Commonwealth Universities Congress in 1948, in terms of a 'cultural crisis'. University teachers tended to see the crisis as an external one, 'affecting the general culture of the society from which we draw our students; affecting the students, therefore, so that they come to us lacking that background and foundation without which the University cannot do its proper work upon them'. The basis that was lacking was 'a matter of habits of mind and habits of life; an emotional rather than an intellectual thing; a faith rather than a philosophy'. Important though that was, the crisis was equally within the university, which was focusing on research and technology to the exclusion of fulfilling its 'cultural function'. There was what he called the 'technological obsession', while what was needed was 'a new conception of a liberal education in which science plays an essential part', and the university needed to become 'the gravitational centre of contemporary cultural life in the community which it serves'.[22] The concept of general or liberal education therefore reached into all corners of the university and the worlds it inhabited. Livingstone had seen a solution in making philosophy part of the curriculum for all students. Moberly had looked at a variety of alternatives to 'one-sidedness', such as courses on philosophy or religion, broad-based general degree courses, honours schools combining science and arts, and most hopefully, widened professional courses, relating occupational and cultural education.[23] Such considerations linked the elements of crisis in the world outside to what Macmurray saw as the deficiencies that students brought with them into the university, but also to what Moberly had seen as the absence of appropriate values on the part of the teachers themselves.

What to teach therefore also incorporated various dimensions of the *purposes* in teaching it. It was the confusions surrounding the interpretations of these that Kneller found so difficult, and yet they were probably amenable to solution, he recognized, through forms of 'balance' in the curriculum: 'a balance of studies is possible and a balance in one's appreciation of human values attainable for the striving'.[24] To achieve such a balance or an understanding of the purposes of a curriculum, however, the problem had to be translated into a variety of vocabularies. In many cases it took the form of advocating particular student outcomes, relating to personality or the achievement of potential. Commonly this linked the content of the curriculum with the ability of students to think autonomously, and therefore incorporated (as it had done for Moberly and others) teaching methods, the uses of the tutorial, the commitment of the teacher. The UGC in 1958 clearly articulated this approach, against the background of an increasingly burdened and specialist-focused curriculum and lack of time. Many students, it believed, now came to the university more concerned about acquiring a qualification than a broad education. Narrowness of outlook could be found in any subject, not just, as was often claimed, in the sciences. Students who were to go on to hold senior positions in various walks of life needed more than specialized knowledge, they needed to become 'educated men and women'. Of the qualities of mind needed the foremost, in the UGC view at that moment, was 'a capacity to think', based no doubt in the acquisition of a body of specialized knowledge – though the latter was not the most important benefit to be derived from university studies. Teaching students to think was the university's 'first duty' and the UGC therefore challenged the universities

> to consider yet again in a fundamental way what it is that they are trying to do with the students entrusted to them. If they are to be turned into well educated people as well as good specialists, what are the qualities of mind which they should develop? Are these qualities sufficiently developed by the courses offered and by the kind of life the student lives? Is there a necessary conflict between the production of a specialist and the production of an educated person? ... thinking on this subject, and fundamental thinking, was never more necessary than it is today.[25]

That the UGC could end its report in 1958 with such a peroration no doubt meant that the questions were exercising the minds not only of its members, but also of the wider community. *Nature* had the previous year, for example, in an article entitled 'Education for modern needs', listed a number of industrial leaders and scientists who had emphasized that what industry was asking of the universities was a supply of graduates from all faculties 'who can think and act for themselves, capable of choosing between truth and falsehood, wisdom and folly, beauty and ugliness'.[26] A balanced curriculum was related to 'modern needs' and a 'fundamental' reappraisal, but both proved less simple than may have been thought.

Some of the shape of the discussion of general education derived from the experience of the American liberal arts college or European patterns of secondary schooling, but most of it came from the difficulties of reinventing what the university could do in its changing environment. The view that it was false to associate a liberal education solely with the humanities was a recurrent theme in the journal literature. The *Journal of Education*, arguing in 1956 for a broadening of scientific and technological studies, was nevertheless clear that 'there is no validity in the equation "non-scientific education equals humane and liberal education" '. It was also true that such an education could not be based exclusively on science.[27] A series of articles in *Universities Quarterly* addressed the issues of what constituted a general education and how it could best be organized. John Fulton, then Principal of University College, Swansea, in 1950 rehearsed the kind of strategies Moberly had previously suggested: probing more deeply from a specialist interest; correcting 'one-sidedness' by a parallel discipline; general lectures or essays. He described the surprise of many people at the Home Universities Conference in December 1949 to find that 'the need for general education won almost unanimous acceptance in a large conference representing university teachers of every grade and faculty, university administrators and lay members of Councils'. In 1952 J.L. Montrose, Professor of Law at Queen's University, Belfast, analyzed the qualities of a specialist education and though important it provided only a particular method of tackling the problems within the discipline, and 'an inadequate university education'. The education he advocated was one that would present students with an outline of 'the main problems which concern mankind', and give them an awareness of methods developed for their solution'. In 1954 Cyril Bibby, of the College of St Mark and St John, then in London, thought that it would be a long time before a solution to the problem of general education would be found. In the meantime he thought it important to build up a file of current practice – and detailed the 'The Common Course' provided at this Church teacher education college. In 1954 Eric Ashby also reviewed a Harvard book on *General Education in Science*, commended the Harvard approach and thought it avoided the fault of British science courses, which tended to be 'mere anthologies of what scientists think are important in their various subjects'.[28] Pressure was increasing for discussion of 'the idea of a technological education' or 'the humanities and the technologist' in the later 1950s. There were at the same time throughout the decade articles, for example, on American and other universities, schools and the teaching of science, which in different ways incorporated problems of and approaches to general education.

The question of university 'purpose' was therefore to a large extent translated into the attention to the curriculum. In 1950 Oakeshott dismissed the idea of 'purpose' altogether, denying that there was any sense in discussing the purpose, mission or function of a university:

> [I]t seems to me an unfortunate way of talking. It assumes that there is something called 'a university', a contrivance of some sort, something you could make another of tomorrow if you had enough money ... A university is not a machine for achieving a particular purpose or producing a particular result; it is a manner of human activity. And it would be necessary for a university to advertise itself as pursuing a particular purpose only if it were talking to people so ignorant that they had to be spoken to in baby language.[29]

Until the later years of the 1950s the question of 'purpose' was treated as too complex and controversial, following the Moberly debates, or was interpreted as other things. In 1957, however, Peter Winch, lecturer in philosophy at Swansea, continued the Oakeshott theme. He registered that 'a lot' was being said about the 'purpose' or 'social function' of a university, and that there were differences of opinion as to what that might mean. There were, however, more important differences between those who thought universities had '*some* purpose', and people like himself who thought they had no purpose whatever:

> [I]t does not even make sense to *ask* what the purpose of a university is, since institutions such as universities belong to a category which does not logically permit the predication of a purpose ... the social philosophy presupposed by the view that institutions ought to fulfil a social purpose is internally incoherent and confused.

There was, he maintained, 'no ulterior purpose' to academic work: 'it would be a mistake to look for the point of academic work *outside* the context of academic work itself'.[30] An important change in the nature of academic and public discussion of 'higher education', as an umbrella description of universities and a new range of institutions, began to take shape, in fact, from 1957–58. It accompanied the establishment of new universities before and after the Robbins report on *Higher Education* in 1963 and resulted in a marked revival of debate.

THE ONLY IMPORTANT EXPERIMENT

Lord Lindsay of Birker, better remembered as A.D. Lindsay, died in 1952. Lindsay, at the age of 72, retired as Master of Balliol College, Oxford, in 1949 and agreed to become Principal of the new University College of North

8. A.D. (Lord) Lindsay, c. 1950. (Courtesy of Keele University Library Archives.)

Staffordshire. The college admitted its first students in 1950, and was to become the University of Keele ten years after Lindsay's death. He had been involved from the outset in attempts to obtain a university in the Potteries. He drew on experience in the Oxford University Delegacy for Extra-Mural Studies and its work for adult education, his ideas about the university as a contribution to democracy, his Christianity, his education in Scotland and long career at Oxford, to formulate a vision for an experiment in university education. He worked closely with the local political and adult education enthusiasts for the new institution, and, as Principal, articulated a scheme that was to become the Foundation Year. The scheme was at the heart of what became known as the Keele 'experiment', and embodied a plan for curricular breadth and a common student experience. This was a different kind of higher education advocacy, combining a practical experiment in curriculum making and a distinct purpose – what W.B. Gallie, the first professor of philosophy appointed, described as Lindsay's thinking of university education 'in terms of service to a democratic community'. The intention was to enable students after graduation to contribute to the community in one way or another, 'playing a leading part, usually as a member of a "free association", in one of those freely cultivated activities that are the leaven of democratic life'. The whole embodied an attempt to reconcile the 'purist' view of the university with a 'utilitarian' one.[31]

That résumé can only be understood with reference to Lindsay's lifelong commitment to adult education and to democracy – between which he saw no separation. He never wrote a book about adult or university education. His reputation was built on his work as a philosopher of democracy, on his work in Oxford, on his articles, addresses and broadcasts, on his socialism and ideas about what became the 'Welfare State', and on the embodiment of his principles and his vision in North Staffs, at the village of Keele near Stoke-on-Trent. The existence of the College owed a great deal to his long involvement specifically with the university tutorial movement in the area, and on his enthusiastic support for the project. Gallie, writing the first book about Lindsay and Keele included 'the Keele experiment' in the title. Michael (later Lord) Young, writing about Keele in 1960 described it as 'the only important experiment in higher education that conservative Britain has managed to produce in the last quarter of a century'. What Lindsay wanted was 'a university not remote from ordinary democratic life'.[32] Discussion of Keele commonly focused on its experimental curriculum and general approach, in the context of the conservatism or traditions of English university education. The UGC, after initially rejecting the application to create the University College, finally agreed, and described three ways in which 'it may be said to be experimental'. First, it gave effect to the educational views of Lindsay. Second, it aimed, in a four-year and not a three-year programme, to offer 'a curriculum of a new type, free from what its founders regard as the excessive specialisation called for by university curricula of the normal type', and it therefore started life, not under the aegis of the University of London's external degrees, but awarding its own degrees under the sponsorship of the Universities of Oxford, Manchester and Birmingham. Third:

> Never before have the founders of a university institution in this country been in a position to dispense with an endowment and put their plans into effect with the backing of the state ... While we would not wish to belittle the contribution which local authorities make to the income of the college, it remains true that the scale and pace of its early development has been determined by the extent to which we have been able to meet the requirements put before us by the college authorities.[33]

The university system therefore had in it at the beginning of the 1950s a newcomer that had seriously broken the traditional mould, and, in the words of the UGC, it was to Lindsay's 'inspiration, more than to any other agency', that it owed 'its life and form'.[34]

Lindsay was a graduate of the University of Glasgow, held a studentship and fellowship at Oxford before and after the First World War, held a chair at Glasgow and in 1924 became Master of Balliol College, Oxford, a position he held for a quarter of a century. He was a member of the Labour Party, and in 1938 stood, unsuccessfully, as a 'Progressive Independent' candidate in an Oxford by-election. Throughout his association with Oxford he was active in University external education, was secretary and later chairman of the Oxford Tutorial Classes Committee and tutored classes and summer schools, including major involvements with the Workers Educational Association and local authorities in Staffordshire and the Potteries. From the late 1920s through the 1940s his publications were mainly in political philosophy, including *The Essentials of Democracy* in 1929 and *The Modern Democratic State* in 1943. His many articles, addresses and broadcasts covered aspects of democracy and its relations to socialism and adult education, and in the 1940s and essentially in his last years, he also focused on the universities, including the idea and practice of the Keele 'experiment'. Democracy, socialism, the Labour Party, adult education, the modernization of the University of Oxford,[35] the breadth and collaborative nature of the curriculum at Keele, his Christianity, were all inter-related elements in his personal philosophy and the range of his activities. Typically, he bracketed together his understandings of democracy and of Christianity:

[T]he inspiration of modern democracy came from men's experience of the entirely satisfactory character of democratic government in the Christian congregation – came therefore especially from the Independents, the Anabaptists, and the Quakers – from the men who had both accepted more wholeheartedly than other Protestants the reformation doctrine of the spiritual priesthood of all believers, and made the small independent congregation the unit of government.[36]

Similarly with democracy and education, he underlined in 1940 that 'a democratic nation to-day has to be a well-educated nation', but education was not confined to the schools, and becoming educated as a nation meant a great extension of adult education: 'The Workers' Educational Assocation has played a very great part in making democracy a reality in England'.[37] Within his affirmation of a vital democracy he shared with Mannheim a belief in the need for planning after the Second World War, seeing that 'planning has come to stay and, indeed, to increase', but the question was: 'Can we have expert planning and keep democratic?'[38] He corresponded with Mannheim and invited him to his home, noting after the latter meeting that they had developed a warm friendship, though: 'I while welcoming and interested in almost all he said, thought him too optimistic, too elaborate, too much of a planner. He thought me too spiritual ...'[39]

When Lindsay turned his attention to the university his instincts pointed him towards what it was best to do for students. In his farewell letter to his colleagues at Balliol he underlined that the College 'exists primarily for the sake of the undergraduates'. Although some of those who taught them were researchers some were 'first and foremost teachers ... The place exists, and I hope always will exist, for the young men'.[40] The priority however, was to escape from the traditional curriculum, with its rigid subject boundaries. His attempt at North Staffs was to link specialization with wider studies and understanding, and though others had trodden that path Lindsay's underlying approach was one of a sense of the organic unity of knowledge, something confirmed for him by Ortega y Gasset's *Mission of the University*. Ortega saw the main function of the university as teaching 'the great cultural disciplines, which he defined in terms of the natural sciences, history, sociology and philosophy.[41] Lindsay's approach to the foundation year was to bring together the humanities, the social and natural sciences in courses on man and the environment and Western civilization. The amalgam was intended to address the unity of knowledge at more levels than other commentators had attempted. It was designed not only to induct students into the broad territories, but also to bring teachers together in joint teaching and tutorials – the learning experience was to be for them also. Lindsay was at the same time exploring combinations of subjects for degree purposes, such as literature and philosophy, and a course reminiscent of Oxford – combining politics, philosophy and economics. Even this, however, was not a blueprint. Writing about English studies in 1950 he indicated his debt to writers like Mannheim and Löwe, and urged that 'we must somehow devise a university education which both gives students understanding of spiritual and social values and allows them to pursue their own particular expertness'.[42]

In 1947 Lindsay had opened a debate on university education in the House of Lords, from the starting point of the great increase in the university population that had taken place and was to continue – expansion inevitably raised 'all sorts of questions about the effect of this revolution on our university system'. The 1944 Education Act was another revolution that had imminent implications for university education, at the same time as there was increasing demand for professionals of many kinds, and the preparation of these did not necessarily have to be to degree level. It was unlikely that institutions would in these circumstances 'preserve their character and their standard if they double their numbers', and the question was whether there should be new institutions which, being small, 'may also be experimental'. He mentioned in this connection that he was familiar with a proposal for such a development from Stoke-on-Trent, and there were other proposals emanating from York, Carlisle, Brighton and other places: 'Is there not room possibly for further experiments?' Adult education was crucial in making appropriate provision. For all of these reasons he was asking the government, which had been generous in funding expansion, to arrange for 'reflection', by appointing a Departmental Committee or by asking the UGC to appoint a subcommittee with extended membership: 'I am not offering answers to these questions; I am only asking that they should be considered.' The UGC could not itself do this since its members would be unwilling to reveal their own weaknesses, and would not be able to look at issues concerning 'the technical colleges and their prospective enlargement into technological institutes' – which were not under the remit of the UGC.[43] The government, it was made clear in the debate, thought any such review was a matter for a committee of the UGC.

Lindsay wanted a review in order to open the door for experiments – his biographer emphasizes that 'what he basically wanted was simply that there should be experiment'.[44] This is what took him to Keele. After it had opened he wrote, in an article for *Nature*, that the new College was 'one practical result of all this fermentation and discussion about universities which has been going on in recent years, notably in this country and in Germany and America'. In the spirit of scientific research it was crucial not just to hand down learning but to investigate. There had to be close links between the university and the mass of the population, and avoiding the isolation of the specialist meant connecting the university with 'the democratic revolution, and the democratic revolution repudiates the notion that power shall be confined to a small and privileged ruling class'. The need for scientific specialists and technical skills had to be combined with general education – something essential for 'an efficient and democratic nation'.[45] There is a central commitment and a continuity in his approach to the universities, to university extension and adult education, and his reputation as an educationist long preceded his connection with the new University College. In 1941 *Picture Post* introduced 'A plan for education' by Lindsay: 'University men look up to him as an outstanding teacher and administrator. One of the leaders of progress in educational ideas.' Christopher Hill compared him to Cromwell, and C.R. Morris in 1951 apologized for asking him when he was ill to review an important book by Raybould on adult education: 'I don't think you will entirely agree with Raybould and you would be listened to in this field more than anyone else.'[46] Eric Ashby wrote a piece for a *Times Supplement* on Keele in 1963, in which he described Lindsay as having three kinds of experience that combined 'to give him a unique insight into post-war problems of higher education; he was

Master of a College which attracted some of the best brains in Britain; he was familiar with the adult-education movement; and he was a socialist'. Lindsay believed in massive expansion, 'not to enlarge such universities as Oxford and Cambridge; nor was it to perpetuate the pattern of benevolent academic colonialism under London' – but by innovation and experiment.[47]

There were to be no more Keeles, but there were to be more experiments from 1957, when the UGC gave approval to go ahead with planning a new University of Sussex, followed by agreement on the creation of six other new universities. All of them received their charters early in the 1960s, and each of them chose distinctive approaches to student learning and living. At the same time calls for a royal commission on the universities were increasingly heard. Such calls had come in parliament from time to time, including Lindsay's – not for a commission but some sort of committee. In 1957 the call was from Michael Stewart, Labour Shadow Minister of Education, appealing for an inquiry into the way in which the universities were meeting the changing needs of the community. This would involve looking at the need for more graduates in such areas as mathematics, the natural sciences and management. Given the increased dependence of the universities on public funds, the community had greater interest in how the universities worked. Stewart had suggested that a commission might estimate the proportion of the population that should enter the universities, based on the proportion of school leavers likely to benefit and the needs of employers. He justified the appointment of a commission, however, on the grounds that the time had come 'to ask afresh what is the real purpose of a university', acknowledging vocational needs but handing on to the next generation 'standards of values and beliefs on which our civilization rests'.[48]

Lord Simon, however, was waging a personal, sustained campaign for a commission, but though he had spoken in the House of Lords debate that Lindsay had opened in 1947 he had not himself pressed for some kind of national review. By the late 1950s he was clearly convinced. When reprinting an article on student numbers, notably technology, where rapid expansion was urgent, he added other material, including on the need for 'a pronouncement of the greatest weight'

> so that Parliament, the Government, the universities, the civil service, and the nation at large shall be persuaded or frightened into vigorous action. Such a pronouncement could probably be made most effectively by a Royal Commission of a few persons of high authority in the scientific and engineering world.[49]

In 1958 he had lunch with Sir Keith Murray, Chairman of the UGC, who poured cold water on Simon's idea of a Royal Commission. Simon noted:

'Keith Murray regards his Committee as a permanent Royal Commission ... the appointment of a Royal Commission might be regarded as critical, both of the U.G.C. and of the Universities'.[50] Later in the year Simon published a lead article in *Universities Quarterly* entitled 'A royal commission on the universities?' The Labour Party, as he now indicated, had agreed to appoint such a commission if returned to power. Although the UGC's report published that year did not concern itself with a royal commission, Simon thought it had addressed similar questions. Simon's article was a curious compendium of questions, covering every aspect of the universities, from the government and the UGC to academic problems, Oxbridge and the other universities. His questions, which he thought the commission could consider, covered the length of the undergraduate course, general education, the relationships between Oxford and Cambridge and their colleges, the work of the UGC, the desirability of more halls of residence, the appropriate scale of government grants to universities, and a swathe of other questions. He thought that any disadvantages of such a commission would be outweighed by 'a thorough and independent study of the whole university system'. The proposal was a criticism neither of the UGC nor of the universities, but was intended to help both to do their work better.[51]

The *Quarterly* invited comments, and though the Principal of Manchester College of Science and Technology lent him support, six other articles – from three English civic universities, one Welsh university college, Oxford and Cambridge – did not. The Vice-Chancellor of the University of Leicester thought Simon had asked so many questions that a royal commission might seem the only way to answer them, but there was already much discussion taking place, Simon was really seeking 'more, and more efficient, national planning of the universities', and a commission was 'a fate I hope we may be spared'. A Reader at Birmingham thought a commission possible only if it considered the question whether to fund the expansion of existing universities or create new ones. A Professor of Education at Leeds thought that 'to have such a solemn, humourless, Benthamite pawing with the basic moral assumptions of university life fills one with horror'. A Senior Lecturer at Cardiff (and President of the AUT) thought all Simon's questions could be dealt with by amending the functions of the UGC and the CVCP, and by recognizing the AUT as speaking for the university teacher. A response from Oxford dealt exclusively with the particular experience of the University, and an assistant tutor at Cambridge thought some of the questions worth while but to be discussed only by 'a predominantly academic committee' of the CVCP type, modified to represent Oxbridge and to contain members other than vice-chancellors.[52]

In May 1960 Simon introduced a resolution in the House of Lords 'to ask Her Majesty's Government to appoint a Committee to inquire and report on the extent and nature of the provisions of full-time education for those over the age of 18, whether in universities or in other educational institutions'. The latter point was something he strongly emphasized, since no parliamentary debate had previously covered both categories. He explored a range of issues, including comparison with student numbers in other countries, size, research, funding and administrative matters, and felt the best way to deal with them was 'by independent persons nominated by the Government' – a committee, committees or a Royal Commission, working for three or four years to consider the next 20 years.[53] He typed a note 12 days later, recording that

> the debate went really well ... Reports in the press were about as good as could reasonably be hoped for; a first leader the Times and a second leader in the [Manchester Guardian]. Most satisfactory ... Hailsham ... did as much as he could to promise serious consideration by the Government ... nearly everybody spoke very highly of the U.G.C. and made it quite clear that they will do nothing to attack them. The universities are complacent, competent and powerful ... Everybody says the universities are free, whereas in fact they are very closely controlled by the U.G.C.[54]

It was reported in September that 'planning for an inquiry is now believed to be in an advanced state and it is expected that, shortly after Parliament reassembles, the Prime Minister will announce its terms'.[55] Simon had had lunch with C.P. Snow a week before the Lords debate, and Snow had been critical of the 'self-satisfaction' of the UGC by comparison with the more self-critical American universities. Snow would like to be a member, and thought Eric Ashby would be the best person to chair a Commission.[56] Ashby had previously written to Simon, suggesting that since 'we regard you as the undisputed Elder-Statesman on University matters', Simon might turn his list of questions for a Commission into an article giving his own opinions.'[57]

The inquiry was in fact not announced when Parliament reassembled in 1960, but in February 1961, when the Committee under Lord Robbins was appointed by the Conservative government 'to review the pattern of full-time higher education in Great Britain and in the light of national needs and resources to advise Her Majesty's Government on what principles its long-term development should be based'. It was to see if there should be any changes in the pattern, whether new types of institutions were desirable, and whether any new planning and co-ordinating arrangements were needed. The Robbins report was presented to Parliament in October 1963.

TECHNOLOGY AND OPINION

One thread that has been largely bypassed in the above discussion of the 1950s, but one that is crucial to an understanding of the decade, is that of technology. At the beginning of the 1950s academic and policy agendas regarding technology in the universities and technical institutions related overwhelmingly to the demand for expert personnel as highlighted by the war. In 1952 Sir John Cockcroft, Director of the Atomic Energy Research Establishment, wrote that 'technological education has been very much discussed in the post-war years', but he was in fact referring to the post-war discussion of its *provision*, productivity, the shortage of technologists and higher technological education in the service of industry and government.[58] From the Percy report on *Higher Technological Education* in 1945 and the Barlow report on *Scientific Man-Power* (also concerned with technology) in 1946, and through other post-war reports and statements, the technology that had proved important in the war became an issue of major policy concern. Evidence to the Percy committee underlined that Britain's industrial position was being endangered by the failure adequately to apply science to industry. The Barlow committee recommended doubling the output of science graduates.[59] The central issue for both science and technology was numbers. Reflecting on the period 1947–52, the UGC commented that 'no subject has been so much discussed as that of technology, not only by industry, professional associations and others bodies and the Press, but by ourselves and our Technology Sub-Committee'. A prominent professor of engineering reported in 1948 that the need for more engineers was so acute, and places so few in the universities, that there were proposals for new universities, for selected technical colleges to award degrees, and for 'shift' working in the universities.[60]

Numbers also meant controversy about whether the education of more technologists should take place in the universities and/or in other institutions. Sir Lawrence Bragg, as we have seen, was arguing in 1949 for building up 'new centres of higher technological education of university rank', though others at the conference supported the expansion of technology in the universities.[61] The following year the AUT argued that technology could train minds as well as mathematics or modern languages, and it was important for technological studies to take place together with the fundamental sciences and alongside the arts. The Dean of the Faculty of Engineering at the University of Bristol thought that the universities should contain 'the genuine engineering scientist' and the idea of reducing pressure on universities by taking technological studies elsewhere was 'peculiarly specious'. However, R.A. Butler, who had been responsible for setting up the Percy Committee, saw the need both for higher technological education alongside research and the establishment of 'higher institutes of technology'[62]. Pressures for new institutions and new qualifications mounted, together with counter-pressures, from this period. In a symposium on 'Higher education in technology' in 1952 one contributor outlined alternative strategies available for higher techno-logical education, including courses at technical colleges approved by a new 'College of Technologists'; the creation of new technological universities; the extension of provision in the universities.[63] The Head of the Department of Engineering at Cambridge reviewed the professional and personal characteristics needed by technologists, and thought that the universities were 'pre-eminently fitted' to develop these.[64] The Vice-Chancellor of the University of Leeds (and editor of *Universities Quarterly*) thought the universities would welcome technological studies, provided these were 'up to the present recognized university standards'.[65] The controversies involved in this search for expansion and its educational implications were taking place at many levels, with frequent reference to 'survival', 'productivity', 'balance', 'standards' or obstacles raised by 'reactionaries'.

Government intervention was also being increasingly directed, as in other countries, to the expansion of higher technology education by policy pressure and funding support, and the mid-1950s were crucial in this respect. Much in the arguments related to evidence of the education of scientists and technologists in other countries – particularly the United States and the Soviet Union.[66] A National Advisory Council on Education for Industry and Commerce had been established in 1947, as we have seen, to advise the Minister of Education on the development of higher-level work in the technical colleges. Its recommendations led to the formation in 1955 of the National Council for Technological Awards (NCTA), an independent body 'to create and administer awards for students in technical colleges who complete … such courses in technology as have been approved by the Governing Body'. By 1958 there were over 2,500 students on 66 courses at 20 colleges studying for the new Diploma in Technology.[67] The NCTA emphasized the importance of 'sandwich courses', combining periods of academic study with substantial work experience, and of including liberal studies (variously interpreted) and the principles of industrial organization in Diploma programmes. This Diploma, said the chair of the NCTA, was going to be the key to rapid development because it was the 'means of raising the standards generally in the technical college world and infusing a new spirit into it … a more liberal atmosphere'.[68] One issue in the debate had now been settled – higher technology education was to be partly in the universities, partly in a new sector of higher education. The Diploma in Technology was an attempt to establish a degree equivalent, and it survived for a decade.

A Government White Paper on *Technical Education* in 1956 devoted a section to the role of the universities, planning to follow up 'with vigour and imagination the impetus which has been developed during the last four or five years'. The plan for technical colleges confirmed the direction taken by the creation of the NCTA and included the development of appropriate independence for the 'Colleges of Advanced Technology' (CATs).[69] Not everyone was happy that the developed colleges were not to award their own degrees: the President of the Engineering Section of the British Association thought that 'the conferment of degree-granting powers on some of our leading technological institutions would greatly encourage young people to choose technology as a career'. Also in 1956 the *Journal of Education* criticized both the universities and the colleges for their narrow, specialist approaches to education. It also offered a dramatis personae of some those contributing to the current debates: 'Professor Zuckermann, Dr Bronowski, the *New Statesman* on "New Minds for the New World", Mr C.P. Snow, their Lordships and others have recently added their individual voices to a number of Government utterances about the urgent need to recruit and train more scientists and technologists.' Improvements were needed in general, the *Journal* believed, away from the 'arrogance and intolerance of specialists' towards 'the civilized humanity of mature adults'.[70]

By the late 1950s it was clear from government and committee statements, policy discussion surrounding the creation and operation of the NCTA and the roles of the universities, the increasing focus of discussion in the *Universities Quarterly* and other journals, and the concerns of a variety of organizations, that technological education had become not only an item on agendas but also a considerable impetus towards the review of 'higher education' that was being either advocated or resisted. Since the Percy report the issues prominently under discussion had widened to include national need and university autonomy, academic standards and the status of technology, budgets, buildings, curricula and pedagogy. The implications were considerable for technologists and non-technologists alike, national policy makers and academics, the universities and the technological institutions. The interpretation of higher technological education and its implications for higher education was most prominently undertaken by Eric Ashby.

NOTES AND REFERENCES

1. 'Notes', *Universities Review*, vol. 22, 1950, p. 134.
2. UGC, *University Development: Report on the Years 1947 to 1952* (London: HMSO, 1953), pp. 7–10.
3. 'Notes', *Universities Quarterly*, vol. 6, 1952, p. 330.
4. UGC, *University Development 1952–1957* (London: HMSO, 1958), pp. 19–20.
5. Pullan, B. and Abendstern, M., *A History of the University of Manchester 1951–73* (Manchester: Manchester University Press, 2000), pp. 30–1.

6. *Universities Quarterly,* vol. 6, 1952, p. 330.
7. Stewart, W.A.C., *Higher Education in Postwar Britain* (London: Macmillan, 1989), p. 62.
8. Caine, S., 'The Congress: a Malayan view', *Universities Quarterly,* vol. 8, 1954, pp. 130–1.
9. Halsey, A.H., 'British universities and intellectual life', *Universities Quarterly,* vol. 12, 1958, pp. 144–6.
10. James, D.G., 'University commentary', *Universities Quarterly,* vol. 10, 1956, pp. 118–19.
11. Morris, C., 'The idea of university education', *Universities Quarterly,* vols 8–9, 1954–55; Bibby, C., 'T.H. Huxley's idea of a university', *Universities Quarterly,* vol. 10, 1956; Winch, P., 'The universities and the state', *Universities Quarterly,* vol. 12, 1957, p. 23.
12. UGC, *University Development: Report on the Years 1947 to 1952,* p. 75.
13. UGC, *University Development 1952–1957,* p. 77.
14. Caine, 'The Congress: a Malayan view', pp. 130–1.
15. 'Notes', *Universities Quarterly,* vol. 4, 1950, p. 115.
16. Ibid., p. 119.
17. Armytage, W.H.G., 'The anatomy of academics', *Education for Teaching,* no. 41, 1956, pp. 54–5.
18. Kneller, G.F., *Higher Learning in Britain* (Berkeley, CA: University of California Press, 1955), pp. 100, 223, 241–2.
19. Morris, C.R., Review of Kneller, *Higher Learning in Britain, Universities Quarterly,* vol. 10, 1956, pp. 391–2.
20. *Journal of Education,* 'Our Reith Lecture', vol. 88, 1956, p. 510.
21. 'Notes', *Universities Review,* vol. 33, 1960, p. 2.
22. Macmurray, J., address at Sixth Congress of the Universities of the British Commonwealth 1948, *Report of Proceedings,* London, Association of Universities of the British Commonwealth, pp. 102–3, 106.
23. Moberly, W., *The Crisis in the University* (London: SCM Press, 1949), pp. 185–92.
24. Kneller, *Higher Learning in Britain,* p. 188.
25. UGC, *University Development 1952–1957,* pp. 37–42.
26. *Nature,* 'Education for modern needs', vol. 180, 1957, p. 1151.
27. *Journal of Education,* 'Our Reith Lecture, p. 510.
28. Fulton, J.S., 'General education', *Universities Quarterly,* vol. 5, 1950, pp. 47–8; Montrose, J.L., 'A specialist approach to general education', *Universities Quarterly,* vol. 7, 1952, pp. 73–5, 78–80; Bibby, C., 'The general education of the specialist student', *Universities Quarterly,* vol. 8, 1954, pp. 369–75; Ashby, E., Review of Cohen and Watson, *General Education in Science, Universities Quarterly,* vol. 8, 1954, pp. 304–8.
29. Oakeshott, M., 'The idea of a university' (*The Listener,* 1950), in T. Fuller (ed.) *The Voice of Liberal Learning: Michael Oakeshott on Education* (New Haven, CT: Yale University Press, 1989), p. 96.
30. Winch, 'The universities and the state', pp. 14, 16.
31. Gallie, W.B., *A New University: A.D. Lindsay and the Keele Experiment* (London, Chatto & Windus, 1960), pp. 43–4.
32. Young, M., 'Nostalgia for Keele', the *Guardian,* 2 December 1960.
33. UGC, *University Development: Report on the Years 1947 to 1952,* p. 10.
34. Ibid.
35. Christopher Hill, historian and a later Master of Balliol College, wrote, in undated notes for an obituary of Lindsay, that he gave a lead 'in modernizing and democratizing Oxford', LP file 145 (1911–1967 Letters, Obits etc.).

36. Lindsay, A.D., *The Essentials of Democracy* (London: Oxford University Press, 1929), p. 20.
37. Lindsay, A.D., *I Believe in Democracy.* Addresses, BBC Empire Programme (London: Oxford University Press, 1940), pp. 34–5.
38. Ibid., p. 28.
39. LP file 204, note.
40. LP file 179, The Master's Letter, September 1949, pp. 2–3.
41. Ortega y Gasset, *Mission of the University* (lectures given at the University of Madrid, 1930) (orig. pub. Princeton University Press, 1944; 1992 edn, New Brunswick, NJ: Transaction Publishers), ch. 4.
42. Lindsay, A.D., 'The place of English studies in British universities', paper given in Oxford 1950, reprinted from Wrenn, C.L. and Bullough, G. (eds), *English Studies Today* (1951) in *Rewley House Papers*, vol. 3, 1961–62, p. 5.
43. Hansard, House of Lords, 14 May 1947, columns 696–703, 707–8, 742.
44. Scott, D., *A.D. Lindsay: A Biography* (Oxford: Blackwell, 1971), p. 349.
45. 'The function of the universities', LP file 209, typescript dated November 1950 of article for *Nature*.
46. *Picture Post*, editorial introduction to Lindsay, 'A plan for education', 4 January 1941, p. 27 (copy in LP file 204); Hill notes, LP file 145 (cf. also Scott, p. xvii); Morris to Lindsay, 1.10.51, LP file 174.
47. Ashby, E., 'Setting the pattern', *Times Supplement* on the University of Keele, 9 October 1963, p. i.
48. Stewart, reported in *Nature*, 'Education for modern needs', vol. 180, 1957, pp. 1149–50.
49. Simon, E., *Future Numbers of University Students: The Desperate Need for Technologists*, (1956) (reprinted from *Universities Quarterly* [with additions], February 1956), p. 15.
50. Simon, note of lunch with Murray 17 April 1958, SP M11/4/31a.
51. Simon, E., 'A royal commission on the universities?', *Universities Quarterly*, vol. 13, 1958, pp. 9–22.
52. Bowden, B.V., 'Too few academic eggs', *Universities Quarterly*, vol. 14, 1959–60, pp. 7–23; Wilson, C., (response), *Universities Quarterly*, vol. 13, 1958, pp. 119–21; Bell, D.A., (response), ibid., pp. 121–4; Walsh, W., (response), ibid., pp. 124–8; Urwin, K. (response), ibid., 128–31. 'Tom Jones', 'A royal commission at Oxford?', ibid., pp. 231–42; Broadbent, J.B. 'Or at Cambridge?', ibid., pp. 243–52.
53. Hansard, House of Lords, 11 May 1960, 'University and other education', columns 615, 617, 622–3.
54. Simon typed note, 23 May 1960, SP M11/11/14.
55. *Technology*, September 1960, cutting in SP M11/11/14.
56. Simon note, 9 May 1960, SP M11/10 (Snow file).
57. Ashby to Simon, 21 August 1958, SP M11/13 (Ashby file).
58. Cockcroft, J., 'Technology and the university', *Universities Quarterly*, vol. 6, 1952, pp. 244–8.
59. *Higher Technological Education* (Percy report) (London: HMSO, 1945); *Scientific Man-Power* (Barlow report) (London: HMSO, 1946).
60. UGC, *University Development 1947 to 1952*, p. 58; Pippard, A.J.S., 'Engineering studies in British universities', *Universities Quarterly*, vol. 2, 1948, p. 167.
61. Bragg, L., 'The place of technological education in university studies', Home Universities Conference, *Report of Proceedings* (London: Association of Commonwealth Universities, 1952).
62. AUT, *Report on the Place of Technology in the Universities* (reprinted from *Universities Review*, vol. 23) (London: AUT, 1950); Rawcliffe, G.H., 'Engineering science

and technology in British universities', *Universities Review*, vol. 22, 1950, pp. 93–107; Butler, R.A., 'The study of technology', *Universities Quarterly*, vol. 1, 1947, pp. 273–5.

63. Sir Frederick Handley Page, Chairman of CGIL Council, 'The higher technology', *Universities Quarterly*, vol. 6, 1952, pp. 125–31.

64. Baker, J.F., 'The universities and post-graduate courses in technology', in ibid., pp. 147–32.

65. Morris, C.R., 'The universities and technology', in ibid., pp. 119–24.

66. An important article on the subject, 'New minds for the new world', was published anonymously in the *New Statesman* on 8 September 1956, pp. 279–82.

67. NCTA, *Declaration of Trust*, London, November 1956; NCTA Press Conference, statement by Lord Hives, London, December 1957; NCTA, *Report for the Period August 1957 to March 1959*, London, p. 1.

68. NCTA, *Report for the Period April 1959 to March 1960*, London, p. 5; NCTA, Press Conference statement by Lord Hives.

69. *Ministry of Education, Technical Education* (London: HMSO, 1956), pp. 12–17.

70. Anderson, D., reported in *Nature*, vol. 180, 1956, p. 1,150; *Journal of Education*, 'Our Reith Lecture', vol. 88, 1956, pp. 510–11.

8

ASHBY: 'THE AGE OF TECHNOLOGY'

VOICE AND AUDIENCES

The development of higher technological education and its impact on higher education can be seen most clearly in the transition of Eric Ashby from research botanist to intensive and thoughtful advocate not only of technology but also of the implications for the internal life of the universities and the higher education system. The focus here is on England, and although Eric Ashby's most formative period was in Northern Ireland, his *Technology and the Academics* published in 1958, was mainly about England. Born and educated in England, including as a botanist at Imperial College, London, he moved to the University of Sydney, became Australian scientific attaché in the Soviet Union for a period during the Second World War, then back to an academic post at the University of Manchester, and with great reluctance accepted the position of President and Vice-Chancellor of Queen's University of Belfast in 1950. The themes of his conference and other addresses in the United Kingdom and worldwide were set in the frameworks of development and ideas that he would have had to address similarly had he become vice-chancellor of an English university. In 1959 he moved to become Master of Clare College, Cambridge, of which university he was also Vice-Chancellor from 1967–75. He had an immense international involvement with universities and by the time he left Belfast he was becoming one of the most important British university voices. The interest here, however, is the emergence of his approach to higher technological education and its implications for democracy, university structures and student experience in higher education.

When he published *Technology and the Academics* he had been at Queen's eight years, and was contributing widely in lectures, addresses, reviews and publications on issues that we have seen emerging in the 1950s. In no sense was he engaged in public debates conducted by other contributors whose voices we have heard, though they formed an important backcloth to the

9. Eric (Lord) Ashby, 1979, Salt Lake City. (Courtesy of Professor Michael Ashby.)

views he was formulating, and he was responsive to the strengths and weaknesses of national policy. He was a member of the editorial board of *Universities Quarterly*, a member from 1950–53 of the Advisory Council on Scientific Policy, and from 1954–60 a member of the Advisory Council of the government's Department of Scientific and Industrial Resarch (DSIR), and grappling at the same time with the implications of the national policies that were intended to increase the number of science and technology students in the universities, including the one of which he was Vice-Chancellor. In going to Queen's, as he wrote in an autobiographical document, he had decided that he was 'more interested in people than in ideas; in teaching and educational issues than in pure science; and in solving problems about people rather than problems about plants'.[1] He continued to be a prominent voice on the implications of technology for the curriculum and life of higher education after he left Queen's, where he became Sir Eric, and then Lord Ashby whilst at Cambridge. The year before he wrote *Technology and the Academics* the decision had been taken to create the new universities, and he had recognized the emergence of a radically changed era to which higher education had to respond. The *New Scientist* began a profile of Ashby in 1958 under the title 'Missionary of the age of technology'. It described his earnestness, enthusiasm and conscience as making him 'something of a missionary, though the mind of the scholar is there to keep these things in proportion'. Among those who spoke and wrote about 'the problems of education in the Age of Technology there are few who do so with more authority or good sense than Sir Eric Ashby'.[2] He had by that stage been widely recognized as an acute analyst of the status quo and proponent of necessary change, one of the most important vice-chancellors and commentators on higher education, gauging his audiences and sharpening his messages about the provision of higher education in general and technological education in particular, but also about outdated thinking and practices in the universities and wider issues of purpose and policy. All of these took clear shape while he was at Queen's University. Though technology and its importance were at the heart of his message, so also was a point to which he was constantly to return: universities were like biological organisms, both having a function to survive, but universities also had a purpose.[3]

Policy making and increased funding by the state during and after the war had, as we have seen, caused anxiety about the universities' ability to defend their autonomy, and Ashby – more than 40 years after the event – described 1946 as the time when they

> passed through a climacteric. For the first time in their history more than 50 per cent of their income came from Parliamentary grants. The Government – to use the jargon of the enterprise culture – had become a majority shareholder in the academic industry.[4]

Although Ashby recognized the national importance of technology he never adopted what Salter and Tapper describe as 'the economic ideology of education', used by the state to bring higher education under its control.[5] That he espoused in his own way the cause of technology was unexpected. After he had been to the Soviet Union during the war he published *Scientist in Russia* in 1947 but in it he discussed only science, not technology. His Australian book the previous year, *Challenge to Education*, had referred to professional and scientific education, but made no mention of technology.[6] At Queen's he became acutely aware of the policy pressures and their implications for the autonomy of the universities and their balance of studies. He did not accept a narrow view of what technology was and what a technological education could be, and approved, for example, of the breadth of the technological curriculum represented by the NCTA and in the development of advanced courses in the technical colleges. He was becoming an increasingly visible university leader. He reflected in an interview in 1990 on his experience as a vice-chancellor (probably covering Cambridge as well as Queen's) that 'I was doing a lot of writing about education then ... and I was regarded as a sort of avant-garde of the British Vice-Chancellors.' Asked if he had become an educational philosopher he answered: 'Yes, but in quotes because philosophers wouldn't have called me that.'[7] It was not on the wider stage, however, but within Queen's that he found and voiced his views.

He began to express views about technology to a limited Belfast audience in 1953. At a graduation ceremony he explained why the University was putting up new buildings, including one to accommodate civil engineering. If war were to break out, he suggested, survival would depend on 'a clear faith in the values we are defending, and a consummate skill in the applications of science and technology to all aspects of defence' – though modern technology was necessary also in peacetime for the survival of industry and agriculture. A shortcoming of life at the University was that it had not given students enough 'respect for practical affairs', and while attempting to make them 'objective thinkers' it had failed to direct them to the sources of ideas about ends and purposes.[8] The following year he came closer, again addressing a graduation ceremony, to relating the issue of technology to the work of the universities. Others in the 1930s and 1940s had discussed the university amid world crises in similar terms: 'we live in precarious times. There is no doubt that the conscience of universities is troubled and they are going through a period of heart searching.' Governments, at Westminster and at Stormont in Northern Ireland, were encouraging 'a great development of higher technology in universities', but there were many in the universities who believed that physicists and engineers 'automatically have a poorer liberal education than classicists and historians'. He expressed what was to become his constant opposition to the belief that the solution lay in devising courses 'to counteract specialism, diluting chemistry with a little philosophy and engineering with a little history'. Graduates were inevitably specialists, and the solution lay in encouraging them to communicate with one another:

'If the universities can restore communication between specialists they need have no fear of technology; indeed technology may already have given the humanities a new lease of life by presenting them with a new challenge.'[9] His conception of the relation between technology and the humanities was to take a different form, but this was his first step towards a fuller treatment of issues that had been surfacing in the debates of the late 1940s and early 1950s.

At the 1955 ceremony Ashby referred to the University's increased teaching and research in technology, setting expansion in a discussion of the importance of the university as a community, embodying what was to be a lifelong commitment: the diffusion of responsibilities in the institution as widely as possible, and the generation of policy, not through 'directives from above but from among the men and women engaged in teaching and research'. Much of the criticism of science and technology he saw as deriving from the failure of the expert to climb 'high enough to see the whole social landscape in which he is working'. He had himself had a university education in science but the rest of his education had been 'ragged and incomplete', since he was 'holding on to Western civilisation by one strand only – science; I had no sure hold on the other three strands of Western civilisation: the Christian tradition, the process of democracy, and the legacy of Greece'.[10] Without direct reference to technology he followed up these latter themes at ceremonies in subsequent years. His university science education had given him a 'kit of tools for his profession' and 'a sort of child's guide to living'. The way studies were organized in a university was 'inimical to wisdom' or 'whole situations', since it concentrated on knowledge in depth.[11] He was turning his attention in a number of directions, ones that he was soon to explore on a national and world stage. From the beginning he considered the University's annual report in need of something more than the formal review of its operations. He began to air a range of views in a preface or a supplement to the annual report entitled 'Prospect for the future'. His first such statement was a plea for the 'privilege of autonomy in university government' – the tradition of 'academic affairs managed by academic people'; in ensuing years he dealt with the domestic issues affecting Queen's – hopes of expansion, narrowing prospects of the financial means of achieving it, and the needs of Northern Ireland – describing the universities in 1954–55 as facing 'a financial east wind'.[12]

His statement for 1955–56 marked a sea change. This was more an essay than a statement for a report, and it is clear that he had discovered within the university and in its outside participants and political supporters an audience to whom he could offer views that reached far beyond, whilst including the issues facing Queen's. Ashby was responding more thoughtfully year by year to the crescendo of demand for more technology graduates. While this was an important point at which the state was reaching out to strengthen its hand on the universities, Ashby accepted this policy direction, while seeking to defend and redefine the university. His vocabulary and tone had changed radically. The UK was facing 'grave economic and international problems' depending for their solution on increased numbers of science and technology graduates, and this was both 'a challenge and an embarrassment to universities'. Russia, as he was frequently to point out, was producing a far higher proportion of such graduates, who had also been studying the humanities and social sciences. Russian education might not be an acceptable model, but it could not be ignored, and the United Kingdom had not shown signs of devising any other or better solutions to 'the problem of the technological age'. Some of his own solutions were 'uncomfortable departures from tradition', but to ignore the 'approaching pattern of society' would be more uncomfortable: 'the truth is that we are at a climacteric of civilisation, when universities must either lead or abdicate'. This argument introduced the tripartite nature of Ashby's thinking that was to suffuse his approach to higher education. First, there was the new technological age, with economic survival depending on industry, and industry depending on experts, many of whom would have to be graduates. Second, there was the impact of technology on what universities taught and how they taught it, the essential problem being:

> how to ensure that those aspects of the humanities which neither science nor technology will ever render obsolete – discussion of moral issues, appreciation of works of imagination, and study of the past – are preserved as an integral part of university work.

Arts faculties could not continue to produce graduates 'innocent of the history and social implications of science and technology', and the humanities needed to be diffused among the future leaders of a technologically based society. It would not be easy to persuade technologists that political institutions mattered as much to them as mechanics, or to convince classicists that the history of electricity was as important as the Principate of Augustus. He emphasized a direct link between the 'technological age' and the breadth of study required for university technology students. Given the creation of the NCTA and the focus on liberal studies in the technical colleges, he regretted that the universities were lagging behind. Third, therefore, there was the question of university structure: he suggested that what was needed was easier communication between faculties 'and more flexibility in the selection of ingredients for a degree'. Circumspect though this was, the meaning was clear. There was too much rigidity in the universities' academic structures (including at Queen's), to the disadvantage of courses of study and students. There would have to be 'some painful renunciation of cherished traditions'. The organization of the university itself was directly related to the age of technology.[13]

Having flexed his muscles Ashby went on the next year to produce a much longer commentary, and then to produce two more before he left the University. His 'essay' in 1957 reviewed the period since 1950, but began with the background of the universities through six centuries of war and social upheaval. Universities had now become 'big business' and given conflicting views within them they had learned how 'to integrate what is permanent with what is contemporary'. Queen's too was preserving a balance, and was not pursuing technology at the expense of the humanities. It needed advice from the faculties and Academic Council on how new decisions might be taken to adapt courses of study, including along lines pioneered by the NCTA. He criticized schools of studies in the humanities for failing to offer any 'civilising influence to the technologist ... What the technologist needs from the humanist is help towards the appreciation of whole situations ... Man does not live by thermodynamics alone.' He considered lay members to be important in university governance and described the Senate as steering by two stars: the ideas and values which for six centuries had accumulated round the word 'university', and the function 'partly traditional, partly novel – which universities are called upon to fill in our place and generation'.[14] The conflict and coalescence of tradition and modernity was to be a constant theme in Ashby's writing, a more penetrating theme and treatment than much of what had previously filled controversies about technology and university expansion.

In his final two contributions to the annual report – when he was finishing and publishing *Technology and the Academics* – he focused on student recruitment for science and technology and university organization and governance. The former was made difficult by school inadequacies and the dismissive attitude of some head teachers, but the University also had to retain a 'vigorous and enterprising' Faculty of Arts. It was important that all members of academic staff had an opportunity to play an effective part in the administration of the University. However, as numbers grew, 'Senate and Academic Council may have to devise measures to protect the University from the benevolent but conservative wisdom of a professorial oligarchy.' By his last 'essay', Ashby's line of argument from technological education to increased numbers and the democratic university had become increasingly clear:

> It is my personal belief that these difficulties of size can be solved only by an increased dispersion of responsibility – and an acceptance of it – among academic members of staff. Even what are commonly thought to be the highest flights of policy cannot be originated by some isolated administrator sitting at a desk...the more the teaching staff share in originating policy in the University, the better the policy is likely to be.[15]

The Ashby of this decade is difficult to detach, on the one hand, from the immediacy of his dedication to Queen's University and its needs and responses to national concerns, and on the other hand from his vision of the world ahead based on science and technology but harnessed to the values and ideals of the traditions of the humanities and social sciences. He had brought with him to Belfast a variety of experience that helped to drive this vision. As a student at Imperial College he had combined his botany with an interest in literature, running a literary society in which he hosted Siegfried Sassoon, Walter de la Mare and Edith Sitwell. He wrote verse, became proficient in German, appeared in several plays and went to concerts.[16] In Russia, despite the glaring weaknesses, argument by 'heresy hunt', 'distortion of truth', state suspicion of foreigners and closed frontiers, all of which he encountered, he was impressed by the way 'Russia has endowed science with the authority of religion'.[17] He brought from these and other experiences a liberalism of attitude towards the running of the University and towards ideas: he was described in 1973 as being 'proud of his pragmatism and happy to be described as an "unrepentant liberal" '.[18] His outlook at Queen's seemed to consist of a combination of science-and-technology with the social mission of higher education, and he was able to think through a variety of issues relating to an expansionist policy, the relationship of tradition to the contemporary and emergent world, and of technology to the humane values he believed to be so important.

THE WIDER STAGE

By 1957 he had agreed to accept the invitation to become 'Master of Clare College, Cambridge, though only if he could defer taking up the appointment until 1959. The comments in his final reports therefore constitute a frank appraisal of what he had learned from his period in Belfast, notably the adaptation of the universities to the technological age, his curricular concerns and the importance of a democratic diffusion of academic responsibilities. By the time he published *Technology and the Academics* and shortly afterwards left for Cambridge, he had also begun what was to become a characteristic, extraordinarily busy period of other public pronouncements – broadcasting, reviewing, lecturing, contributing to conferences and publishing. His involvement in international university affairs was to make him a prominent contributor to universities and the literature of higher education in Africa, India and the United States in particular. In 1951–52 in print and in a conference address he discussed the issue of universities providing adequate facilities for students living at home, in order to enable them to be 'full-time students' – views that became widely cited and discussed.[19] In 1954 a

Committee on the Organisation and Finance of Adult Education, which he chaired, published its report.[20] His most important 'public' year while at Queen's, however, was 1956, the year in which he turned his annual report contributions into 'essays'.

In that year he delivered an 'oration' at Goldsmiths' College, University of London, explaining it was the first oration he had ever given – though 'lectures, addresses, speeches, votes of thanks ... are part of my daily routine'. He chose as his topic 'The teacher in an age of automation', reflecting on the aspects of 'tomorrow's world' likely to be important to teachers, and he gave some indication of the kind of things he was reading and thinking about – books on contemporary economics and on automation, including one published by the DSIR, of which he was a Council member.[21] In *Universities Quarterly* he opposed the government's decision for the Public Accounts Committee to scrutinize university accounts, since he believed that lay membership of governing bodies was already a sufficient safeguard. This was part of his dedication to what he wrote about in an article on 'Self-government in modern British universities' in the same year. This concerned university constitutions, emphasizing that although governing bodies held sovereignty and academic members were not in a majority there, the conditions for academic freedom were delegated to the senior academic body. University government by consent was secured by ensuring 'that there is an upward and not a downward flow of business and policy making'.[22]

In an article on 'Function and survival in British universities' he discussed the changing functions of universities and what he saw as three of their stable features – their government, their identity as coherent societies (focusing on student residence in Britain, unlike in other European countries), and the importance attached to research. 'Unstable' features included the difficulties associated with specialization, and 'the invasion of technology'. Though one-third of students were studying technology in British universities (including medicine, 'which is *par excellence* a technology') it had not been *'assimilated* into university life' (his italics). It was treated as narrow and having nothing intrinsic to offer to the university, yet the survival of British universities could depend on how they assimilated technology. Classical humanism, concerned though it was with such important issues as good and evil, justice and taste, no longer reached into 'the bloodstream of society'. It was fallacious to assume that technology could not embrace the humanities:

> Humanism is concerned with the creative acts of man: these include aeroplanes as well as gothic churches, and textiles as well as poetry. It is true that aeronautics and textile technology are frequently taught in such a way as to miss all the humanism essential to a mastery of these subjects; but that is not an inherent weakness in technology: it is

a weakness of technologists. It is deplorable, but no worse than the narrow philological study of Shakespeare, or the pedantic editing of some third-rate poet.

The future lay in creating a technological humanism. Technology was the application of science to social needs, and 'it cannot be understood unless social needs are understood'. The technologist was bound to take account of human values, 'taste in design, justice in labour relations; even the problems of good and evil'. Making the issues of humanism an integral part of technology would thereby enable them 'to reach the bloodstream of our inevitably technological civilization: and that is the greatest educational need of our time'.[23]

Ashby was exploring the history, sociology and morphology of the university, and his analysis was rooted in the policies and university circumstances he was experiencing. At a conference he looked sceptically at the topic he had been invited to discuss: 'Impact on the universities of the government's policy for the expansion of technological education'. He did not believe that there was such an impact, 'in the sense that an impact is a short sharp shock'. Over the previous 18 years the percentage of students studying technology in British universities had increased only from 10.5 to 12.9. There were precedents for most problems arising from government policy: new institutions were being established, as they had been in the nineteenth century; the redistribution of finance amongst faculties was nothing new; the policy would make universities more expensive to run and therefore more dependent on the state – again, nothing new in international experience, given that American state universities and European universities had relied for a century or more on public finance. The *new* problems lay in the need to find continuing roles for faculties of arts, and the relationship between the humanities and technology. New courses and course combinations had to be designed, and central to this effort was the way faculties of arts could offer humane courses to technology that were 'integral', not 'extraneous' to it. He gave an example of how this could be done:

From the study of metallurgy (for example) it is a natural step to the history of industry since the seventeenth century, and from there to the sociology and ethics of industrial societies ... those who profess history, social philosophy, political institutions, and jurisprudence would have a vital contribution to make to undergraduate courses in technology.

To this he added an important rider: 'if only the chronic intellectual costiveness of faculty boards could be purged ... if only the ivory curtains between faculties were raised'. This was a bitter reflection on one aspect of his years in university education, as much as a plea for the future of arts faculties, by contributing to the teaching of technology.[24] He returned to the fray on two occasions the following year. In a lecture to the Institute of Metals he re-affirmed his conception of technological humanism. In an article he accused the British universities of having a split personality, accepting the invitation to produce more technologists, but apprehensive about the effect on a liberal education. Again, he emphasized that the technologist needed help towards 'the appreciation of whole situations', and if faculties of arts failed to help and to resume 'something of their mediaeval function in the university' the universities would not fulfil their 'traditional purpose in society'.[25]

The strength of Ashby's commitment to these views was illustrated in his last year at Queen's, in the unlikely context of an issue of the *Belfast News-Letter* commemorating the first half century of the University (from 1849 it had been a college in a federal university, receiving its charter in 1909). In an extensive leading article, after celebrating the history, he turned to post-war expansion. Increased attention to science and technology had led some people to raise the 'imaginary problem' that this would be at the expense of 'what they vaguely describe as the humanities'. What they meant by that had something to do with art and music, Shakespeare and Racine, or emendation of corrupt Greek texts or the quarrels of Shelley with his wife in 1814. But, and it was a strong 'but', science and technology were humanities: 'By some diehards they are not yet admitted as humanities, but then neither was Greek regarded as a humanity before the Renaissance (though astronomy was); nor was English a humanity until the nineteenth century ... humanism is indivisible.' At Queen's he indicated, in forthright language for a celebratory essay, 'these mischievous barriers between studies' had begun to be broken down. Tomorrow's world did not mean, as some imagined, a demand for narrow experts, but 'for civilised people who can blend expertise with the art of living'.[26] The UGC was at the same time expressing the view that applied science should be taught where it was in close touch with the pure sciences and humanities, 'many of whose disciplines are becoming increasingly recog-nised as a necessary part of the education of the technologist'.[27] Ashby was shortly to join the UGC, but he had developed a more dynamic approach to the issue.

TECHNOLOGY AND THE ACADEMICS

In 1957 Ashby had also delivered the Ballard-Mathews Lectures at the University College of North Wales, Bangor. Although *Technology and the Academics*, published the following year, was based primarily on the Bangor lectures, it extended them and incorporated a good deal of his other publications – their ideas and arguments, spirit and direct extracts. Much was modified, much added, and all was encapsulated in his tripartite response to the 'technological age' that had overarched his addresses and publications from 1954, and especially his 1955–56 'essay': the 'invasion' of technology; the universities' response to the teaching of technology and his own commitment to 'technological humanism'; the implications of expansion and expensive technology for dependence on the state and university autonomy and governance. The book was part history, part curriculum and pedagogy, part social philosophy. Its unifying theme, however, was what he considered the most important aspects of the arrival of technology in the affairs of the nation and the consciousness and practices of the university. He explained why science had been so long delayed 'crossing the Channel', and the social and academic reasons for its late acceptance in the universities in the nineteenth century. This moral tale underlined the problems attending the arrival of technology and the universities' failure completely to understand and accept it. Higher technology had not been 'assimilated into the ethos of the universities, which have adapted themselves considerably to the scientific revolution, but in adaptation to technology ... they have not yet reached equilibrium'. The panoramic argument he conducted again covered six centuries of the universities and their identity; the pragmatic adaptation of the British universities to science in the nineteenth century; the role of science in democratizing the academic world; the tension in the civic universities between a traditional liberal education and utilitarian needs; the pressures on universities to respond to the industrial competition associated with developments in higher education in Europe and the United States.[28]

Ashby's account of the English universities' relationship with science directly fed his underlying argument for a different, more coherent, more fundamental understanding of technology and the technological age. The book sought ways of arriving at a series of changes – in the interpretation of a liberal education, the ways in which universities were governed and made decisions, and the position of the arts and humanities, which needed to be strengthened. He questioned whether faculties of arts, as 'custodians of Renaissance humanism', could save the universities from the present 'danger of maladaptation'. He was not only a botanist turned vice-chancellor, he had also become a natural scientist turned social scientist and historian with his sights set on a range of specific, crucial questions. *Technology and the Academics* was the most public of all the pronouncements on the technological age that he had made in this period at Belfast, seeking to implement national policy at Queen's and taking part in the forums of which he was becoming an active and increasingly sought-after member. He pursued the same questions in other national contexts, and adaptation was the central concept in his presentations to and involvement with universities in other countries.

It was important to Ashby's career after he left Belfast that in the 1950s he had already visited India, Uganda, Ghana, France and the United States with various international bodies, and he had accepted an invitation to chair a Carnegie Corporation commission on higher education in Nigeria only on condition that the start was postponed until he arrived in Cambridge.[29]

Against the historical chapters of the book he set his central concerns with technological humanism and the self-government and internal democracy of universities (a message he carried with him in his international activities). He was clearly aware of the cumulative effect of the developments and debates of the 1940s and his early years in Belfast, but he did not refer back to them directly. He will have been aware of relevant commentaries in *Universities Quarterly*. J.S. Fulton's outline of different approaches to 'general education' in 1950 had included the specialist being 'persuaded by his developing interest in his own subject not only to probe more deeply but also to follow that interest into kindred or complementary fields'. He will have followed the discussion in the journal and elsewhere of the salient issues resulting from the policies of expansion. He will have been aware of the accelerating interest in the relationship between engineering and 'humanistic studies' in the United States and commentaries by some engineering educators in Britain regarding the need for the engineer to acquire 'some appreciation of the social implications of his creative effort' and to understand the historical interaction of science and engineering with 'social customs, relations and institutions'.[30] He commented on developments in the Colleges of Advanced Technology and although he may have drawn from other sources inspiration or confidence for his commitment to 'technology in its completeness', on that central aspect of his approach he had constructed while at Queen's a strong personal philosophy of higher education:

> I believe it could be achieved by making specialist studies (whatever they are: metallurgy or dentistry or Norse philology) the core around which are grouped liberal studies which are relevant to these specialist studies. But they must be relevant; the path to culture should be through a man's specialism, not by bypassing it.

He had used such examples in his previous publications, and here he elaborated on the example of brewing, in terms that were to become a familiar part of the Ashby canon: general culture for the student was not by 'diluting brewing courses with popular lectures on architecture, social history, and ethics, but by making brewing the core of his studies'. From the wish to make beer it was a natural step to biology, microbiology, chemistry, the marketing of beer, the design and architecture of public houses, the history of beer drinking, its relationship to religion and ethics. A student who could weave his technology into the fabric of society could 'claim to have a liberal education'. A student who could not do this could not 'claim even to be a good technologist'.[31]

Ashby at the end of the 1950s had a philosophy of education, and he was to be critical of the 1963 Robbins report on higher education for not having one – and for not tackling necessary curricular reforms.[32] As a vice-chancellor facing the challenges of expansion he was a willing expansionist, accepting, as we have seen, that the universities had to make 'some painful renunciation of cherished traditions ... either lead or abdicate'. He had now articulated his view of the universities in terms of an essential overhaul: 'If technology were to become the core of a new twentieth-century humanism (as Greek became the core of a new fifteenth-century humanism), several adaptations would be necessary in British universities', including above all a reassessment of the curriculum and the contribution of the humanities. Subtle 'adaptations in academic thought' would be necessary, by professors of both technology and the arts.[33] His acceptance of technology and such radical implications did not, however, mean that he held a crude view of what the economy required from the university and the implications for university control. The case for technology was for him the same case as the one for the self-critical, adaptive, democratic university. By the end of his period at Queen's he was seen nationally and internationally as representing a liberal response to the pressures on the universities. The process of his *becoming* a missionary for technology, or more precisely for new approaches to higher education in a technological age, was now complete. From the end of the 1950s he would continue to reassert and amplify his mission, lecturing, writing, warning.

IN THE VIEW OF THE PUBLIC

In 1969 Ashby gave written and oral evidence to a Select Committee of the House of Commons looking at the relationships of students to their universities and colleges. He told the committee:

> The difference that I have seen in my career as a university teacher I think is that universities have moved from being institutions in which the public had comparatively little interest. They did not appear in the Press and therefore they went on from year to year not greatly affected by public opinion because public opinion was not expressed in clear forms. We have now moved into an entirely different situation where universities are very much in the view of the public, being watched all the time, criticised, and where demands are being made of them of the kind that certainly were not made when I began my academic career.[34]

The first few years of the 1960s were significant in marking this shift in the relationship between the universities and public opinion. The number of universities was rapidly expanding, public debate about science and technology and the responsibilities of the universities was sharpening. From 1961 to 1963 all the stakeholders in higher education were giving evidence to the Robbins committee (and in many cases publishing their evidence) and the Robbins report in 1963 marked an important transition from the influence of the kinds of advocates we have discussed to opinion making by governments, committees, official reports and those who spoke on their behalf. Ashby himself gave written and oral evidence. The parliamentary committee to which Ashby was speaking in 1969 reflected the change, and his description of the shift in attitudes towards higher education that had been taking place under a different kind of public pressure represents a crucial change in the focus of our discussion here.

In the early 1960s Ashby confirmed the position he had established for himself. He was Master of a Cambridge college and a member of some of the most important bodies relating to higher education. He was the first non-American to chair a Carnegie Committee panel in West Africa, and he was attacking apartheid and defending academic freedom in a lecture at Witwaterswand University in South Africa. He was lecturing and publishing at the remarkable rate that he was to maintain until his death in 1992. In these activities in the early 1960s he constantly reiterated some of his basic themes. When he published *Technology and the Academics* an engineering academic who reviewed it complained that he had previously, in journals of the Institute of Metals and the Institution of Electrical Engineers, given brief accounts of his views on the place of technology in the universities. The book was disappointing because he did not provide a more extensive analysis of the important matters with which he was dealing.[35] This missed the point that Ashby needed to disseminate his messages about technology and about the conduct and underlying values of higher education. What had been said in two professional journals needed a wider audience, and into the 1960s he continued to face different audiences with versions of his central ideas, and to draw for his ideas on what he saw as a world community of universities. Reviewing the comparative analysis of these universities in a higher education edition of *The Year Book of Education* he saw it as 'a reassuring witness to the vigorous spirit of self-criticism in the Higher Learning, and to the great powers which universities have for self-improvement and adaptation to the contemporary world'.[36] This was not a view he was able to sustain with such confidence in future decades. In 1974, bringing together some of this work in *Adapting Universities to a Technological Society*, he was still addressing the 'unprecedented crisis' of Western industrial nations, emphasizing that their institutions were 'not adapting themselves fast enough to the consequences of technological change; and what does not adapt does not survive'.[37] He did, however, sustain a view of the university no less committed than that of Moberly or Lindsay or an earlier generation of commentators, but with the range of emphases that derived both from his experience and from his concern with the issues he had associated with the transition to the technological age. He was able to confront contemporary dilemmas in the context of tradition and adaptation, deriving an approach to these contexts from his biological background – the need of organisms to adapt in order to survive. Social institutions, however, were concerned about survival for defined or assumed purposes, and tradition was therefore a concept he found it important to view through the lens of new situations and purposes – whether technological, social or educational. Through the various themes and vocabularies he encompassed from the 1960s onwards there is this unifying thread.

To the Robbins committee in 1961 he argued that diplomas in technology and teacher education should be replaced by degrees, a move that would deprive the degree of

> a spurious status-value and make it what it ought to be: a statement certifying that its holder has had a liberal and coherent education (for degrees – even in technology or commerce or teaching – should be granted only on curricula which do constitute a liberal education).[38]

The following year, in South Africa, he gave powerful support to the struggle against segregation, to a university 'under siege'. He also argued that 'it is one of the tasks of a new era still to preserve Man's continuity with his past. On the other hand a university must not remain a mere replica of its ancestors, transmitting a petrified culture.'[39] Throughout the 1960s he was pursuing the ideas he had begun to develop in Belfast about the need for universities to break down their departmental and faculty barriers and to develop their internal democracy. At Queen's he had argued against the power of the professoriate. In 1963, in a sociological publication, he discussed decision making in the academic world, including in the new universities, whose constitutions were 'as conventional in design as violins are'. 'Radical mutation' was needed instead of preserving departments as 'the loci of concentration of power in civic universities'. At its worst the department was 'a cell of anarchy and autocracy', and given the undefined limits of its power there was a great need 'to provide constitutional safeguards for democratic government *within* departments'.[40] All the weaknesses in higher education related to its difficulty in addressing issues of what should be preserved and what needed to be changed. In Germany as in South Africa he addressed the problems of interpreting the university in the state, its freedoms and responsibilities, and in Australia as in Oxford he looked back over the unplanned changes in attitudes to teaching duties, a 'flight from teaching', a 'schizophrenic and disintegrating profession' in the face of research and other pressures. He wondered why there was no 'Hippocratic oath' or ethical code for the academic as for the legal and medical professions.[41] The tone of his advocacy when talking about change was consistent, exemplified by his Oxford lecture on the academic profession amidst the changing demands and expectations of the younger generation:

> [W]hat really unites members of the academic profession is not an interest in one another's scholarship; it is our common participation in the mechanism of intellectual heredity. Our duty is to perpetuate the stability of tradition coupled with the potential for changing tradition; to transmit a corpus of orthodoxy coupled with a technique for constructive dissent from orthodoxy. This is a prime use of academic freedom.[42]

In formulating this tension between stability and change the biological image was constantly to hand: 'universities as well as organisms adapt themselves to new environments and yet preserve a historical identity'.[43]

It is not necessary here to trace all the directions – geographical and intellectual – in which he went from the 1960s, combining the two in an 'informal' history he published in 1963 of the Association of Universities of the British Commonwealth.[44] He wrote authoritatively and influentially, for example, on Africa, India and the United States, and was a consistently thoughtful advocate, not of tinkering or reacting or resisting, but of attention to basic issues. In many respects his sustained analysis of the university was pioneering. He repeatedly pointed out that there was little or no research on the universities themselves, and as he wrote in 1963 'to make decisions in the British academic world is still to travel without maps'. Although the UGC and the CVCP collected some empirical data,

> until we have some foundation or institution for systematic study of higher education, to provide continuity of effort and constancy of purpose, the corridors of academic power will continue to be ill-lit and the men who walk in them ill-informed.[45]

With research on university government still in its infancy in the early 1970s, it could still be said that to anyone studying it, 'as to anyone interested in universities, the most valuable publications are the books, articles, and lectures of Sir Eric Ashby which are unrivalled for their sustained scholarship and insight'.[46]

He continued to pursue the university processes, aims and contexts thrown into sharp relief by the issues surrounding higher technology education,

consistently advocating greater involvement of academic staff in the government of universities and in the responsibilities of departments. Although
he resisted the 1960s student demands for representation on university
governing bodies he was immensely sympathetic. They did not have the
expertise to run universities, 'for the art of academic government ... needs a
long and austere apprenticeship'. Students did, however, 'know how they
want universities to be run'. A lifetime in universities had led him to consider
that their ideas 'by and large sound viable'.[47] It was this sentiment that led
him and his co-author, Mary Anderson, to explore in detail the history of
student organization in *The Rise of the Student Estate in Britain*, and in a
parallel set of lectures in Canada, published as *Masters and Scholars*, both in
1970. By this stage Ashby had come to agree with the principle in a Charter
published by the National Union of Students in 1940, that students had a right
to participate in university government and administration. Nevertheless, 'the
Scholars come to learn and the Masters are there to teach. Any pattern of
participation which weakens this authority of the university must be
resisted.'[48] The radical student movement (discussed in Chapter 9 below) had
by the late 1960s become a determining context for serious reflection on
university governance and purposes.

Ashby's continuing view of higher education from the 1960s could be
presented as two overlapping circles labelled 'technological humanism' and
'autonomy'. We have traced the genesis of the former in his addresses and
reports of the 1950s, pointing as they also did to the issue of institutional
adaptation. The second circle encapsulates his awareness that such adaptation
takes place, or fails to take place, internationally as the universities seek to
preserve their autonomy, their academic freedom and their traditions in the
face of state pressures. Ashby was aware that the difficulty was not an
arbitrary one, but one that resulted from the state's *dependence* on the
universities, requiring university reciprocity: 'As states come to depend more
on universities, these traditional rights will be all the harder to defend.'[49] The
implications for universities in Africa and elsewhere were a crucial part of the
argument, academic freedom and university autonomy were 'essential to a
university if it is to fulfil its function in society',[50] a symbiotic relationship he
had explored in *Technology and the Academics*, emphasizing the crucially
critical role that universities needed to play in the relationship:

> They are essential to society, yet they must from time to time threaten
> the stability of society ... it has become their duty to generate ideas
> which may change our way of life ... Universities must of necessity be
> committed to society, but the commitment should be on their own
> terms.[51]

Hence the inter-related preoccupations regarding governance and structure, social and university purposes and values, as essential elements in the battle over tradition and adaptation. He was confident of the origins of the issues, and of the directions of renewal. In the 1950s and early 1960s he was writing and speaking at a time of popularity and prestige of the universities, but also a time when they and their ecology were changing dramatically.

His discussion of the concept of university 'community' in 1973 at a centenary celebration of the University of Canterbury, New Zealand, shows his approach to past and present. If community meant a 'cosy consensus about common interests, the modern university is not a community'. It was an appropriate concept only if it was used to mean people with diverse interests and goals, 'working on the same campus, sharing the same central heating and catering facilities ... Even so, it may be less of a community than (say) a brewery ... No. Universities today are communities only in an attenuated sense of that word.' They had once had more community spirit because they were smaller, shared a modest lifestyle and religious faith, often uniting them against 'an indifferent and sometimes hostile secular world'. The erosion of shared beliefs had taken a long time to be recognized, and once they were seen to be vanishing a 'sort of ethical vacuum' remained. Anticipating the kind of research that was to take place in the United States and Britain from the 1980s in particular, Ashby also saw the homogeneity of the university being fractured by its members looking beyond it 'for recognition and acclaim'. The judgement of the vice-chancellor was for many young academics less important than that of colleagues in the discipline, those 'who edit journals, or sit on committees distributing research funds, or elect men to the honours of scientific communities'. Ashby appealed for the restoration of some sense of commonality and community for the benefit of students and staff alike – a sense of membership for and by all, self-government, the maximum dispersal of authority, the idea of a university, not as 'a community but as a constellation of communities, based on groups of people who really *are* united by a cement of common interest'. A department or faculty was not automatically such a body, since everyone must be enabled to feel they have a stake in the welfare of the group, and all (academics, technicians, secretaries, cleaners) must be on familiar terms and aware of one another's needs. The 'prime purpose' of it all was the students, who had demonstrated in the period of unrest a 'hunger for a community spirit'.[52] Community, liberal values, curriculum and the organization and decision making of the university continued to be at the core of his concern for change in the interests of its members, not least its students. Expansion had led a number of countries to review their higher education provision, including the growing presence of non-university higher education, but in 1973 Ashby was critical of both the Robbins report and of the array of volumes under the auspices of the Carnegie Commission on Higher Education in the United States (he had himself contributed one of the volumes, *Any Person, Any Study*, two years earlier). He described the Carnegie reports as a 'colossal encyclopedia', but in the thousands of pages of these volumes as in Robbins he saw something missing:

> They go into great detail about increase in size of the system, about how the enlarged system shall be financed, about the way to make the system easier of access to all who need to enter it, about the cost-effectiveness of the system and its efficiency. But they have comparatively little to say about whether the system should change and what is to be its function in the society of tomorrow. To me it is clear that the system will have to change in all countries which undertake mass higher education. 'More' does not mean 'worse', but undoubtedly 'more' means 'different'.

The future therefore lay not in lowering standards but in understanding the meaning of 'different' in the configuration of higher education.[53] He pointed similar criticisms at both the CVCP and the UGC. Eleven years of attendance at their meetings had left him with 'one outstanding impression: we rarely, on either committee, dealt with educational problems'. University teachers had also 'done precious little corporate thinking about the consequences of the present trends'.[54]

Ashby's explorations of what higher education had become and needed to become continued some of the debates of earlier decades, as reflected particularly in the Moot and in Moberly's *The Crisis in the University*. His portraiture of the system and his commitment to change were different, however, and confronted features of an age that had not been visible to his predecessors. He was the last of the twentieth century's major advocates, with a widening audience to whom his messages of change were addressed, rooted in a constant insider's analysis and re-analysis of the institutions, their histories, their strengths and deficiencies. His ideas were widely cited and discussed, his services were widely sought as a commentator on fundamental aspects of higher education and the era of social change. When, in 1960, Lord Robbins was invited by R.A. Butler to chair the enquiry into higher education, he hesitated, one reason being that he had 'always been rather bored by abstract statements on this subject by Vice-Chancellors and prominent educationalists, Sir Eric Ashby always excepted'.[55]

NOTES AND REFERENCES

1. Ashby, E., (n.d.) Notes towards a biography (100-page typed document lodged before his death with the Royal Society and Clare College, Cambridge, p. 47.
2. *New Scientist*, 'Sir Eric Ashby: missionary of the age of technology', 23 October 1958, pp. 1112–13.
3. Ashby, E., *Technology and the Academics: An Essay on Universities and the Technological Revolution* (London: Macmillan, 1963, orig. pub. 1958); Ashby, E., 'Function and survival in British universities', *University of Toronto Quarterly*, vol. 25, 1956, pp. 220–9.
4. Ashby, E., 'A voluntary club', *Times Higher Education Supplement*, 20 October 1989, p. 17.
5. Salter, B. and Tapper, T., *The State and Higher Education* (Ilford: Woburn Press, 1994), p. 12.
6. Ashby, E., *Scientist in Russia* (Harmondsworth: Penguin, 1947); *Challenge to Education* (Sydney: Angus & Robertson, 1946).
7. Interview by Alf McCreary, Information Director, Queen's University of Belfast, December 1990, transcript, p. 9.
8. Ashby, E., 'Valedictory Address', *Annual Record of the Queen's University Association*, Summer 1953, pp. 30–1 (copies are in the Special Collections Library of Queen's University).
9. 'Address', December 1954, pp. 6–7.
10. 'Address', Summer 1955, pp. 18–20.
11. 'Address', Summer 1956, p. 17; 'Address', Winter 1958, p. 41.
12. Vice-Chancellor's Report for the year 1950–51, pp. 203–4; 1951–52, p. 168; 1952–53, pp. 174–5; 1954–55, p. 168 (he did not include a statement in 1953–54).
13. Report 1955–56, pp. 163–5.
14. Report 1956–57, pp. 164–8.
15. Report 1957–58, pp. 194–6; 1958–59, p. 254.
16. Notes towards a biography, pp. 16–16a.
17. Ashby, E., *Scientist in Russia* (Harmondsworth: Penguin, 1947), pp. 11–16, 111, 116, 202.
18. Hennessy, P., in *Change*, 1973, pp. 23–5.
19. Ashby, E., 'A note on an alternative to halls of residence', *Universities Quarterly*, vol. 5, pp. 150–4; 'Halls of residence and student amenities', Home Universities Conference, *Proceedings 1952*, London, Association of Universities of the British Commonwealth , pp. 14–20.
20. Stephens, M.D. (ed.), *Ashby Report on Adult Education* (1954), reprinted with Foreword and Introductory Essays by Lord Ashby *et al.* (Nottingham: University of Nottingham Department of Adult Education, 1990).
21. Ashby, E., *The Teacher in an Age of Automation* (London: Goldsmiths' College, 1956).
22. Ashby, E., 'University commentary', *Universities Quarterly*, vol. 11, 1956, pp. 9–11; 'Self-government in modern British universities', *Science and Freedom*, vol. 7, 1956, pp. 3–10.
23. Ashby, 'Function and survival in British universities', pp. 200–9.
24. Ashby, E., 'Impact on the universities of the government's policy for the expansion of technological education', address to the Home Universities Conference, *Proceedings 1956*, London, Association of Universities of the British Commonwealth, pp. 68–73.
25. Ashby, E., 'Technological humanism', *Journal of the Institute of Metals*, vol. 85, 2, 1957; 'The educational framework of an industrial society: the influence of technology on the British universities', *Research*, December 1957, pp. 454–7.

26. Ashby, E., 'Fifty years of an Ulster university. Memorable academic milestone', *Belfast News-Letter, Queen's University Gold Jubilee Supplement*, April 9 1959.
27. UGC, *University Development 1952–1957*, p. 53.
28. Ashby, *Technology and the Academics*, chs 1–3, p. 88.
29. Ashby listed the impressive range of his international activities in his 'Notes towards a biography'.
30. Fulton, 'General Education', *Universities Quarterly*, vol. 5, 1950, p. 47; Willis Jackson, 'A note on electrical engineering', *Universities Quarterly*, vol. 2, 1948, pp. 175–6.
31. Ashby, *Technology and the Academics*, pp. 84–5.
32. Hennessy in *Change*, pp. 23–5.
33. Report 1955–56, p. 165; *Technology and the Academics*, pp. 85–8.
34. Select Committee on Education and Science. Session 1968–69: *Student Relations*, vol. 2 (London: HMSO, 1969), p. 276.
35. Allanson, J.T., Review in *Universities Review*, vol. 31, 1959, pp. 69–70.
36. Ashby, E., Review of Bereday and Lauwerys (eds), *The Year Book of Education, 1959. Higher Education*, in *Universities Quarterly*, vol. 14, 1960, p. 206.
37. Ashby, E., *Adapting Universities to a Technological Society* (San Francisco, CA: Jossey-Bass, 1974), p. vii.
38. Ashby, E., 'Memorandum', in Committee on Higher Education, *Higher Education*, Evidence – part one, vol. E, (London: HMSO, 1963), p. 1,671.
39. Ashby, E., 'Universities under siege', *Minerva*, vol. 1, 1962, pp. 22–5.
40. Ashby, E., 'Decision-making in the academic world', *Sociological Studies in British University Education* (*Sociological Review*, Monograph No. 7, 1963), pp. 10–11.
41. Ashby, E., 'The future of the nineteenth century idea of a university', *Minerva*, vol. 6, 1967, pp. 15–16; 'A Hippocratic oath for the academic profession', *Minerva*, vol. 7, 1969, pp. 64–6 (abridged address at the Association of Commonwealth Universities Congress, Australia, 1968); A Hippocratic oath for the academic profession (interview, 1974) in Urban, G.R. (ed.), *Hazards of Learning* (London: Temple Smith, 1977); *The Academic Profession* (London: Oxford University Press, 1969), pp. 6–13.
42. Ibid., p. 14.
43. Ashby, E., 'What a university should be' (address to the Centennial Convocation of Cornell University), *Cornell Alumni News*, vol. 64, 1964, p. 12.
44. Ashby, E., *Community of Universities: An Informal Portrait of the Association of Universities of the British Commonwealth 1913–1963* (London: Association of Commonwealth Universities, 1963).
45. Ashby, 'Decision-making in the academic world', p. 13. Cf. also Ashby, E., *University Hierarchies* (London: Imperial College, 1976) arguing for a rigorous study of hierarchies and control.
46. Moodie, G.C., 'University government', in Butcher, H.J. and Rudd, E., *Contemporary Problems in Higher Education: An Account of Research* (Maidenhead: McGraw-Hill, 1972), p. 264.
47. Ashby, E., ... *And Scholars* (London: London School of Economics and Political Science, 1965), pp. 11–12.
48. Ashby, E. and Anderson, M., *The Rise of the Student Estate in Britain* (London: Macmillan, 1970); Ashby, E., *Masters and Scholars: Reflections on the Rights and Responsibilities of Students* (London: Oxford University Press, 1970), pp. 62–3.
49. Ashby, 'What a university should be', p. 15.
50. Ashby, E. and Anderson, M., 'Autonomy and academic freedom in Britain and in English-speaking countries of tropical Africa', *Minerva*, vol. 3, 1966, p. 317.
51. Ashby, *Technology and the Academics*, pp. 92–4.

52. Ashby, E., 'Is the university a community?', in Ashby, E. *et al.*, *The University on Trial* (Christchurch, New Zealand: University of Canterbury, 1973), pp. 59–71.
53. Ashby, E., 'The structure of higher education: a world view', *Higher Education*, vol. 2, 1973, pp. 142–5.
54. Ashby, E., 'The academic establishment: bottleneck or pump?, *Times Higher Education Supplement*, 15 October 1971, p. 17.
55. Quoted from Robbins's autobiography in Moser, C., 'The Robbins report 25 years after – and the future of the universities', *Oxford Review of Education*, vol. 14, 1988, p. 5. Robbins also described most modern books on education as very heavy going, 'with the exception of Lord Ashby's and one or two others', in Lord Robbins, *Higher Education Revisited* (London: Macmillan, 1980), p. 2.

PART III

A NATIONAL PURPOSE

9

1960s: 'EXPANSIONISM'

ROBBINS

What we have traced to this point is both the growth of a system and the changing articulation of direction, purpose and change by a series of advocates who sought to influence opinion about higher education. From the promoters of institutions in the early decades of the twentieth century, to those who reflected on the roles of universities in the social and international upheavals of the mid-century, and to those who sought values and relevance alongside concerns about the state-as-financier, we have seen shifting relationships amongst advocates, institutions, policies and the system. The 'opinion' towards which advocates directed their messages was variously that of political and social elites, the leadership of the institutions, academe in general, national and international publics. From the early 1960s, however, the meaning of 'advocates' and 'opinion' changed, the direction from which influential messages and policies were coming was different, and past agendas that included autonomy, purpose, values or scale and community, were either intensified or radically altered.

In England the crucial feature of the system in the early 1960s was expansion. The seven new universities were being planned before the Robbins committee on higher education was appointed in 1961, and they were opening either before it reported in 1963 or soon afterwards. The CATs were rapidly increasing their degree-level work under the auspices of the NCTA. The teacher training colleges were raising their entry standards and turning their two- into three-year courses. Sir Edward Boyle opened a conference in 1961 by wondering how many people realized the speed of change. Immediately after the war full-time higher education was 'almost entirely confined to the system of universities which existed at that time, by 1970 there may well be 100 institutions substantially engaged in providing full-time higher education'. He also reflected long after the event that although the Robbins committee had been intended to further university expansion, the central reason for appointing the committee was 'the consciousness, particularly within the Ministry of Education, of the lack of any coherent policy for the emerging pattern of higher education'.[1] The new 'green fields' or 'plate glass' universities, with their new locations, new architecture, new curricular profiles, helped to raise the level of public awareness of university provision, and pointed to the possibility of more such developments. The numbers of students, 50,000 in 1939, had doubled by 1959, under all of the pressures towards science and technology, demography and greater access. The old universities were growing in size, and the generations of students entering them and the new universities had grown up in a changed world. The students were described by W.R. Niblett in 1962, in *The Expanding University*, as 'differently orientated from their predecessors. They have different attitudes to work, to politics, to the future of Britain, to religion, from those of yesterday.'[2] By this date Moberly's *The Crisis in the University* was in its fifth edition, and though many were still aware of the issues and directions to which Moberly had pointed, proponents were attempting to adjust to a new climate. *The Expanding University* was overwhelmingly concerned with the needs, the problems, the threat of the new university order: 'Society, as never before, is eager to take hold of its universities and to use them for its own purposes ... people see them as indispensable to the national economy. They have become public institutions.'[3]

There were, of course, those who could not accept that it was possible to increase the student population without standards being lowered, and the most clamorous rallying cry was that of Kingsley Amis. His opposition to 'catching up' with America and Russia 'by building *more* colleges which will turn out *more* graduates and so give us *more* technologists (especially them) and more school teachers' was briefly expressed in *Encounter* in 1960, in the middle of an article entitled 'Lone voices'. He followed that statement with a call that was to ring out around debate on higher education. He wished he could have a 'tape-and-loudspeaker' sewn in the binding of the magazine to 'bawl out' his message, but he had to resort to various sizes of block capitals: 'MORE WILL MEAN WORSE'. He was 'quite sure that a university admissions policy demanding even less than it now demands – for that is what a larger intake means – will wreck academic standards beyond repair'. He had no wish to teach in something called a university that was really 'a rather less glamorous and authentic training college', or to live in a society 'which has abandoned the notion of the university as a centre of learning'.[4] Not all the critics used capital letters and the same vocabulary, but the underlying appeal on behalf of a tradition in danger was to continue to be heard more or less distinctly throughout the century.

Into the confusions of the new order came the Robbins committee. While it was still deliberating the Labour Party set up its own study group on higher education, which published a pamphlet in 1962 entitled *The Years of Crisis*.

Kingsley Amis

le on behalf
comatose or
elves. There
ld-age pen-
les, not to
who cannot
se are fewer
a splendid
trend-hound
directed out-
wash (as an
alled it) who
han all those
in honorary
consciously
the stuff on
vould sound
: song were
rather than
f some in-
and-fish-and-

do my best
ial vexation,
disquiet-mis-
ich altruistic
etail my own
ertising has

The trouble is not just illiteracy, even understanding this as including unsteady grasp of the fundamentals of a subject as well as unsteadiness with hard words like *goes* and *its*. But for the moment I want to drum the fact of that illiteracy into those who are playing what I have heard called the university numbers racket, those quantitative thinkers who believe that Britain is *falling behind* America and Russia by not producing as many university graduates per head, and that she must *catch up* by building *more* colleges which will turn out *more* graduates and so give us *more* technologists (especially them) and *more* school-teachers. I wish I could have a little tape-and-loudspeaker arrangement sewn into the binding of this magazine, to be triggered off by the light reflected from the reader's eyes on to this part of the page, and set to bawl out at several bels: MORE WILL MEAN WORSE.

I do not know whether it is better to have three really bad school-teachers where formerly there were two mediocre ones, and I have no information about what can be expected to happen to technologists, but I am quite sure that a university admissions policy demanding even less than it now demands—for that is what a larger intake means—will wreck academic standards beyond repair.

10. 'Lone Voices: Views of the "Fifties"', by Kingsley Amis, *Encounter*, July 1960.

This Taylor committee had the remit to prepare a statement of policy on higher education, and it did so with the main target of continuing the expansion of higher education, 'on a scale never before contemplated'. It envisaged about 70 universities in England and Wales and about ten in Scotland. Though it contained paragraphs on the right to higher education and the future diversity of form and function of the universities, the document was overwhelmingly focused on the birth-rate and potential university entry, the demand for skilled manpower, resources, the range of higher education institutions, and the administration of government finance and control.[5] Given the background to the modest Taylor review and the considerable Robbins investigation it is not surprising that they shared similar priority topics. The Taylor report reflected the restive Labour interest in expansion of the late 1950s and pointed towards its continued policy effort when it came to office in 1964. The Conservative decision to appoint the Robbins committee reflected the expansionist intentions of ministers like David Eccles and Edward Boyle, and the committee was invited

> to review the pattern of full-time higher education in Great Britain and in the light of national needs and resources to advise Her Majesty's Government on what principles its long-term development should be based. In particular, to advise, in the light of these principles, whether there should be any changes in that pattern.[6]

Shortly before his death in 1984 Robbins was asked in an interview why as 'a proto-Thatcherite economist' he had nevertheless supported expansion, at the time seen as a radical cause: 'He told me he had been persuaded by a remark by R. H. Tawney, who said of the United States that you could not underestimate the benefits America had received because so many of her people had had at least "the smell of a higher education" '.[7] Whatever Robbins's economics, he and the committee had been plunged into a review of a national situation, aware that 'no such instructions have been given to any committee or commission in the past'. The situation they were examining reflected increased educational opportunity in the schools and developments in various sectors of post-school education, alongside concern about the failure of higher education adequately to support the national economy in a highly competitive world. Robbins himself had looked at the nature of higher education as 'a public service', and had concluded that he saw 'no escape from the necessity of very considerable dependence' on income from the state. Private enterprise alone could not 'provide all that is desirable in this respect'. There were dangers, and the committee had addressed them.[8]

The report did, however, devote a chapter to 'academic freedom and its scope', focusing on what it called 'the most difficult of all the problems we

11. Lionel (Lord) Robbins. (Courtesy of London School of Economics and Political Science Archives.)

have had to consider – what machinery of government is appropriate for a national system of higher education in this country?' This, now intensified, was a problem that had haunted writers on higher education from the mid-1940s – the time of what Ashby had called a 'climacteric'. The committee was faced with the issue of how to keep a balance between 'the necessity of freedom for academic institutions and the necessity that they should serve the nation's needs'. It recognized the anxieties associated with limitations on the independence of higher education institutions, but equally recognized that 'subvention involves allocation and that allocation may involve co-ordination and certain controls; and it is not felt that such measures need be an improper encroachment on legitimate academic freedoms'. The UGC was the device that had been invented to make such improper encroachments 'less probable'.[9] This discussion was not so much about academic freedom as about the machinery in which it had been and should be embodied – in line with the terms of reference given to the committee. The report did have a chapter on 'Aims and principles', which was to achieve considerable publicity and to be cited in discussions of higher education for decades to come. The committee here set out four aims, objectives or purposes (it used all of these as synonyms) to be served by higher education, having agreed that there was as yet no 'system' in the sense of 'a consciously co-ordinated organisation'. The country had been served well enough by the

> largely unco-ordinated activities and initiatives of the past ... [but] ... from now on these are not good enough ... the needs of the present and still more of the future demand that there should be a system ... we are not demanding that all the activities concerned should be planned and controlled from the centre ... where there is common provision, there should be co-ordinating principles.

These were: instruction in 'skills suitable to play a part in the general division of labour'; teaching in such a way as to 'promote the general powers of the mind'; 'the advancement of learning' (which raised difficult questions about the balance between teaching and research); 'the transmission of a common culture and common standards of citizenship'. The latter part of the chapter also set out some principles that had guided the committee's work, but these did not flow from the previous objectives, consisting of such matters as numbers and eligibility, the status of institutions, the organization of higher education and the maintenance of standards.[10]

The difference between the two parts of the chapter also reflects a difference between the discussion of objectives and the rest of the report. Responding to its remit, the committee addressed issues relating to types of institution, courses in universities, the teacher training colleges (as they were still called), the CATs and the technical colleges, the future demand for and pattern of higher education. It considered the implications for staffing, teaching methods, finance and the internal government of institutions of higher education. The report and the substantial volumes of appendices indicated not only the extent of national and international evidence the committee had gathered, but also the research evidence it had collected in relation to the so-called 'pool of ability'. The committee rejected the idea of such a pool and its alleged limits, and declared the principle that 'courses of higher education should be available for all those who are qualified by ability and attainment to pursue them and who wish to do so'.[11] Its own research and that of key sociological and psychological witnesses convinced it that there were 'reserves of untapped ability', explained by social class and family background. Witnesses like psychologist P.E. Vernon, for example, were adamant in their messages to the committee:

> This Memorandum contests the view – widespread among educationists – that there exists in the population a fixed distribution or 'pool' of intelligence, which limits either the numbers of individuals capable of

higher education, or the educational standards that can be achieved by groups of pupils or students of given I.Q. level.[12]

The committee's conception of entry to higher education by all those qualified to do so, and its use of the most recent sociological and psychological research, were prominent and influential features of its report.

It very soon became clear that the committee had under-estimated the demand for places, but the important point here is that it validated the current trend in relevant research and heavily underlined justifications for expansion. The fact that the door had been opened in the late 1950s and that the new universities had been created did not diminish the importance of the committee's weight behind continuing expansion. It proposed that the CATs should become universities, that new Special Institutions for Scientific and Technological Education and Research (SISTERS) should be created, and that existing regional colleges (which had been designated to conduct advanced work) might become parts of universities or in the future attain university status. The training colleges, now to be called 'colleges of education', should have some form of academic collaboration with the universities, and their certificates should become B.Ed. degrees. All of these, together with the committee's consideration of specialist institutions of other kinds, pointed towards the machinery for planning and co-ordination that its terms of reference had invited it to consider. It rejected the idea of overall responsibility for all branches of education under a Secretary of State for Education, and recommended that 'autonomous' higher education (not the colleges that would remain under local authority control) should come under a new Minister of Arts and Science. The structures adopted by the Labour government from 1964 did not follow the committee's proposed directions for the regional colleges, the colleges of education, or ministerial responsibilities.

If the bulk of the report was not derived from its stated 'aims and principles', there was also, as A.H. Halsey pointed out shortly after its publication, an 'asymmetrical' relationship between its use of social science research for the expansionist issue 'and the kind of research that went into the shape of higher education that would follow from expansion'. He concluded that on the purpose of a university, its size, content and administration, the report seemed based 'on a more primitive kind of evidence collection – more primitive in the sense of asking the wise men for their opinions and distilling out of them what appears to be the most coherent, plausible or politically viable statement'. The report sometimes became 'a not terribly well-informed intellectual discussion'.[13] The difference between the substantive report and its 'aims and principles' was later picked up at the University of Lancaster by a research unit on aims and objectives in higher education. The Robbins report had based its projections on the fundamental criterion of the likely demand for higher education places, and the early statement of aims therefore took the form simply of 'a preamble which has no direct implications for the substance of the report to follow'. The statements of aims had remained 'at a high level of generality. Nothing obviously follows from them; whether the university, for example, can change, is changing or should change is not clear.' This report also quoted Sir Edward Boyle, former Minister of State at the Department of Education and Science (DES), saying in 1968 that the Conservative Party intended to set up a policy commitee that might study 'the rationale of the universities – Robbins was rather short on this'.[14]

The central importance of the Robbins report for the story here lies in the fact that it happened at all, and that it came to represent more or less the end of the kinds of advocacy, audience search and opinion making that we have traced. The committee and the report were indeed meshed into audiences. The committee received representations from an enormous number of organizations and individuals (including Ashby), and it found a ready audience for the report and its appendices. It not only *advocated* (as its terms of reference had done) a new version of 'system', it *represented* that new version. Initiative for change and a crucial measure of co-ordination and control over the system and direction for its component parts were now being recommended by a government-appointed committee, and the underlying principle was accepted by governments. A Conservative government accepted the report and this and related implications, and a Labour government – while rejecting some of the detail – did likewise. The ways in which advocacy and campaign, economic and popular demand had influenced the system were now to be replaced to a large extent by governments' perceptions of the needs of the state. Stuart Maclure described the change pointedly three years after the report:

> When Mr. Harold Macmillan set up the Committee on Higher Education in 1961, he was consciously or unconsciously ending a cycle of English academic history. Till Robbins the pretence was that because universities were autonomous, the main policy of government towards higher education should be to have no policy. Effectively the universities stood outside the educational system ... To include the universities within any articulated national system of education was to threaten all that had become sacred.[15]

Maclure's point related to a national system of 'education', but it was equally relevant to a national system of 'higher education' and to how change was beginning to be driven.

The symbolic importance of the committee's work and report was lost in the popular eagerness to see a further rapid development of higher education. In the late 1950s and early 1960s all the signs pointed to expansion that required the kind of commitment that the creation of the new universities and the Robbins report represented. The commitment was important for teacher education and technology as well as for universities existing and to come. The issues following the publication of the report had to do mainly with implementation, though questions of 'more means worse' had not been laid to rest. Robbins himself was angered by the Conservative government's lack of urgency to act as well as to accept principles. In December, two months after the report appeared, the government promised action in the spring, and in the House of Lords Robbins, in the words of the *Guardian*, 'harangued the Government front bench, warning them that unless they heeded his words all their fine talk about expansion would be gone in the wind', and he declared: 'If the Government mean business they mustn't wait for the spring. They must take some quick decision here and now.'[16] There was controversy over where ministerial responsibility should lie, and over what was soon to become Crosland's 'binary' policy, creating the polytechnics as a second sector of higher education. Argument over expansion by enlarging old or by creating new universities rumbled on during and after the committee's deliberations. The AUT told the committee that the size of universities was already too great to retain the quality of academic life for staff and for students, 'and we believe that more universities rather than larger universities is the better policy'. Lord Hailsham, then Minister for Science, told a conference in 1960 that Oxford and Cambridge, by their very excellence,

> exercised a baleful influence on the whole system, discouraged the formation of an adequate number of new institutions by attracting, no doubt, a predominance of private benefactions ... and depreciating the achievements and limiting the growth at a healthy rate of university institutions locally placed to meet the demand.

The UGC came out in favour of new universities having a minimum target of 3,000 full-time students and 200 acres. With Keele and the recent new universities in mind it argued in its 1964 report that:

> [T]here is need for constant experiment in the organisation of university teaching and the design of university curricula. New institutions, starting without traditions with which the innovator must come to terms, might well be more favourably situated for such experimentation than established universities.

Robbins, however, told a conference after the committee's report was published that he did not believe 'that expansion can be well served by the proliferation of an additional number of university institutions of small size'.[17]

Spring too far behind for Lord Robbins

Government's lack of urgency

By NORMAN SHRAPNEL, our Parliamentary Correspondent

In the Lords, you are often very close to the horse's mouth—as close as listening to Lord Robbins on the Robbins Report, as we did yesterday; but a lot of people must have felt themselves uncomfortably near the horse's hooves as well.

Lord Robbins—eager to demolish a host of dangerous misunderstandings that he believes to have sprung up over his report and also to stimulate the Government to act as well as just accept principles—found it necessary to make a highly aggressive speech.

Both ends of Lord Robbins were dangerous, you might say. He took sharp bites at those who had attacked his expansion policy, and a lusty kick at the Government for what he evidently regarded as a perilous lack of any proper sense of urgency.

He was convinced that the universities could win through in the colossal task ahead of them, but not without immediate assurance that adequate Government help will be forthcoming. They needed to be satisfied now about the 1964-65 grants, but all the Government would say about this was that the situation would be reviewed in the spring.

Must not wait

The spring! Lord Robbins seemed to regard this as rather like telling a starving garrison that its request for supplies would be reviewed after the forthcoming harvest. Spring, to Lord Robbins, was too far behind. And so it was, he felt sure, for many a young graduate who was of vital importance in the expansion scheme. His fear was that they might not wait, in planning their careers, for the Government's financial thinking to ripen.

"If the Government mean business they mustn't wait for the spring. They must take some quick decisions here and now—before we adjourn for Christmas."

It was in terms like these that he harangued the Government front bench, warning them that unless they heeded his words all their fine talk about expansion would be gone in the wind. In fact, there were, in a sense, two Government front benches. There was the conventional one—now so severely depleted—in its usual place, and there were also Mr Quintin Hogg and Sir Edward Boyle sitting side by side on the steps of the throne.

They could make no promises from there; and Lord Bessborough, who has inherited Mr Hogg's educational responsibilities in the Lords, sounded unlikely to have anything to say before they did. Yet they looked an entirely friendly Tweedledum and Tweedledee, and showed no response to Lord Morrison of Lambeth's sly expectation that they are about to have a battle.

Two Ministers or one? The question was touched on several times. Mr Hogg and Sir Edward continued to look obstinately divisible—and just possibly a little comforted by Lord Robbins's belief that two Ministries are better than one.

There seemed little else to comfort them. Speaking as "a working vice-chancellor," Lord James of Rusholme sprang purposefully into the Robbins saddle and joined in the charge. He spoke of disquiet in the universities, of suspicions that the Government is "willing the ends without the means," and of the urgent need, at the very least, for an immediate increase in the grant for postgraduate work.

The debate goes on today, and since Lord Eccles is due to speak this may not be any happier a day for the Government; for it was this former Minister of Education who first threw down the challenge for a positive and immediate commitment.

(Report, page 2)

12. 'Spring too far behind for Lord Robbins', the *Guardian*, 12 December 1963.

Amidst these kinds of issues relating to practicalities and emergencies the implications for the relationship between higher education and the state were not heard as directly and in the same forms as they had been in the previous two decades.

ONE SYSTEM OR TWO?

The government's immediately issued statement accepted the principle of the Robbins report that higher education should be available 'for all those who are qualified by ability and attainment' and wished to enter it. Most of the detailed proposals, the government statement indicated, were 'a matter for the academic world, but it is for the Government to take decisions on a number of the most important recommendations'.[18] It was in fact the incoming Labour government that was to make the decision of most importance here, affecting both the system and future student numbers. Robbins recommended that the new generation of non-university higher education institutions (following the absorption of the CATs into the university sector) should have the possibility of graduating to university status individually 'as they develop'.[19] Eric Robinson, who had been prominent in the Association of Teachers in Technical Institutions (ATTI), pilloried this 'ducklings' and 'swans' recommendation. The ATTI, he explained, had considered the Robbins recommendations and prospects for higher education and had been faced with a choice between 'a planned and coherent development outside the universities and an unplanned conglomeration'. It had therefore produced a discussion paper which opted for a binary system based on the advanced work of the regional colleges, which would form a 'public system in parallel with the university system'. Robbins had ruled out the idea of a unitary system of higher education: 'Under Robbins a small number of the colleges might eventually become universities. They were the ducklings of higher education and some of them might grow into swans. We are suggesting that ducklings should grow into ducks.'[20] Anthony Crosland, the Labour government's Secretary of State for Education and Science, drawing on the ATTI discussion document and advice from within the Civil Service, propounded what became the binary policy, freezing an alternative, parallel, non-university sector of higher education. The technical college tradition and the pioneering work of the NCTA, together with the political targets of Crosland and the Labour government, were to generate a new sector of higher education based on the elevation of suitable regional colleges to 'polytechnic' status.

Crosland announced the policy in a speech at Woolwich Polytechnic in April 1965, emphasizing Britain's two traditions, embodied in what he called the 'autonomous sector' and the 'public sector', a dual system preferred by the government to

> a unitary system, hierarchically arranged on the 'ladder' principle, with the Universities at the top and the other institutions down below. Such a system would be characterized by a continuous rat-race to reach the First or University Division ... Let us now move away from our snobbish caste-ridden hierarchical obsession with University status.

The polytechnics were to have distinctive features – the provision of full- and part-time courses, their vocational tradition, their greater interest in 'applying knowledge to the solution of problems than in pursuing learning for its own sake'. There was to be no new university or accession to university status for ten years. Significantly he added that the colleges of education should remain under the control of the local authorities.[21] The speech raised many anxieties, particularly in the universities, and Crosland later regretted having made it, as 'an appalling blunder', without adequate reflection.[22] He attempted to allay the anxieties in a speech at Lancaster University in January 1967, emphasizing not only the two traditions, but also the possibilities of co-operation across the sectors, withdrawing the implication that the universities were not 'socially responsive', and again – in opposition to the Robbins proposal to associate the colleges of education with the universities – insisting that 'the local authorities should maintain a stake in higher education' by retaining control of them.[23] John Carswell, from experience of university affairs at the Treasury, the DES and the UGC, later described the 'polytechnic policy' as Crosland's response to a narrow political imperative – 'the impossibility, as he saw it, of a Labour Secretary of State taking institutions from urban local education authorities which were predominantly controlled by Labour, and bringing them under the same regime as the universities'.[24] Some of the origins of the binary policy are therefore clear. It was seen as historically correct, as providing a body of institutions more responsive to national economic and social needs, and as indicating the government's support for the local authorities. It was also strongly commended to Crosland by voices within the Department of Education and Science, notably that of Toby Weaver, Deputy Under-Secretary of State, who is often credited with being the most serious progenitor of the policy.[25]

There were mixed views in the universities and amongst those who spoke for them. On the one hand the new sector might protect the universities from excessive student numbers and overbalance towards technology, but on the other hand the policy did not take account of the universities' engagement with areas highlighted as specific to the 'public' sector. Robbins was dismayed. In the House of Lords, several months after the Woolwich speech, he pointed out that despite protests from 'the romantics and the traditionalists, technology has long been part of the university system here', and talked of the 'abracadabra of this precious Binary system'. In his autobiography he later commented: 'What I do not understand was the ultimate philosophy inspiring the idea of the binary system – the eternal separation of two rival sectors.'[26] Crosland's Woolwich speech, in Maclure's view, sowed the seeds of an unreal debate, but it was also 'a measure of the work that the Robbins Committee didn't do, that so much misunderstanding and spleen could be generated so easily. The Robbins report was a mixture of reticence and revelation.'[27] Between 1963 and 1965 priorities had been reshuffled. In Carswell's metaphor, Robbins had left 'the ladder from the technical college to paradise … leaning against the wall.'[28] Priority was now attached to the construction of an additional paradise.

The government, of course, had every intention of continuing expansion, and the binary policy – however presented – underpinned that intention. The Robbins committee had endorsed the view that there was no limited pool of ability, a view that had in fact been part of the post-war landscape of views about education. A Nuffield College group (including Lord Lindsay) that produced a report on British universities in 1948, had, for example, assumed 'that there exists a great reserve of uncultivated capacity'.[29] Crosland had no doubt shared much of the post-war search for ways of providing for this reserve, and though before and immediately after assuming office his preoccupation was with the schools, there were implications for higher education. In 1961 he indicated that 'we now know that measured intelligence is *not* a purely innate characteristic; it is at least partly an acquired one. With this knowledge, the whole discussion of "equal opportunity" takes on a new aspect', and with a 'strong' definition of equal opportunity in mind 'every child should have the same opportunity for *acquiring* measured intelligence'.[30] It was not a difficult step for him, therefore, when he looked at higher education, to see advantages in a sector that had already established its potential for part-time, mature and sandwich, as well as full-time, students. These were opportunities not readily available in the universities and more easily developed in a parallel sector of polytechnics. Gerald Fowler, who had recently been a Labour Minister of State in the DES, and was in 1972 Assistant Director at Hatfield, one of the new polytechnics, summarized what he saw as the intentions of the binary developments:

> The early advocates were thus seeking, not to create a depressed, second-class, and under-financed sector of higher education, as their opponents sometimes contend, but to give recognition to the possibility that there might be more than one valid philosophy of higher education, or such differences of emphasis within a philosophy as to require more

than one institutional model. They wished less to create a new pecking order of colleges than to question the right of all universities to be above all non-university establishments in the order.[31]

The new model of institution and sector, nevertheless, embodied not just a philosophy for higher education, but also a philosophy for the role of government. Much of the concern about universities in previous decades had focused on the related issues of institutional autonomy, state finance and the protective mechanism that the UGC had come to represent since the First World War. Neither the UGC nor any similar funding body was proposed, however, for the new sector, and anxieties lay ahead therefore for both sectors: 'The polytechnics resented the autonomy of the universities: the universities saw the regulated status of the polytechnics as a threat.'[32]

Crosland announced in April 1967 the list of the first 28 polytechnics to be designated, and two more were to follow. Together with the list the DES issued 'Notes for guidance' on the organization of polytechnics. One paragraph importantly indicated the proposed relationships between the Secretary of State, the local education authorities and the newly designated institutions. Together with the appointment and report of the Robbins committee and Crosland's policy pronouncements, the paragraph revealed clearly the profound change that had now taken place in the concept of higher education and in the directions from which controlling policies and new versions of advocacy were to come:

> The Polytechnics must of course operate within national policies and within limits set by the financial and legal responsibilities of the local education authority. It must rest with the Secretary of State, for example, to determine the number of Polytechnics and to co-ordinate developments throughout the system as a whole through his control of building programmes and the approval of courses. He must continue to set and enforce minimum standards. Salary and grading structures for the academic staff will also continue to be settled under national arrangements. A number of important responsibilities must similarly be discharged by the local education authorities. Within national policies they must settle the broad range of courses to be provided, and the Polytechnics must continue to be subject to controls in financial and administrative matters such as the approval of estimates, capital development and the level of fees.

These were essentially the existing controlling principles of the colleges being elevated, re-presented in terms of a new relationship with national government. Since the polytechnics were to parallel the universities in terms of the standards of courses and the development of research, the possible future threat to the universities was a real one. The paragraph setting out these responsibilities and constraints also stressed the importance for the polytechnics 'that, within the limits necessitated by national policy and their dependence on public funds for financial support, they shall be given all possible freedom in managing themselves with the minimum of detailed control by the main-taining authorities'.[33] The stage was set for the tensions that were bound to arise as the polytechnics worked with the local authorities but sought maximum freedom from control by them. The real significance of this passage, how-ever, is its silence on the relationship between the polytechnics and the state, other than that of 'limits' and 'dependence'. Fowler's bland reference to 'more than one institutional model' in fact meant that the new institutions were not to share in the degree of autonomy available to the universities.

The most serious deficiency of the polytechnics was their limited resource base compared with that of the universities, and much argument around the polytechnics focused on this weakness. In his 1968 book, *The New Polytechnics*, Eric Robinson, described as 'one of the leading apostles of the polytechnic',[34] underlined the potential of the new state system, but also the inevitability of the lion's share of resources and public esteem going to the universities, at least in the short run. In 1970 Margaret Thatcher, then Opposition spokesman on education, defended the roles of the polytechnics and their 'enormous potential', but emphasized that they would not achieve what was wanted of them on the basis of the Labour government's current spending plans.[35] From their formal designation in the late 1960s and early 1970s the polytechnics struggled to define their identities, matched against their own histories and profiles, the interpretations of government and local authority, the universities' position and plans for expansion and change, and the diversity of aspirations within and beyond the polytechnics. In 1972, seven years after launching the policy and four years after he had ceased to have government responsibility for education, Crosland described three ways in which the polytechnics had developed. Some had sought to become more like universities, others had defined their role more in terms of meeting regional needs in technical subjects, and a minority were pursuing a distinctive polytechnic 'ideal' – focusing on regional needs, community links, part-time courses and continuing education.[36] Also in 1972, in a memorandum to a parliamentary committee, the new Committee of Directors of Polytechnics (CDP) broadly summarized its view of the present and potential of the institutions. At this early stage of their existence and development it was an important statement:

Polytechnics should develop as a distinctive sector in higher education, as local authority colleges. This does not mean, however, that academic relationships should remain as they are, in which Polytechnics have no power to award their degrees and are largely dependent upon external bodies for the award of their Diplomas and other qualifications. In our view, Polytechnics should be encouraged towards academic independence by granting to them the right to award degrees and other qualifications. We do not think it necessary that all Polytechnics should be granted this right simultaneously; they are at different stages of development and have different histories.

The CDP argued that degree-awarding powers should be acquired by all of them within ten years, since they had shown themselves to be 'mature and responsible academically' and could only suffer if a system of 'academic tutelage' to external bodies continued beyond the point when it was necessary.[37] The thrust of this argument was clearly directed not against government policy or relationships with local authorities, but against *academic* dependence on 'external bodies'. Although the CDP did not name it in this connection, this predominantly meant the Council for National Academic Awards. The Robbins committee had proposed its creation, to replace the NCTA, to be established under royal charter to award degrees in non-university institutions, and to extend the science and technology areas that had been the remit of the NCTA. The CNAA was set up in 1964.

Its charter defined the purposes of the CNAA as 'the advancement of knowledge and learning, the diffusion and extension of the arts, sciences and technologies and the promotion of liberal, scientific and technological, professional industrial and commercial education', and it would have the power to 'confer academic awards and distinctions on persons who have successfully pursued courses of study at educational establishments other than Universities'. Awards made were to be 'comparable in standards to awards granted and conferred by Universities',[38] and indeed for many years the majority of external examiners of CNAA-validated courses came from the universities. The role of the CNAA was to be crucial in helping to produce what could be interpreted as two systems of higher education or as one system arbitrarily divided. The CNAA became the main 'external body' for the polytechnics, although some universities were involved in 'validating' courses, and other technical and specialist organizations did likewise. The CNAA and its associated institutions began to alter the face of higher education. They developed a system of approval of institutions and validation of courses which responded to the requirement not only that courses be similar in standard to those of universities, but also that the institutions have appropriate resources and academic procedures in order to implement such a standard. Although the CNAA was 'external' it did not prescribe syllabuses and forms of examination. In its first report it made it clear to the institutions that there was 'a great measure of freedom afforded to them in courses leading to the Council's degrees', and although external examiners were important 'the ultimate standards achieved by students in the course and their final examinations will depend in greatest measure on the ability and initiative of the teaching staff'.[39] From the outset degrees were approved in subjects that were rare or non-existent in the universities, outstandingly in business studies, but also in such fields as building economics, estate management, food science and photographic technology, and increasingly in areas of education, arts and social studies, including modern languages and sociology. By 1967 the Council was approving courses based on what it called 'newly evolving disciplines, or interfacial areas between established disciplines' (in 1967–68 it reported degree courses in environmental engineering, engineering geology and geotechnics, statistics and computing). M.Sc. courses were rapidly being approved in areas relevant to industrial research and development (such as diesel engine design, molecular science of materials and operational research).[40] Although Crosland had been cautious about the development of research, the CNAA set out to allow the institutions 'to develop research in the way that they wish'.[41]

A historian of the 'polytechnic experiment' has explored the extent to which such trends involved tensions between these academic developments and commitment to preserving and enhancing their traditional provision for part-time and continuing education at levels associated with further education and not normally available in universities.[42] The sights of the CNAA were set primarily on the standards of institutional and course procedures. Although the CVCP, however informally, *represented* the universities, the quality control and developmental roles of the CNAA meant that it *engaged* with the polytechnics and spoke for a sector in ways unlike the CVCP. The parallel body to the CVCP was in fact the CDP, which itself often reflected the diverse commitments and aspirations of the polytechnics. The CNAA spoke a new language, that of course validation – eventually, as the pressures for greater independence mounted, 'partnership in validation' and institutional 'accreditation'. The Council embodied a new version of accountability, involving more and more academic staff from its constituent institutions in its operations – ones which dissidents inside the sector and critics outside it often saw as increasing and unnecessary bureaucracy. At different times it reorganized its procedures and involved larger numbers of its constituent institutions in its operations, delegating more powers to the institutions themselves – which could not but raise their aspirations even higher.

The two sectors continued to reflect their traditions and different modes of funding and accountability, but the CNAA model of quality scrutiny was to be echoed from the 1980s in developments in the universities, and then from 1992 in national bodies overseeing the unified system of higher education.

Reports on EDUCATION

ISSUED BY THE DEPARTMENT OF EDUCATION AND SCIENCE, CURZON STREET, LONDON, W.1

No. 30 June 1966

The Council for National Academic Awards

Nearly two years ago a royal charter was granted to a new educational institution, the Council for National Academic Awards (or the C.N.A.A.). Its purpose is to provide degrees of university standard to students in technical and other colleges outside the university system. The Council is now a going concern.

The Council's Charter

For many years colleges of technology and commerce have been providing courses at degree level. These courses have normally led to a Diploma in Technology, a London University external degree, or a college diploma. College diplomas have varied in standard from college to college and, while satisfying admirably the needs of local industry in the area of the college, do not necessarily have a national standing. The Diploma in Technology was restricted in each case for students to sandwich courses of honours degree level. With the exception the London University external degree has usually been the qualification aimed at in courses at degree level in colleges, and it is not possible to over-estimate the contribution of the London University external degree system to the development of higher education over the last century. Under this system syllabuses are devised by London University and students are examined externally by the University.

Maintaining Standards

The Council for National Academic Awards was set up as an independent institution by Royal Charter in 1964 on the recommendation of the Robbins Committee, which saw the need for an alternative degree system in whose administration the colleges could participate. The Robbins Committee recommended that the universities should participate in the work of the new Council in 'giving important assistance in establishing standards and generally helping the colleges in their academic progress', and this recommendation was followed in the provisions for Council membership. The Charter empowers the Council to grant awards to students who successfully complete approved courses in colleges of technology and commerce and other non-university institutions without their own degree awarding powers. At present the Council awards the degrees of B.A., B.Sc., M.A., M.Sc., M.Phil. and Ph.D.

The Council's Royal Charter requires it to act so as to give colleges three freedoms, subject to the Council being satisfied about standards:

(i) The college is free to devise its own curriculum and syllabuses and to teach its students according to these syllabuses.

(ii) Subject only to certain minimum requirements, the college settles its own admission standards.

(iii) Students are internally examined in the colleges with the help of external examiners approved by the Council.

These freedoms are substantial and if the Council is to retain the guardian of standards then it must obviously be satisfied that the courses which gain its approval are likely to reach the standards required by its Charter. For this reason proposed courses are examined in detail before being approved. Two aspects are considered: the college and the course.

13. 'The Council for National Academic Awards', *Reports on Education*, June 1966.

The CNAA was massively engaged in working with the polytechnics to strengthen their higher education definition. Eric Robinson, as early as 1968, commented that:

> Lord Robbins has subsequently explained that this Council was to have a very limited function. It was to concentrate on colleges which were

clearly *en route* to full university status. It is likely that, in common with most of his university colleagues inside and outside the Committee, he failed to appreciate the potential of this instrument.[43]

The CNAA and its associated institutions were, in fact, to become major components in the developing pattern of higher education.[44] The CNAA became not merely a figure in a changing system, but also a major contributor to change, concerned with widening access to higher education and maintaining and raising standards. It extended and reinterpreted the curricula of higher education. It addressed the difficult balance between exercising responsibilities and enabling institutions to shoulder theirs. It took a process of peer validation and review pioneered by the NCTA and developed it into an instrument that worked for institutions and courses serving a majority of the country's higher education students – an instrument adapted from the late 1980s to a new configuration of higher education. It was concerned not only with the standards of individual courses, but also with questions of desirable 'balance' and the relationship of students' experience of courses to their employment intentions and opportunities – including a continuous commitment to sandwich courses. The CNAA's approach to validation assumed that employment opportunities should be a direct concern of institutions in appraising their course proposals and implementation. Many of these characteristics were important to some extent to some universities, but the explicit aims and procedures of the polytechnic sector were distinctive of the CNAA.

The Robbins committee, Crosland and the binary policy, the polytechnics and the CNAA formed a transition to the agendas of the extraordinarily strengthened position of the state in its dealing with higher education. Salter and Tapper ascribe the transition to Crosland and his Woolwich speech:

> His speech was a clear and unequivocal statement of the new educational ideology. It recognised that 'there is an ever-increasing need and demand for vocational, professional and industrially based courses in higher education', that a 'public' sector of education, separate from the universities, was required to promote such courses, and 'that a substantial part of the higher education system should be under social control, and directly responsive to social needs' ... The important political step had thus been taken to legitimise state intervention in higher education.[45]

There is no doubting the importance of the Crosland policy, but this interpretation is only partially true. It is likely that the bridge to greater state intervention would also have been established by the Robbins recommendations, which involved, for example, the creation of the CNAA and government decisions on transitions to university status. The crucial sequence, however, begins with the NCTA and most importantly with the appointment of the Robbins committee itself. The committee, as we have seen, was appointed to advise the government on the principles on which higher education should be based, 'in the light of national needs and resources'. The committee was asked to advise whether 'any new types of institution are desirable' and what changes might be necessary in planning and co-ordinating the development of 'the various types of institution'. It is arguable that it was therefore the terms of reference of the committee that opened the door to 'legitimising state intervention'. The Robbins terms of reference themselves, presented to the committee by a Conservative government, announced the presupposed need for new institutions responding to national needs. The existence of the NCTA and government intervention to define the regional colleges and their advanced work dated from the mid-1950s. The CNAA charter had invited it to make appropriate arrangements 'for training and experience in industry or commerce', as the NCTA had done. The Woolwich speech was simply a further step in 'legitimising state intervention'.

'CRITERION OF RESPECTABILITY'

Before the Robbins committee reported, Boris Ford, from the new University of Sussex, caustically suggested that 'in some academic circles ... "expansionism" has become the criterion of respectability'. The Robbins committee were 'firm expansionists' and the universities were committed to 'a fairly impressive expansion', though academics were confused about student numbers, believing that more students would mean poorer students. There were important issues of the pattern of higher education and the nature of the 'intellectual and academic responsibilities of universities *towards* higher education' – the question being whether colleges of education and other institutions of higher education should be brought under the universities' umbrella.[46] This was not the only issue in 'expansionism'. Size, community, staff-student contact, standards and resources surfaced for the new universities of the late 1950s and 1960s, and in one way or another for the older universities and the colleges that were soon to become polytechnics.

The numbers themselves seemed intractable and daunting. The number of students roughly doubled again in the universities during the 1960s and as the CVCP pointed out in 1969, on the basis of the Robbins principle of admitting school-leavers qualified for entry, the numbers in universities would double again to 450,000 in the next decade:

> A basic question posed for the government is whether it is to continue with policies based on the assumption that all those qualified and

wishing to enter full-time higher education should have the opportunity to do so. If so, the cost implications are substantial. If not, the political and social implications are no less severe.[47]

UNIVERSITY DEVELOPMENT IN THE 1970s

Introduction

The postwar history of higher educational development in the United Kingdom has been one of a constant upward revision of estimates of demand for places and of need for facilities. The 1970s are likely to prove no exception and the opening of the decade was heralded with new projections of numbers of prospective applicants much larger than any previously canvassed officially. One of the factors which has served as much as any other to falsify predictions in the past has been the increasing appetite for educational advancement. This continued development into the 1970s raises important issues for all those concerned with matters of educational policy. But whatever the problems which may emerge, the desire of an ever-growing proportion of young people to take advantage of the intellectual enrichment to be gained from furthering their education is, we believe, a development to be welcomed and in all possible ways to be encouraged. The greater personal fulfilment which results and the stimulus imparted to the life of the community as a whole are important elements in the worthwhile development of any modern society.

2. The Committee of Vice-Chancellors and Principals has discussed the issues which may be expected to arise in the context of a great increase in the demand for higher education in the 1970s, and in particular it has considered the problems for the universities. In the course of its deliberations the Committee has been in consultation with the universities individually, and their views have formed a basis for the observations which follow. They are put forward against a background of an impressive record by the universities of expansion to meet the greatly increased demand over the past decade and a wide-spread confidence in the universities in their ability, given the diversity and adaptability of the university system, to meet the new needs and changing circumstances of the future.

The Role of the Universities

3. Experience since the war has shown that, as the general educational standard of the country improves, and the horizons of opportunity are widened, the proportion of young people admitted to universities can be increased without perceptible fall in the intellectual ability or awareness of those gaining entry. Over the same period the need for university educated people has similarly increased. Some professions which formerly recruited for the most part non-graduates and trained them entirely in service now expect all or almost all their recruits to have a degree. Also, the occupations particularly in science in which for a long time a degree has been a pre-requisite now include a much larger part of the total working population than they did a generation ago. In addition, a number of entirely new professions calling for university education have appeared. The universities as educational institutions, therefore, play a far more central and significant role in society than would have been the case even ten years ago. The same is true of the universities as centres of learning and research. They have always seen themselves as

3

14. 'University Development in the 1970s', by The Committee of Vice-Chancellors and Principals of the Universities of the United Kingdom, April 1970.

The government's 1972 White Paper, *Education: A Framework for Expansion* suggested that on current estimates the non-university institutions would have the 'formidable task of providing ... for some 335,000 full-time and sandwich students in England and Wales in 1981 ... a net expansion of some 130,000'. The polytechnics would play the 'key role', but the colleges of education and other colleges would play their part. The government's longer-term aim at that time was 750,000 full-time and sandwich students.[48] The polytechnic and CNAA developments had become a crucial element in national numbers planning. At the beginning of its first full year of operation (1965–66) the CNAA had just over 4,000 students enrolled on 89 degree courses. Three years later student numbers had risen to nearly 20,000. In 1980–81 there were more than 123,000 undergraduates and over 35,000 students on masters and other postgraduate courses and on research degrees.[49]

The 'public sector' of higher education was growing rapidly, partly by the new numbers resulting from demographic and democratic change, partly by the amalgamation of new institutions into the sector. As Carswell phrased it, the numbers were 'brigaded into polytechnics and sent over the top, rather like a last line of reserves, towards the terrain into which the colleges of advanced technology had marched, and disappeared into the mist'. The polytechnics had contributed most to this massive expansion, the total numbers of which were greater than Robbins and his colleagues 'could have imagined in their most euphoric dreams'.[50] Other factors affected the rise in student numbers, one being the 1962 Education Act, introducing a standard system of grants to students accepted for first degree courses. A second was the availability of part-time courses and the consequent increase in mature student numbers. In the 1970s, for example, part-time student enrolments outstripped the growth rate of full-time students three-fold, representing 30 per cent of all student numbers in higher education in 1975.[51]

'Expansionists', notably in the universities, also had doubts about excessive expansion of individual institutions and addressed the issue of desirable size. For the new universities something of the order of 3,000 students was widely held to be a suitable norm. John Fulton, Principal of the University College of Sussex and then its Vice-Chancellor when it received its charter, was the strongest advocate of such a target. In 1960 he told a conference it was an extravagant use of staff to keep new universities too small, and a 'community of scholars' of less than 300 would be inadequate for the purposes of scholarship and teaching, and a matching student population would be 3,000. This would not be too large, and he thought 'we would all confess to a feeling of uneasiness about a student community which has got beyond a certain size'. Two years later he argued that the question of 'How big shall we be?' had now become paramount and he repeated the previous arithmetic. Yet again in 1963 he was emphasizing that 'the size of universities is ... by long tradition associated in this country with the quality of undergraduate life'. The larger the university, the more difficult it was to provide student residence, social amenities and frequent contact with academic staff. Rapid expansion made 'the problems of achieving social cohesion assume formidable dimensions'.[52] As the new universities diversified their degree programmes, particularly through cross-disciplinary opportunities, they emphasized their commitment to maintaining traditional university standards. One sociologist included student standards in a list of 'myths' commonly associated with fears about university expansion.[53]

Margaret Thatcher's 1972 White Paper, while looking at issues of expansion overall, was a programme of contraction for teacher education. Forecasts of initial training places suggested that the current figure of 114,000 places should be reduced to 60,000–70,000 by the end of the decade. As a result some colleges, singly or jointly, might become major institutions of higher education adding the arts and human sciences to their programmes – and in this way a new grouping (part of the 'public' sector) came into being, the 'Colleges of Higher Education'. Other colleges were encouraged to combine with polytechnics, and 'some may need to close'.[54] A period of considerable difficulty followed, mirrored in David Hencke's 1978 book on the period entitled *Colleges in Crisis*. The Principal of one of the new colleges, in the same year, described the basis of confusion in many people's minds about the similarities and differences of the various types of higher education:

> ... all offer under-graduate programmes, all have been judged by national standards, and have generally a high level of resources. Most have some residential accommodation and can attract students from all parts of the country and from overseas. All have strong interests in maintaining academic freedom and in encouraging the independence of teaching staff. All aspire to standards of academic excellence, reflected by the sometimes mystical standards of a university or CNAA degree.[55]

With their own different traditions, these colleges were often in rural or suburban locations, generally with a higher proportion of students in residence, and smaller than the polytechnics and universities. They were now, if remaining separate institutions, having to compete for students in new or related subject areas, or if combining with polytechnics (or in a small number of cases, universities) having to adapt to the requirements and opportunities of their new identities.

The final and highly significant example of 'expansionism' in this period was the creation of the Open University (OU). The Robbins committee terms of reference had restricted it to 'the pattern of full-time higher education'. In 1962, however, the Labour Party's Taylor committee recommended, apart from the expansion of and innovations in, other adult education, that 'as an experiment, the B.B.C. sound radio and television and the [Independent Television Authority] should be required to co-operate in organising a "University of the Air" for serious planned adult education'.[56] Before the Robbins committee reported Michael (later Lord) Young was also arguing the case for such a national university. The Prime Minister, Harold Wilson, made a speech in 1963 supporting the possible development of a 'university of the air', and the government set up an advisory committee under Jennie Lee to consider the proposal. A White Paper appeared in 1966 and the 'Open University' followed, with a charter in 1969. Its first intake, 25,000 part-time students, was in 1971 and it was progressively to become the largest university in the United Kingdom, as measured by enrolments. The overwhelming majority of its students have been over the age of 25. An editorial in the *Times Higher Education Supplement* in 1972 bracketed the OU with the CNAA as 'unqualified success stories in higher education'.[57]

The significant features of the OU were obviously seen to be those associated with the features of distance education it pioneered:

> From the beginning, the OU incorporated 'multimedia' in its teaching – though on a small scale – television, radio, computers and audio cassettes were all exploited. However, it was the process in which these aspects were all developed which was thought to be innovative at that time'

– notably the course team, bringing together academic staff, BBC producers and educational technologists. Course teams were 'at the core of the teaching and learning "engine" ', but regional part-time tutors provided face-to-face and phone counselling and tuition.[58] Distance education was later to be adopted by other universities and to become a basis of national 'e-university' planning, although at the end of the century, with over 150,000 undergraduates and 50,000 students and 'customers' of other kinds, the OU accounted for 22 per cent of all part-time higher education students in the United Kingdom. The polytechnics, or 'new universities' from 1992, accounted for a high proportion of the remainder, though many of the 'old universities' had also by then moved in mainly limited ways into part-time higher education.

The system (or 'systems') being advocated and built across the twentieth century had therefore by its last quarter become closely and increasingly enmeshed with state funding and planning, guidance and control. Expansion was associated with change, and whether under the UGC or local authorities and the CNAA, the institutions came to *expect* government or government-directed intervention, to respond to or anticipate external changes, to see expansion as a 'criterion of respectability' but also as a slippery slope to the next zigzag of government financing and policy. There remained, of course, hierarchies of institutions and differential impacts of government policy or social pressures. The Universities of Oxford and Cambridge shared only slowly in the upward trend of student numbers. Oxford, for example, appointed a Commission of Inquiry under Lord Franks to consider the 'recommendations and criticisms in the Robbins Report', and the part which Oxford played and should play in the system of higher education. The Commission reported in 1966 that the University had long made changes under pressure, but had not 'fully understood the change in direction which has been involved' and its 'explanation of itself lacks coherence ... the mists through which Oxford permits itself to be seen obscure much more than its statistics'. In the late 1940s, 1950s and early 1960s undergraduate numbers fell, while postgraduate numbers increased. Evidence to the Commission envisaged 'a fairly static' number of undergraduates. The 7,300 in 1963–4 might increase, with the addition of 400 reading applied science and clinical medicine and 700 more women, to 8,500–9,000 in 15 to 20 years.[59] The Commission commented, in relation to total student numbers, and in response to the University's evidence:

> A decision to plan Oxford's future as a medium-sized university is the choice of a pattern of life and involves a conscious control of the forces of expansion. The Hebdomadal Council told us ... that in its view a total student population of about 10,000 in the next ten years would be right. The numbers in the first term of the academic year 1965–66 were about 9,800. We have thought in terms of about 13,000 over the next 15 to 20 years ... This figure is still within the medium-size range: it represents a determination to slacken the recent rate of growth.[60]

The 'pattern of life' was collegiate and academically heavily reliant on the personal tutorial. These total numbers included not only the more rapidly increasing postgraduate numbers, but also some 500 'recognized students' doing short professional courses. At this period Oxford not only did not share the prevalent 'expansionism' of higher education, it set its face against the 'forces of expansion' in order to protect its social and academic patterns. The older universities in general moved with various degrees of enthusiasm or ambivalence along the expansionist road, though permanently alarmed about how it was to be resourced – finding from the 1980s that the alarms could be worse than they feared.

'ALIENATION AND REVOLT'

The period of expansion in the 1960s coincided with the entry on stage of student protest movements. Student revolt and radicalism have erupted in various forms since the earliest history of the universities. Lord Robbins told a Canadian audience in 1968 of his memories of student grievances and action in the inter-war period, and he had also been re-reading Turgenev's *Fathers and Sons*. The novel dealt with the same problem of 'alienation and revolt among the younger generation. Indeed, I am inclined to argue that there are profound psychological reasons why this should be a more or less permanent feature of the human situation.'[61] Whether the movements of the 1960s were within some such continuity or were basically different from their predecessors is less important than the fact that student revolts internationally were *seen* as new, and the voices of students were *heard* as a new incursion into debate about higher education. It is important that 'voices' is in the plural since the messages and demands were extremely varied, even though the political and social causes of student disaffection were relatively few. Students were dissatisfied with aspects of their institutions, and suspicious of or antagonistic to the wider political arenas in which their institutions were situated. A significant feature of these movements is that in the 1960s and 1970s they paralleled and to some extent replaced other forms of advocacy. With whatever differences and confusions, they had things to propose: they wanted to remove the dangers and anxieties that the adult world had bequeathed to them, they wanted something better than what Robbins, analyzing their 'distress', called 'the empty clichés, the misleading generalities, the appeals to the gallery, the utter fourth-ratedness of it all'.[62] They wanted something better from their institutions and their society.

Disturbances in England began in the second half of the 1960s, at institutions as diverse as the London School of Economics, Hornsey School of Art and universities old and new. Sit-ins and the occupation of administrative and other premises by substantial proportions of the student bodies, the issue of manifestos, deputations and public discussion were some of the features of the campaigns. Like student protesters in other countries the declared aims were diverse – and contested amongst students themselves. At one end of a spectrum aims were couched in revolutionary slogans. What they were *against* included bourgeois, liberal ideology, in general and as manifest in their institutions and experience. The target was authority, to be confronted directly, because dominant ideas 'are invariably produced, or reproduced, within the university itself'.[63] No aspect of capitalist society was immune from the attack, underpinned by revolutionary theory derived from Mao or Che Guevara, Marcuse or the revolutionary proclamations that accompanied much student revolt everywhere. What this version of student revolt was *for* was most frequently encapsulated in the concept of 'student power'. At the other – unquestionably majority – end of the spectrum, the hostility was directed variously against poor institutional conditions and services, poor teaching, lack of contact between students and academic staff, failure to match up to students' prior expectations, unimaginative curricula, disregard for the interests of students, and the lack of adequate student participation in the decision-making procedures of the institutions.[64] Some of this hostility could be related briefly or enduringly to particular national political or policy targets and might be expressed with different degrees of vigour. The tendency at this end of the spectrum, however, was to accept the possibilities of institutional reform, while still mistrusting the controlling power and mechanisms of the authorities. The concepts of 'participation' and 'representation', rather than 'power', and the interpretation of the concepts, were therefore central to the way these latter students' demands were formulated.

The leaders of the NUS in the late 1960s were strongly in favour of the 'middle way' of student representation in governance, between consultation and power, the latter of which Jack Straw, then Deputy President of the NUS, described in 1968 as one of a number of 'inexplicit and meaningless phrases'. Straw, advocating representative participation, linked it importantly with the internal 'accountability' of the authorities: many of the 'sit-ins' had been concerned not so much with participation itself, but with the accountability of authorities' actions to the rest of the community. It was essential to change the basis of university government because, as at present constituted, administrators could make token concessions and take decisions elsewhere: 'the nearer one thinks one is getting to the centre of power, on this committee or that, the farther away in reality it goes'.[65] Two years later Straw described the universities as 'the last great unreformed institutions of our time', accusing them of failure to apply their own ideals to themselves and so blinkered by power that they 'cannot see, much less respond to, the fact that our whole society is changing'. Having made 'paper concessions' to the students, they had ensured power remained in the same hands: 'the façade of government has changed but the reality has not'. The Vice-Chancellor of the University of Essex, Albert Sloman, on the same occasion, reflected on the targets of international student protest: 'Sometimes the protest has been directed against the institution itself: its anachronistic curricula, its indifferent teachers, even its imperfect administrators! Often it has been directed against society at large: its failure to prevent war and famine.' Those students who saw universities as merely reflections of society and needing to be destroyed or turned into centres of social revolution had been 'totally dwarfed by ... the very much larger number who are concerned as never before about the quality of their own institution and are demanding a say in determining that quality'.[66]

The reception of the student messages – including by vice-chancellors – involved extensive negotiation, as well as confrontation, with students locally and nationally, either informally or in the establishment of joint working parties to plan for change.[67] The position in some institutions deteriorated to a point that made such negotiation impossible, or at least long delayed. An account of what happened at the Polytechnic of North London described it as 'the making of an oligarchy', and the Director of the Polytechnic from 1971 talked of 'these student guerrillas of the Fascist left'.[68] Researchers, in Britain as in the United States, had begun to study the students, their backgrounds, their aims. It was widely felt that the student protest movement in British institutions would have long-term effects, including at the art colleges on the curriculum in art and design. It was equally widely felt that the impact would be minimal, and that student representation would have neutral or only marginally beneficial influences. Research on students, their movements and institutional events soon produced a thriving literature.[69] Like attempts we have previously discussed to advocate change and shape opinion, the student movement brought the nature and purpose of the university and other higher education on to discussion agendas in forums of many kinds, including parliament and the press, meetings of vice-chancellors or university teachers, academic and political conferences. The 'student' had historically been subject to many changing images, and from the 1960s 'students' and 'their' movement captured public attention.

The image of the student changed at the same time as, and had strong connections with, the changing image of 'youth', particularly in its many manifestations of 'youth culture'. In 1965, before the British student movement had taken off, Bryan Wilson wrote a piece entitled 'The needs of students', in which he approached the link between university students and their 'generational' world outside:

> It is still vaguely assumed that scholarly values should be inhaled from the atmosphere of universities. But the atmosphere has changed: the clientele itself has radically affected it. In the past it seems that people brought with them to the university values which were much less dissonant with the university's business than is now the case. At the time adult society was *still* respected, and the accumulated knowledge of society was esteemed, so that those who entered universities, even if not always desperately keen to learn themselves, were not root-and-branch opposed to what learning stood for. There was not then a generational sub-culture, promoted by mass-media, with values largely alien to those of the academic and cultural tradition of our society.[70]

Wilson's analysis therefore encompassed not only students and their changes, but also the sub-culture with which they could be identified, thereby diminishing the importance of the threshold to the university and enhancing the importance of atmosphere both inside and outside the institution. Much discussion about students therefore focused not only the stances they took, but also on the status that helped to explain them. Were they adolescents or adults, were they 'visitors' to the university or 'members' of it? Within what parameters could their demands for change be justified, or even understood? The difficulty in answering such questions lay not only in different ideologies of change, but also in the different situations of students themselves. As one analysis of student residence pointed out, they did not necessarily – even if one postulated a common student culture – 'share a wide range of common norms; it implies rather that they share a common situation in life, a common consciousness, and a common identity'.[71] What commentators were to realize was that the movements were less about differences generated by background and experience than about the ways situation, consciousness and identity provided platforms on which dissatisfactions could be articulated, messages communicated, and targets defined.

It is no coincidence, therefore, that as student energies were being harnessed to protest, the Latey report on *The Age of Majority* was being published and its implications being considered. The report argued, in 1967, that the historical reasons for 21 being the age of majority were no longer relevant. It made an abundantly clear case for change, italicizing its central theme: *'we feel extremely strongly that to keep responsibility from those who are ready and able to take it on is much more likely to make them irresponsible than to help them'*. There were implications for the age at which young people could marry without parental permission or make binding contracts (for example, for hire purchase). It concluded

> that by 18 most young people are ready for these responsibilities and rights and would greatly profit by them as would the teaching authorities, the business community, the administration of justice, and the community as a whole ... We therefore recommend that the need for parental or Court consent to marry should cease at the age of 18.

The Committee did not take evidence on the appropriateness of 21 as the voting age, or as the age for jury service, although in the latter case it confessed that 'it would not actually keep us awake at night if people under 21 were to serve on a jury'.[72] In 1969 parliament enacted a reduction of the age of majority to 18, including for the purposes of voting. These developments, together with the sub-cultural and wider social changes, contributed to the sense of unrecognized adulthood that was part of student disaffection. Although the old position of the university as being 'in loco parentis' had now changed, institutional structures and attitudes were not changing sufficiently rapidly to satisfy the aspirations of students to participate and to be represented.

Ashby, as we have seen, was arguing before an audience at the LSE for change on the basis of the common seal of the University of Cambridge, which was used on behalf of the 'Chancellor, Masters and Scholars', all being co-equal. The students (or 'scholars') and their organizations seemed to him in 1964 to have reached a great deal of maturity. Although he argued that students did not have the expertise to run universities (which needed a 'long and austere apprenticeship'), students did know how they wanted universities to be run. There would be great difficulties in implementing the 'trinity' proclaimed in the Cambridge seal, 'but (for a start) could we not place greater emphasis than we do on the fact that a university is a society of Chancellor, Masters, and Scholars, coequal in importance?'[73] Certainly in the later 1960s and into the 1970s there were many students who felt this need for membership and 'co-equality', but who also felt that their dissatisfactions and visions of how a university should be run could only be demonstrated by being represented in academic government. After all, the generations which had served the 'austere apprenticeship' had produced neither institutions nor societies that embodied the justice, democracy and spirit of community that were targets of much of the student dissent.

Although the strength of the student movement ebbed in the early 1970s, in the conditions of the 1970s and 1980s students found new issues on which, however briefly, to revive the radical energies of the late 1960s. They campaigned against war and injustice, apartheid and the directions of university investments, and with particular vigour addressed the conditions of 'studenthood' – economic, social and political. Student *movements*, however, were increasingly inhibited by the changing social values and economic realities of Thatcherite Britain, the growing dominance of the need to succeed in relation to potential employment, the competitive arenas in which they and their institutions had been more and more strongly placed. The ethos and events of the late 1960s left decreasing echoes within the British student body, as they did also in other countries. They left perhaps a more permanent effect on public opinion and the 'image' of students. The effect on the institutions took time to diminish, but diminish it did. In the United States, where student rebellion had impacted more widely on institutions, the already considerable literature on 'crisis', 'campus war' or 'revolt' of the 1960s continued to grow. The interpretation of the influence of the movement internationally on higher education was ambivalent. An international conference of academics on the future of the university held in Venice in 1973 reflected the varied degrees of 'reform', 'transition' or 'strain' that were present in many countries at this time. The book that came out of the conference began with a statement by an eminent American lawyer on university aims and standards, the opening sentences of which read:

All of us must bear wounds inflicted by life in the universities of the Western world during the decade of the 1960s. So do our institutions.

Some of our wounds are grave, some less so. None I believe were superficial, though few if any were fatal.[74]

The book ended with reflections by an eminent philosopher and educational administrator. He judged the experience of recent years to have left the imagination of the higher education community focused 'not on the problems of possibilities of the future, but on the unpleasantnesses of the recent past ... In the minds of most university teachers and administrators ... something like a civil war has taken place, and they are living through its aftermath.'[75] A British commentary on events adduced evidence that the troubles were nearly over, which did not mean that they could not flare up again, but if so they would 'become economic and be powered by the new national strength of the National Union of Students'.[76] The aftermath seemed to point ambiguously in various directions. The trajectory of higher education from the 1970s contained, internationally as in Britain, other profound elements of change.

NOTES AND REFERENCES

1. Boyle, E., 'Intellectual responsibilities in higher education', *Universities Quarterly*, vol. 16, 1962, p. 127; Boyle, E., *Government, Parliament and the Robbins Report* (London: College of Preceptors, 1979), p. 4.
2. Niblett, W.R., *The Expanding University: A Report* (London: Faber & Faber, 1962), p. 13.
3. Ibid., p. 11.
4. Amis, K., 'Lone voices. Views of the 'fifties', *Encounter*, vol. 15, 1960, pp. 8–9.
5. Labour Party's Study Group on Higher Education, *The Years of Crisis* (London: Labour Party, 1962), passim.
6. Committee on Higher Education, *Higher Education: Report* (London: HMSO, 1963), p. iii.
7. Scott, P. in *Education Guardian*, 4 December 2001.
8. Committee on Higher Education, *Report,* pp. 4–5; Robbins, L., 'Recent discussion of the problems of higher education in Great Britain' (1964), in his *The University in the Modern World* (London: Macmillan, 1966), pp. 32–3.
9. Committee on Higher Education, *Report*, pp. 228, 233–5.
10. Ibid., ch. 2 passim.
11. Ibid., p. 8.
12. Appendix One, Part 2, Section 2 ('The influence of family background'); Vernon, P.E., *Memorandum in Evidence – Part Two*, p. 170.
13. Quoted in report of a discussion entitled 'Discussing Robbins' in November 1963, *Universities Quarterly*, vol. 18, 1964, pp. 158–9.
14. Entwistle, N.J., Percy, K.A. and Nisbet, J., report to the Joseph Rowntree Memorial Trust on 'Educational Objectives and Academic Performance in Higher Education', vol. 2: 'Aims and objectives', University of Lancaster [1971?], pp. 9/4–9/6. The quotation from Boyle is from the *Times Educational Supplement*, 18 October 1968.
15. Maclure, S., in a symposium on 'Who killed Cock Robbins?', *Twentieth Century*, vol. 174, 1966, p. 40.

16. The *Guardian*, Report on debate in the House of Lords, 12 December 1963, p. 1; Committee on Higher Education, *Report*, p. 276.
17. Association of University Teachers, *Submissions to the Committee on Higher Education*, AUT (1961), p. 4; Lord Hailsham, opening a conference on 'New and larger universities?', *Universities Quarterly*, vol. 15, 1961, p. 125; UGC, *University Development 1957–1962* (London: HMSO, 1964), pp. 93–4; Lord Robbins, address on 'Universities and the future pattern of higher education', Home Universities Conference, *Proceedings 1963*, p. 19.
18. *Government Statement on the Report of the Committee under the Chairmanship of Lord Robbins* (London: HMSO, 1963), p. 3.
19. Committee on Higher Education, *Report*, p. 149.
20. Robinson, E., 'Coherence or conglomeration?', *Education*, 7 May 1965.
21. Crosland, A., Woolwich speech, in Pratt, J. and Burgess, T., *Polytechnics: A Report* (London: Pitman, 1974), pp. 203–7.
22. Boyle, E. and Crosland, A., in conversation with Kogan, M., *The Politics of Education* (Harmondsworth: Penguin, 1971), p. 193.
23. Crosland, A., 'The structure and development of higher education', in Robinson, E., *The New Polytechnics* (London: Cornmarket, 1968), pp. 193–6.
24. Carswell, J., *Government and the Universities in Britain: Programme and Performance 1960–1980* (Cambridge: Cambridge University Press, 1985), p. 93.
25. See particularly Godwin, C.D., 'The origin of the binary system', *History of Education*, vol. 27, 1998, pp. 171–91; Pratt, J., *The Polytechnic Experiment 1965–1992*, Buckingham (1997), ch. 2.
26. Speech in the House of Lords, 1 December 1965, in Robbins, *The University in the Modern World*, p. 149; Robbins, L. *Autobiography of an Economist* (London: Macmillan, 1971), p. 281.
27. Maclure, in 'Who killed Cock Robbins?', p. 40.
28. Carswell, *Government and the Universities in Britain*, p. 67.
29. Nuffield College, *The Problem Facing British Universities* (London: Oxford University Press, 1948), p. 92.
30. Crosland, C.A.R., 'Some thoughts on English education', *Encounter*, July 1961, p. 52.
31. Fowler, G.T., 'The binary policy in England and Wales', in Niblett, W.R. and Butts, R.F.(eds) *Universities Facing the Future* (San Francisco, CA: Jossey-Bass, 1972), pp. 271–2.
32. Carswell, *Government and the Universities in Britain*, p. 127.
33. Department of Education and Science, 'Government and Academic Organisation of Polytechnics: Notes for Guidance', typescript [1967], pp. 1–2.
34. MacArthur, B. 'Role of the polytechnics is defined', *The Times*, 2 March 1968.
35. Thatcher, M., 'The role of the polytechnics', the *Guardian*, 17 February 1970.
36. Whitburn, J., Mealing, M. and Cox, C., *People in Polytechnics; A Survey of Polytechnic Staff and Students 1972–3* (Guildford: Society for Research into Higher Education, 1976), p. 6.
37. CDP, Memorandum of Evidence to the House of Commons Expenditure Committee (Education and Arts Sub-Committee) (London: HMSO, 1968), p. 133.
38. CNAA, *Charter and Statutes*, pp. 3, 11.
39. CNAA, *Report for the Period 30 September 1964 to 30 September 1965*, p. 11.
40. CNAA, *1967–8 Report*, pp. 8–9.
41. CNAA, *1966–7 Report*, p. 10.
42. Pratt, *The Polytechnic Experiment*.
43. Robinson, *The New Polytechnics*, p. 25.
44. The following summary is based on Silver, H., *A Higher Education: the Council for*

National Academic Awards and British Higher Education 1964–1989 (Basingstoke: Falmer, 1990), ch. 11.

45. Salter, B. and Tapper, T., *The State and Higher Education* (Ilford: Woburn Press, 1994), p. 15.

46. Ford, B. 'The universities' role in higher education', *Sociological Studies in British Higher Education (Sociological Review Monograph* no. 7), (1963), p. 172.

47. CVCP, University Development in the 1970s, typescript (1969), p. 1.

48. Secretary of State, *Education: A Framework for Expansion* (London: HMSO, 1972), pp. 34–5, 41.

49. CNAA, *Report for the Period 30 September 1964 to 30 September 1965*, p. 5; *Report for 1968–1969*, pp. 15–16; *Annual Report 1980*, pp. 24–40.

50. Carswell, *Government and the Universities in Britain*, pp. 73–4, 126–7.

51. Bourner, T. et al., *Part-time Students and their Experience of Higher Education* (Buckingham: Open University Press, 1991), p. 3.

52. Fulton, J.S., address on 'New universities', Home Universities Conference, *Proceedings 1960*, pp. 47–8; 'The shape of universities', in Niblett, *The Expanding University*, pp. 53–4; *Experiment in Higher Education* (London: Tavistock, 1963), p. 8.

53. Little, A.N., 'Some myths of university expansion', *Sociological Studies in British Universities (Sociological Review Monograph* No. 7) (1963), p. 185.

54. *Education: A Framework for Expansion*, pp. 43–4.

55. Porter, P., 'Expanding in the eighties', the *Guardian*, 6 June 1978, p. 15.

56. Labour Party, *The Years of Crisis*, p. 34.

57. Times Higher Education Supplement, 4 August 1972.

58. English, S., 'The Process of Change in Teaching and Learning in Higher Education: Integrating Information and Communication Technology', University of Plymouth Ph.D. thesis (2001), p. 124.

59. University of Oxford, *Report of Commission of Inquiry* (Oxford: Clarendon Press, 1966), vol. 1, p.18; vol. 2, pp. 4, 12, 40.

60. Ibid., vol. 1, p. 46.

61. Lord Robbins, 'Present discontents of the student age group', in House of Commons Select Committee on Education and Science, *Student Relations*, vol. 7 (London: HMSO, 1969), p. 182.

62. Ibid., p. 188.

63. Blackburn, R., 'A brief guide to bourgeois ideology', in Cockburn, A. and Blackburn, R. (eds), *Student Power: Problems, Diagnosis, Action* (Harmondsworth: Penguin, 1969), p. 163.

64. Cf., for example, Startup, R., 'Why students wish to reform university government', *Research in Education*, no. 11, 1974, pp. 68–82; Blackstone, T. *et al.*, *Students in Conflict: L.S.E. in 1967* (London: Weidenfeld & Nicolson, 1970), p 1.

65. Straw, J., 'Participation in practice', in Crouch, C. *et al.*, *Students Today* (London: Fabian Society, 1968), pp. 22–6.

66. Straw, J., 'Student participation in higher education: education for democracy and technology' and Sloman, A.,'British universities and their students', in Straw, J., Sloman, A. and Doty, P., *Universities: Boundaries of Change* (London: Panther, 1970), pp. 7, 29–30.

67. The major national document was the *Joint Statement from the Committee of Vice-Chancellors and Principals and the National Union of Students*, published jointly by the two organizations in 1968.

68. Campell, F.J., *High Command: The Making of an Oligarchy at the Polytechnic of North London. 1970–74* (London: 'Time Out', [1974?], passim and p. 125.

69. Cf., for example, Biggs, D.A., 'Recent research on British students: a brief analysis',

Research in Education, no. 15, 1976, pp. 79–96; Hanson, A.H., 'Some literature on student revolt', *University of Leeds Review*, vol. 12, 1969, pp. 123–39; Lipset, S.M., *Rebellion in the University: A History of Student Activism in America* (London: Routledge & Kegan Paul, 1972); Blackstone *et al.*, *Students in Conflict: L.S.E. in 1967*; Startup, 'Why students wish to reform university government'.

70. In Wilson, B., *The Youth Culture and the Universities* (London: Faber & Faber, 1970), pp. 123–4.
71. Hatch, S., 'Student culture and the impact of institutions', in Brothers, J. and Hatch, S. (eds), *Residence and Student Life: A Sociological Inquiry into Residence in Higher Education* (London: Tavistock, 1971), p. 191.
72. *Report of the Committee on the Age of Majority* (London: HMSO, 1967), pp. 15, 17, 42, 51.
73. Ashby, E., '... *And Scholars*' (London: London School of Economics and Political Science, 1965), pp. 3, 14.
74. Bickel, A.M., 'The aims of education and the proper standards of the university', in Seabury, P. (ed.) *Universities in the Western World* (New York: Free Press, 1975), p. 3.
75. Frankel, C., 'Epilogue: reflections on a worn-out model', in ibid., p. 279.
76. MacRae, D., 'The British position', in ibid., p. 179.

10

FINAL DECADES: 'PAINFUL TRANSFORMATION'

'OH YES WE WILL!'

Features of the voices for higher education up to the 1960s were vision and the confident anticipation of and planning for a bigger or better or different future. In the 1970s and 1980s the controlling hand of government placed both the institutions and the voices that spoke for them in postures of increasingly guarded analysis and defence. The confidence expressed by a Moberly or an Ashby that the limited but necessary boundaries of government expectation and involvement would not be overstepped diminished sharply as these were seen from higher education as requirement and intervention. After Robbins and the binary policy the next policy indication of the extent of the move from state oversight to state leverage of change was the 1972 White Paper. Demography and the economy largely dictated the numbers, organizational and financial planning, but reflected in the arithmetic were also political and social assumptions about the future of the system. These applied not only to assumptions about teacher education. The lion's share of the expansion of student numbers generally was to be borne by the polytechnics, and the government intended 'to arrest the tendency of unit costs to rise (at constant prices) from year to year' in the universities, thus slowing down the previous rate of expansion. Assumptions about the university student population were based on the government having taken into account the estimated numbers of qualified school leavers, though with minimal account of part-time students and no consideration of the possible entry of mature or other groups of potential students.[1] Niblett drew attention to the difficulties and lack of defined purposes for higher education in what he described as 'a jolting document for all institutions of higher education', containing 'abundant matter ... to rouse us sharply from the peace into which we seemed to be drifting'. Though it offered opportunities, to take them was 'not going to be easy for anyone'.[2]

From now on government policy documents on higher education were to contain new vocabularies or redirected old ones – contraction and closure, amalgamation, cost effectiveness, efficiency, selectivity, concentration, standards, quality – all acting as proxy for the parent vocabulary of (greater) accountability. Constraint on further expansion became increasingly clear as the birth rate declined from 1964, pointing to an impact that would be felt in higher education at the beginning of the 1980s. *Higher Education into the 1990s. A Discussion Document* was issued by the DES and the Scottish Department in 1978 emphasizing that student numbers in British higher education – 520,000 full-time and 230,000 part-time – had tripled since 1960. (Operational planning did not, however, take account of part-time and Open University numbers.) The increase would continue for several years, but the decline was expected to begin in 1982–83 and to fall more steeply from 1990–91. The percentage of the 18-year-old age group had stabilized at about 14 per cent, 'but there is no certainty (nor can there be) about the proportion of the age group likely to be suitably qualified for and willing to embark on higher education courses' (echoing the principle on which the Robbins forecasts had been made). The document offered five models of possible policies that would tackle the resource and other difficulties involved, and raised for discussion various possibilities of temporary and longer-term measures, the abandonment of the Robbins principle, more efficient use of resources, the cessation of expansion, institutional contraction, and different approaches for the universities and other higher education.[3]

Reactions in higher education ranged from confusion to alarm. There were implications for building and staffing, for principle and logistics. If there was going to be an increase before the decline, could 'additional resources be acquired quickly enough to meet the upsurge and then be shed painlessly in the trough that will follow?'[4] There were, however, doubts about the validity of the figures, let alone the options. The peaks and troughs might turn out to be on the less dramatic side of the calculations. Even more difficult to understand, as a group of academics from Bradford University pointed out, was the 'interplay of socially predetermined factors and central policy'. Many of the assumptions in the discussion document were wrong. Were the outcomes of demographic change *inevitable?* In the recent past a period of decline in the 18-year-old group had been accompanied by a significant *increase* in higher education enrolments. The analysis suggested that the discussion document was not about demography but about government policy and its failure to see the potential for greater recruitment into higher education:

> These major policy questions of how much higher education is desirable, how to widen the socio-cultural base of intake, and how to broaden participation throughout life remain of vital importance. They

will not be solved solely by policies directed towards reforms in the institutions ... The correct approach to them must be through an active study of those barriers which probably eliminate any aspiration to higher education and hence the motivation for attainment from the majority of the population.[5]

Richard Hoggart, who chaired the Advisory Council for Adult and Higher Education, elaborated, a month after the publication of the discussion paper, the core meaning of 'participation throughout life', pointing out that the universities needed 'to think more about their links with age groups other than the eighteen-plus ... "continuing education" has a good claim to become the main point of growth within education in the eighties'. The existing concentration of the universities on full-time, 18-plus students did not match 'the range of needs'.[6] There was a host of responses to *Higher Education into the 1990s*, voicing such criticisms of the assumptions and policy underpinning of the document, or in other ways defending the institutions and their purposes. The fact that they were *responses* is an important point here. Different or sterner policies or more of the same were to evince parallel responses. Higher education was being placed in a posture with which in previous generations it had not been very familiar – that of defensiveness, not against change, but against what were seen as narrow, damaging or wrong policies. The posture was to become most uncomfortable in 1985.

In that year Sir Keith Joseph issued a Green Paper on *The Development of Higher Education into the 1990s*. The tenor of the paper was set by an introduction on 'The Government's main concerns', focusing on implications of the United Kingdom's disappointing economic performance since 1945, compared to other countries. Higher education establishments needed to 'beware of "anti-business" snobbery. The entrepreneurial spirit is essential for the maintenance and improvement of employment, prosperity and public services'. Effective research needed to be concentrated, and therefore research policy over the next few years would be towards 'selectivity and concentration'. Because of the decline in student numbers it was 'not improbable that some institutions of higher education will need to be closed or merged at some point during the next ten years'. Other changes might be in the student support system, but primarily in attitudes that needed to be shaped by the situation in the economy:

> ... there is continuing concern that higher education does not always respond sufficiently to changing economic needs. This may be due in part to disincentives to change within higher education, including over-dependence on public funding ... In higher education the Government believes it right to maintain a distinct emphasis on technological and directly vocational courses at all levels.

1.5 The shortage of appropriately qualified manpower can be made good only if higher education is sufficiently flexible to respond quickly to new needs. As the UGC has said, the universities in particular need to develop greater ability to adapt to change. The report of a Steering Committee established by the Committee of Vice-Chancellors and Principals (CVCP) under the chairmanship of Sir Alex Jarratt (the Jarratt Report) recognises this and recommends developments in universities' management structures and practice which merit early and careful consideration. For the public sector the Government has asked the NAB to undertake a study of efficiency and management practice.

1.6 In addition to developing the flexibility needed to be able to respond to future change, our higher education establishments need:

— to be concerned with attitudes to the world outside higher education, and in particular to industry and commerce, and to beware of "anti-business" snobbery. The entrepreneurial spirit is essential for the maintenance and improvement of employment, prosperity and public services. Higher education should be alert to the hazard of blunting it and should seek opportunities to encourage it. More generally, higher education needs to foster positive attitudes to work. Most students will have to be able to work co-operatively in groups as well as individually; they will need to be able to show leadership and to respond to it.

— to go out to develop their links with industry and commerce. Many techniques and arrangements are in place already, for example, industrial contracts; consultancy; appointment of businessmen to the governing bodies of academic institutions; joint academic appointments with business and other employers; updating and sandwich courses; the sponsorship of individual students by employers; and the appointment of Industrial Liaison Officers. More recent innovations which bear particularly on the transfer of technology include teaching companies, science parks, business clubs and industrial professorships.

— strong connections with their local communities. The development of closer links with local industry and commerce are of prime importance, especially with actual or potential employers of their students, but the extension of artistic, cultural and recreational facilities to members of the local community can also be valuable.

1.7 The Government attaches great importance to raising standards. In part this is a matter of appropriate procedures and mechanisms. Last year, the Government established an enquiry into academic validation in the public sector* and gave its full backing to the setting up by the CVCP of its own enquiry into the procedures for ensuring quality in the universities. But, if standards are to be raised, individual academic staff and those with responsibility for management and leadership in institutions need to pay continuing attention to the quality of teaching.

---

*The report of this enquiry, undertaken by a committee chaired by Sir Norman Lindop, was published in April 1985, titled "Academic Validation in Public Sector Higher Education" (HMSO, Cmnd 9501).

4

15. 'The Development of Higher Education into the 1990s', by the Secretary of State for Education and Science and the Secretaries of State for Scotland, Wales and Northern Ireland, 1985, p. 4.

Although there were gestures towards 'liberal institutions' and the importance of the arts, 'arts provision should to some extent be concentrated in the interests of cost-effectiveness', mainly in the university sector for the sake of quality: 'the proportion of arts places in higher education as a whole can be expected to shrink'. Academic staff felt threatened by the tone as much as by the content. There were references to the raising of standards being dependent on 'continuing attention to the quality of teaching', quality of outcomes being dependent on 'the quality, competence and attitudes of the academic staff'. Tenure was attacked as an 'impediment', hindering adaptation to change. Other proposals echoed loud around the system, including a proposal to review the role, structure and staffing of the UGC.[7]

As Secretary of State for Education and Science, it was Sir Keith Joseph whose voice was most heard in the Green Paper. As a leading Conservative advocate of a liberalized economic market place he had the paradoxical role of propelling higher education towards a place in it, and at the same time sternly laying down the rules and requirements for the diverse operations of the universities and the other institutions. The Green Paper was an advance on the 1978 planning options in that it saw the longer-term as dependent not only on the proportion of school-leavers, which it thought might now rise as a result of the Government's policies for schools, but also on increased demand from women and mature students. All of this was within the search for increased economy and efficiency, including 'the further rationalisation of provision'. The underlying thrust of the Green Paper and some of its salient messages were also heard in the Secretary of State's public pronouncements. Three months before the Green Paper was published he had told the North of England Education Conference that 'In higher education, to the extent that the quality of teaching is inadequate – I do not think there can really be any doubt that this is sometimes the case – both staff themselves and institutions must work together to see that standards are improved.'[8] At a conference on the Green Paper two months after its publication he argued that 'more needs to be done – and can be done – to provide public reassurance about teaching and examination standards and to develop programmes of staff appraisal and development' (this latter having emerged after the Green Paper as a result of pressure, mainly from the AUT). This tone was again prominent when he continued: 'Preservation of standards in quality and examinations is something which, under present arrangements, I can only urge the universities to tackle for themselves. But I shall ask them with increasing frequency to demonstrate to me that they are doing so.'[9] The next year, however, he was replaced as Secretary of State by Kenneth Baker, someone thought to be less likely to hector all sections of the teaching profession. Whatever grains of truth there might have been in the Green Paper, it had been received as a high-handed or arrogant approach to the issues at stake.

Furious responses to the Green Paper and to Sir Keith's interventions were widespread. One such response, by Robin Marris, Professor of Economics at Birkbeck College, University of London, accused him of ignoring the international respect for the positive features and efficiency of British higher education, and of deliberately attempting to thwart upward social mobility. If there were a suitable judicial process Sir Keith 'would be convicted of treason for systematically trying to degrade the national's higher education system'. The article was entitled 'Why Sir Keith should be impeached'. Marris also published a lecture originally intended for a Conservative policy forum. In it he described the Green Paper as 'probably the worst state paper in British history'. It had been 'almost universally condemned, and not only among the intellectual elite'. The London Broadcasting Company had organized a debate on the motion 'The Government's higher education policy is a recipe for national decline' – a motion carried by a margin of about five to one of those who voted by telephone.[10] Not all the responses from higher education were as confrontational, but most were so to a degree, in line with the general perception of government policies – not only Sir Keith's – on higher education as narrow (some said 'philistine') and dangerous. More conciliatory policy attitudes followed in 1986, with the new Secretary of State adopting a different line on some of the key issues. He told the CVCP that there would be no closures and that the Government had been converted to expansion after years of talk and action to do with contraction. Although the number of 18–19 year-olds would still fall by about a third in a decade, industry and commerce would be increasing its manpower demands. Universities would need to sell themselves to a new clientele: 'You must not only be ready to admit, but must be ready positively to encourage young people with non-traditional qualifications and older people who may lack all formal qualifications.'[11] A White Paper followed.

From the early 1960s there had been a continuity of growing government ascendancy over policy, action and argument. The White Paper of 1987, *Higher Education: Meeting the Challenge,* and the Act of the following year confirmed, if confirmation were needed, that ascendancy. In many respects the White Paper and government intentions were more liberal than most of their immediate predecessors. Although there were to be rewards for bringing higher education closer to the world of business, it endorsed British higher education as among the best of the world, and 'the encouragement of a high level of scholarship in the arts, humanities and social sciences is an essential feature of a civilised and cultured country ... Meeting the needs of the economy is not the sole purpose of higher education.' The particular ideas or ideology are not at this point, however, as important to our argument as the fact of increased government control. Student numbers were to rise. Quality and efficiency were focal points of the paper. It was no longer appropriate for polytechnics and other colleges predominantly offering higher education to be controlled by local authorities, and they were therefore to be freed from local constraints, given corporate status and funded centrally through a Polytechnics and Colleges Funding Council (PCFC). The UGC was to be replaced by a Universities Funding Council (UFC).[12] A crucial stage in the remodelling of the higher education system had been passed (without more demands for anyone's impeachment!), a process that would be taken further in the early 1990s.

The universities' reactions to this constant process of government intervention, particularly in relation to student numbers, was described retrospectively at the beginning of the 1990s by Stewart Sutherland, at the time Vice-Chancellor of the University of London, as a kind of pantomime:

1960s and 1970s
Government: You will expand!
Universities: Oh no we won't!
Government: Oh yes you will, or we shall give all the money to the Colleges of Advanced Technology (CATS) and the new universities!
Universities: Oh yes we will!

1981 to 1988
Government: You will stop expanding!
Universities: Oh no we won't!
Government: Oh yes you will, or we shall fine you for each student over quota whom you admit!
Universities: Oh yes we will!

1988 to 1992
Government: You will expand!
Universities: Oh no we won't!
Government: Oh yes you will, or we shall give all the extra money to the polytechnics!
Universities: Oh yes we will!

1992–
Government: You will stop expanding!
Universities: Oh no we probably won't!
Government: Oh yes you will, or ...[13]

'DONNISH DEPRESSION'

The pantomime as seen by Sutherland gave rise to other interpretations at the time. In an address in 1975 Michael Shattock, Academic Registrar of the University of Warwick, described the effects of the 'financial screws ... tightened in successive jerks over the last few years'. Planned expansion was curtailed in 1972–73, 'the first major disruption of universities' plans'. Given the cuts and consultations on expansion, the brakes were applied only to be followed by decisions to expand – again rescinded, funding announced and spent but not delivered. By the middle of the 1970s universities were trying with difficulty to plan for survival. Not only was sensible planning either difficult or impossible, but internal consultative processes had also been disrupted, amidst the unpredictable changes coming from the government and the UGC:

> Planning and allocations committees inevitably have to choose between competing claims and even in normal years compromises are made, understanding reached and assurances given as part of the necessary cycle of decision taking. In the last three years however the normal cycles have constantly been disrupted, foreshortened or even abandoned as central government staggers from crisis to crisis ... How does a vice-chancellor, or a development committee chairman retain credibility when he has to announce cuts on one day and then seek approval for an expansion plan on the next? ... The result has been that throughout the university system trust has increasingly been eroded in the elaborate participative processes of decision-taking laboriously set up over the years.

In many cases the intensity of the cuts had meant 'rapid and ruthless pruning of academic budgets with the minimum of consultation'. The result had been accusations of 'democratic centralism' and 'personal odium that has been collected by vice-chancellors and chairmen of key committees'. Over the previous three years the universities' autonomy and internal self-government had been weakened and they had been 'harnessed more and more directly to Government policy to the detriment of our intellectual role in society'. In 1975, when Shattock gave this address, he expressed pessimism about the future, and by the time it was published the following year events had 'amply justified my fears'.[14]

Other commentators, with other emphases and explanations, also dwelled on the damage to relationships of trust and the sense of academic community. In 1973 Sir Derman Christopherson, Vice-Chancellor of the University of Durham (and recently chair of the CVCP) published *The University at Work*, with a chapter on 'The sense of community'. His focus was community for the student, who, when a member of a real 'academic community', is learning

> not just in the hours spent in the lecture room, the tutorial class and the laboratory, but continuously ... The university community, like any other, has to be a natural one, in which people are brought together to achieve common purposes, not an artificial one.

Analyzing the difficulties and disturbances of recent years, notably the tensions between students on the one hand and staff and the institution on the other hand, Christopherson – not unlike Moberly – looked to the Christian contribution. The individual Christian could do little to change national policies on major issues, but

> what he can do to unify the university society so that its voice can be clearly heard, and its advice appreciated, can be a great deal. And the problem of unifying a society, in a university context as elsewhere, is in the end a matter of the creation of a sense of community.[15]

Following the example of the German 'Gesamthochschule' there were small currents of European interest in the idea of a 'comprehensive university'. The German model attracted an international seminar in 1971, and Roy Niblett described the model as having much in common with 'that which in so many countries is lapping at, even knocking down, the walls of the conventional university – if any university anywhere can any longer be described as "conventional" '.[16] The British binary system ran counter to such a trend, and from its inception there were critics who held out the prospect of a 'comprehensive' alternative – though not necessarily accepting the Robbins view of a traditional university sector. Robin Pedley's inaugural lecture as Professor of Education at Exeter attacked the 'separatist' policy, favouring the application of something like the secondary comprehensive school principle to 'the whole field of post-school education'.[17] In 1977, following the teacher education crisis, he set out a detailed plan with the objective of developing 'the comprehensive, collegiate university ... without alarms or destruction', bringing together all the existing institutions of higher and further education in 'natural social areas'. This did not mean that 'the devastation of existing educational communities, which now lays waste the world of teacher training, must continue', and the theme of·institutional and wider community was salient in the argument.[18] Other versions of 'higher education for everyone' fed into debate.[19]

Throughout the 1970s higher education, and particularly the universities, were scampering in search of clear direction as their expansion and expectations lost momentum, academics became disillusioned and public opinion became less supportive. A crucial feature of the decade, therefore, was pervasive doubt about how far universities, and to a lesser extent the 'alternative' polytechnic sector, needed, wished and could legitimately be expected to adapt to the changed economic and political contexts in which they had to operate and survive. For their vice-chancellors universities were beginning to look more seriously not for liberal educators, philosophers or visionaries, but for managers and associates of the corridors of power. The system was too preoccupied with immediate challenges to take part in debate about the parameters of change and adaptation. Looking ahead to the 1980s a conference in 1973 considered a paper written by the Vice-Chancellor of the University of Bristol, suggesting that 'unless we go in for the long look rather more often than we do now, then we, our students and ultimately society are going to suffer for it'.[20] How successfully governments were fashioning the agendas for discussion of higher education was to become even clearer in the 1980s, as was the difficulty of higher education in fashioning any kind of coherent response. The institutions were being fractured by the many pressures, by the student protest movement, by the divided loyalties of staff to their institution and to their discipline. The *Times Higher Education Supplement* had come into existence in 1971 and a contributor to the first issue ended his somewhat caustic reflections in welcoming the new publication:

> Among academics in the 'tertiary sector', and particularly in the universities, there is encouragingly little sense of belonging to the kind of higher education community which the sociologist has it in him to describe. On the whole their commitments remain with their own particular branch of learning, and with the particular institutions around which the life of education defines itself. Now they have acquired a weekly newspaper to mirror their commendable professional disunity. Long may they both continue.[21]

Also in the first issue, and on the same page, Ashby contributed an article on 'The academic establishment', signalling another 'climacteric': 'Unprecedented changes have been taking place for the past 30 years and more are to come.'[22] The drama of higher education was seen here through two different lenses, and it was to become particularly intense when, in 1981, what had seemed a disaster in the early 1970s became more of a cataclysm. A.H. Halsey described 1981 as the year when 'the universities were rudely summoned ... to the experiment of strength through starvation of public funding.' The *Times Higher Education Supplement* had become 'a Friday catalogue of donnish depression'.[23]

The 'starvation' to which the universities (most acutely the Universities of Aston, Bradford and Salford) were suddenly and dramatically subjected resulted from the decision of Mrs Thatcher's government substantially to cut the budget of the UGC in real terms. The UGC in turn imposed differential cuts on the universities and the government's decision, in the words of a new vice-chancellor at Salford from 1981, 'destabilised the British university system' and initiated long-term changes, making the universities 'amenable to change in ways to which it had hitherto been resistant'.[24] The retiring head of the Department of Educational Enquiry at Aston, a department closed following the cuts, called these 'vandalistic external circumstances'.[25] For the three-year period from 1981 the universities' grant for home students was cut by 8.5 per cent. Similar cuts for what was now called 'local authority higher education' followed. The overall policy, in the words of the Parliamentary Under-Secretary for Higher Education at a conference in 1983, was one of 'restraint' and required 'substantial reductions in academic staffing' – reductions that were expected to continue.[26] There is no doubt that the cuts were driven not only by economic circumstances but also by the wish to compel higher education to seek increased private funding. This was to be heard most clearly in Keith Joseph's 1985 Green Paper reference to 'over-dependence on public funding'.[27] The effect was a transition from 'donnish depression' to sustained anxiety and vituperation, at individual and systemic levels. At the end of the 1980s, critical of attitudes on both sides, the Head of Education Policy Group at the Confederation of British Industry, summarized the decade in the following terms:

> The last decade has been a disaster for higher education in the United Kingdom. Resources have been depleted, morale shattered, all sense of clear purpose and direction abandoned. Response to threats to higher education and doubts about its value have not prompted a spirited defence of the academic ethos by its guardians or a vision of the future by its leaders but an inward-looking, truculent trench mentality.[28]

The difficulty of framing 'clear purpose and direction' in the 1970s had been intensified by the events of the early 1980s, bringing some institutions to the brink of bankruptcy and closure (rescued in fact by innovative approaches to the market) and the system as a whole to a kind of impotence.

Much of the impotence was born of confusion. Was there really an aim of achieving the 'mass higher education' that Trow had defined and, amongst others, Annan had seen as relevant to the British condition? Moving from small-scale to mass higher education meant that 'the customs, ideals, organisation and behaviour' of institutions had to change, and the state, once a 'benevolent and distant provider of funds' became implicated in their planning.[29] How far would it be implicated? How could higher education respond to the conflict between financial cuts and desirable growth? How could standards be upheld? What was a desirable stance for higher education faced with uncertainties and inevitabilities? One 'inevitable' answer was provided in 1985 by the Jarratt Report on efficiency studies in universities, proposing the development of a range of performance indicators. A joint working group of the CVCP and the UGC produced a first statement on this proposal the following year, discussing indicators that would 'assist universities in the internal management of their affairs ... the availability of sound management information is necessary for the effective running and financing of any large and complex organisation'. The key issues were 'value for money and accountability'.[30] Embattled, the universities were accepting the management solution, and their vice-chancellors were now to be, and often to be called, chief executives. If universities (and to some extent the polytechnics also) were not engaged in trench warfare, they were at least learning to locate the parapet.

Within higher education there were, however, different responses. Ashby and others had in previous decades understood the strength of the disciplinary loyalties of academic staff, and there was an international – especially American – literature describing and analysing these loyalties, of academics in general and of separate disciplinary groups in particular. The role of the discipline was thrust into discussion of higher education in Britain most notably in 1989 by *Tribes and Territories* by Tony Becher, Professor of Education at the University of Sussex. The book was the outcome not only of research on a range of research departments in British universities, but also of familiarity with the American work on the disciplines by Burton Clark, Martin Trow and others. Becher had himself also contributed to the literature earlier in the decade. The book tackled disciplinary territories and the values that underpinned them as perceived by researchers themselves, established a typology of disciplines, and probed the strong, even dominant, roles that disciplines, their subject packages and departments played in higher education as it had been and was becoming.[31] Becher's research reflected and confirmed the experience of academics in universities, polytechnics and colleges. The discipline and the department or subject group had always been important in the professional lives of academics, but they were now becoming more so as they saw the impact of national policy strategies on the management and operation of their institutions. Sir Christopher Ball, who had until the previous year been Warden of Keble College, Oxford, wrote in 1989 that 'for most of us it remains true that our first loyalty is to our discipline, to the single honours degree and to research. We find it difficult (and uncongenial) to raise our eyes from the particularities of disciplines.'[32] More and more the reputation, status and income of departments depended on success in disciplinary research, and individual careers depended on it. The department, as a proxy for the discipline and the disciplinary culture to which the academic belonged, became more of a retreat from the hostile national and institutional worlds. As polytechnics increasingly struggled for comparability with the universities their departments and academics also found their disciplinary loyalty taking greater precedence over their institutional one.

It is difficult, therefore, to identify a strong thread of advocacy in the conditions of the 1980s. The focus was on what was happening, how things worked, how the situation had been arrived at. The academic press and the growing number of conferences reflected the agendas contained or implied in the national policy directions. Research and discussion focused on higher education and work, the sandwich course, competences, staff development, institutional change, accountability. At the heart of what was, and what was not, on these agendas was the state. Maurice Kogan, Professor of Government at Brunel University, told a Canadian audience in 1986 of the break up of 'established relationships between the state and higher education ... Government in Britain is more unrestrained in its power than in virtually any other democratic country.'[33] Niblett, in 1990, described what were perceived as current urgencies, including finance, student funding, co-operation with industry and the construction of science parks: 'What becomes clearer and clearer is that the agenda for the discussion of issues in higher education is now one which the government itself has chosen. The larger and longer term purposes of higher education are not subjects much attended to.'[34] Much had changed even since Sir Frederick Dainton, former Vice-Chancellor of the University of Nottingham, told a Cambridge audience cautiously in 1981 that he wished to 'make some observations on universities in Britain which I believe to be relevant to their future health and which touch on their relationship with the State, a matter of some delicacy at the present time'.[35] It was indicative of the times that in 1983 a spoof government memorandum could be written, as of ten years later,

> ... to coincide with the closure of the last of Britain's universities. It is worth recalling that only ten years ago it was universally assumed that these anachronistic institutions would continue indefinitely. The last decade has seen their unnecessary activities brought to an end with a speed and efficiency which rival the disposal-rates of other terminations of unwanted institutions like the House of Lords.[36]

Christopher Ball reflected in 1989 that UK higher education had been faced from the middle of the twentieth century with the fundamental challenge of how to adapt 'an elite system to provide a popular model; when the history of higher education in the present century comes to be written, I believe that the painful transformation to a popular system will prove to be the key theme'.[37] Transformation was certainly not new in the 1970s and 1980s, but the pain had been particularly intense.

'OBEISANCE IN RETURN'

Profoundly different though higher education systems are in many ways, the underlying trends in expansion and the relationship between higher education and the state that we have traced were in evidence in many other countries in the second half of the twentieth century. The procedures of review, policy formulation and systemic and institutional change were often very similar, with the same kind of motivation and purposes. For example, the Robbins report was paralleled in roughly the same period by investigations and policy reviews and proposals. In Australia, the three volumes of the Martin report of 1964–65 on *Tertiary Education in Australia* included recommendations for raising the status of the technical and other colleges, resulting in the creation of the Colleges of Advanced Education. In Canada the Duff-Berdahl report of 1966 on *University Government in Canada* (commissioned by the Association of University Teachers and the Association of Universities and Colleges) coincided with intensive debate about the federal–provincial relation in the provision of higher education. At a 1966 conference the Prime Minister recognized the responsibility of the provinces for education, but also that

> the federal government accepts primary responsibility for employment and economic activity generally in the country ... It is ... the responsibility of the federal government to devise and apply national policies and measures that are necessary to ensure that the economy of Canada will continue to expand.[38]

From this period changes in higher education, invariably in the name of reform, in Europe and elsewhere pointed towards stronger national direction of higher education as a whole. Burton Clark, from a later vantage point, citing Norway as an example, described the general trend: 'All were planned at the top, debated, and enacted at the national centre. Goals were stated at the highest level with the system as a whole in mind. Central personnel of a formal encompassing system had a hand in implementation.'[39] The predominant literature of this trend was therefore the review and policy-oriented output of the commissions and committees that addressed the 'system as a whole'.

Of a somewhat different kind was the stream of publications that emerged in the United States from the Carnegie Commission on Higher Education, 1967–73 (followed by those of the Carnegie Council on Higher Education). Given the very different situation in American higher education what reform pointed towards was to some extent federal involvement (particularly in the funding of research), but also forms of co-ordination particularly at state and regional level. In 1972, James Perkins set American higher education in the international scene. Increased student numbers and rapidly rising costs were resulting in new organizations 'that are changing the educational landscape. The traditional independence and autonomy of institutions is giving way to state or national coordinating bodies.' Although the American system was different, the expanding federal involvement was clear, ranging from education of the disadvantaged to medical education and university standards: 'The expanding federal role puts the most severe pressure on the public and private universities to evolve national organizations and programs of their own that will act as both counterparts and counterweights to the new federal interest.'[40] 'Co-ordination' in the United States was not entirely different in principle and purpose from 'national centre' planning and implementation in Europe. An American historian pointed out in 1965 that national involvement in higher education had been intensified in the United States during the Second World War as it had in other countries, drawing ever more heavily on

> the trained personnel of universities and colleges for advice on strategy, propaganda, intelligence, or economics ... During the war and since, however, the universities of the country, and to a much smaller extent the colleges, have been employed in a different and more critical service for the government: to conduct a number of vast programs of scientific research and development ... The impact has been far-reaching, and both beneficial and detrimental ... The major question now is whether ... the universities can regain control of their own purposes and future.[41]

Such a process of federal engagement in the United States, and governments' higher education policy making, internationally accelerated at many levels through the following decades. Clark Kerr described the 1960s and early 1970s as 'the greatest period of attempted reform of institutions of higher education in the Western world in eight hundred years'.[42] 'Reform' in this context meant all the policy-making, programming, planning and funding strategies that we have discussed, intended to secure the kinds of directions and outcomes that would satisfy national aspirations. Australia, for example, embarked on a long sequence of such policies and decisions, culminating in 1988 in a policy statement on higher education in the Commonwealth, aiming to make coherent the trends evident in the Martin and other reports about the shape of the system, its control and funding mechanisms from the 1960s. The 1988 statement was issued by the Minister for Employment, Education and Training (vocabularies similar to those in the various transmutations of British government organization), and it made crystal clear the 'unified national system' to be superimposed on existing institutions:

> Commonwealth support for growth and reform in higher education will focus on those institutions which make up the unified national system of higher education. This system will consist of a range of higher education institutions with specific missions agreed with, and funded by, the Commonwealth. Under the new system there will be fewer and larger institutions than at present, and there will be more effective co-ordination between them on issues such as course provision, disciplinary specialisation and credit transfer ... Size is not an end in itself; rather, in most cases, it is a necessary condition for educational effectiveness and financial efficiency.[43]

Such aims for the systematization of higher education became increasingly clearly and powerfully expressed from the 1960s through the 1980s even, as in Australia, where regions or states within a federal framework had strong historical oversight of their higher education institutions. The model that was being developed in Australia was one that applied in other countries also – diversity, flexibility and competition for resources, within a framework over which government and its agencies had control.

In all of these examples the balance between public accountability and institutional autonomy was at stake, a balance that in all the cases resulted from the growing need for government funding and the reciprocity involved. No less than its European and other counterparts, the United States, though 'blessed with decentralization and diversity', was also

> hankering after the promised virtues: economy, efficiency, elimination of overlap, less redundancy, better articulation, transferability, accountability, equity, and equality. Our dominant line of reform since World War II has been to impose on the disorder of a market system of higher education new levels of coordination that promise administered order. We continue to do this at an accelerating rate.[44]

In these and other examples in the Western and the developing world the intervention of governments was related to funding and accountability, student numbers, the sharpening demands of economic competition.

The impacts on institutions and systems from the 1970s through the 1990s were everywhere, as in Britain, shaped by the switchback of economic fortune. The President of the University of Notre Dame in the United States, at the beginning of the 1970s, opened a conference on universities in a changing world by emphasizing their importance in changing society, but also asking the question whether they could 'adapt themselves rapidly enough to survive amid all the changes they have stimulated?' He had been a faculty member and administrator at Notre Dame for 25 years, and he opened his closing remarks to the conference with the reflection: 'I can think of no period more difficult than the present. Never before has the university taken on more tasks – and been asked to undertake many more – while the sources of support, both public and private, both moral and financial, seem to be drying up.'[45] In all of these countries, as in Britain, it often seemed that the climate could not become any colder or drier – only to discover that it could. Experiencing greater state support, in whatever national tradition, might diminish one set of problems and help to accomplish such positive aims as wider access and equity, only to exacerbate the difficulties of adaptation and to diminish the prospects of survival in a recognizable form. Daniel Moynihan, New York Senator, wrote in 1980 that all the well-intentioned American policies to expand and support higher education carried a cost: 'It is in the nature of universities to require patrons, in the nature of patrons to require certain forms of obeisance in return.'[46]

PYRAMIDS

Through the policy directions and vicissitudes of higher education in the second half of the twentieth century we have seen the increasingly firm establishment of a national or nationalized system. Although the pressures and stimuli were economic, ideological and political they, and the responses, were not the monopoly of any government or political party. Nor were they insularly British. The system as it took shape did not eliminate institutional autonomy or diversity. It threatened and in many respects seriously diminished the former, but in the latter case it made inroads into the pattern of diversity among institutions and sectors without basically undermining the diversity based on historical characteristics. In the final decade of the century the former polytechnics remained a distinctive grouping within the unified university system, even while nominally sharing its features and also retaining amongst themselves different emphases in their interpretation of mission. Expansion and national frameworks of quality assurance or national policies for greater equality of access did not undermine the historical bases of the privileges associated with Oxford and Cambridge. League tables reflecting research income and activity separated off almost exactly the pre-1992 and post-1992 universities. Resource levels continued to reflect the identities of institutions that had become members of the 'system' in different waves of 'new' colleges and universities in the nineteenth and twentieth centuries. It was only in responses to national requirements for the quality assurance of teaching, research and institutional procedures that universities old and new resembled one another more closely, though by no means totally.

By the 1990s higher education was in fundamental respects an instrument of state planning, with a level of institutional autonomy not dissimilar from what was now considered appropriate for schools or hospitals. Higher education continued to proclaim a unique commitment to academic values, but operationally its differences from other public sectors lay in such matters as its ability to attract non-public funding, notably for research. The essential similarity lay in state funding, regulation or guidelines, and the monitoring and evaluation of performance. Within the institutions, as we have seen, academics could retain some sense of academic independence by retreating into their departmental, disciplinary and research identities, relating to their professional or disciplinary organizations and their email and Internet communities. There were mixed feelings amongst academics in the 1990s about the value and impact of the assessment of teaching quality or research, if for no other reason than that timetables for the preparation and conduct of external and internal review conflicted with academics' traditional and preferred priorities. They felt the mounting demands on them from student numbers and depleted staffing, nationally set criteria of various kinds, student development profiles, and the rapid growth and adoption of Communications and Information Technology (C&IT).

Our story has been less concerned with the details of teaching and learning, research expectations and assessment than with the shape and nature of the system, the voices speaking for it, and the content of their messages. Commentaries in the 1990s were largely governed by what Martin Trow called 'the withdrawal of trust in its universities by the British government'. As a consequence the government had been

> forced to create bureaucratic machinery and formulas to steer and manage the universities from outside the system. In the absence of an effective competitive market, effectively precluded by government policies, bureaucratic institutions and their mechanisms are the alternative to a relationship of trust between state and universities.

The result was performance criteria, rules and policy requirements or guidelines. Trow's explanation of the Thatcher government's approach (one that was not to change in spirit and intention under the Labour government from 1997) suggested that it was based on a view of the universities as 'backward, conservative, self-serving' and partly responsible for Britain's poor performance in international markets. The universities were therefore seen as in need of reform, which had to be forced on them from outside. Trow identified the first major step as the radical cutting of their budgets from 1981, impelling them towards new sources of funding, greater efficiency and responsiveness to the market. The replacement of the UGC in 1992 by the Higher Education Funding Council for England (HEFCE) and similar bodies for Scotland and Wales (and continuing a different arrangement in Northern Ireland) created 'an arm of government, an instrument for the implementation of government policy on universities'.[47]

These interpretations and trends comprehensively dominated policies in the 1990s. The control and direction of higher education through new mechanisms, the vagaries and limitations of funding, the new managerialism and the formulation of priority economic outcomes for the institutions, were encapsulated in the 'withdrawal of trust' and drove the policy agendas of the final decade of the century. In 1988, following the White Paper of the previous year, the polytechnics had been transferred from local authority control to national funding. The 1991 White Paper proposed the abolition of the binary line and in 1992 the two sectors were brought under the new single funding mechanism of the funding councils. Trow's explanation of the origins of the new managerialism also largely accounts for the unification of the system at this stage: unification provided government with a single national means of driving more than 100 higher education institutions towards its economic and political goals. The 1991 White Paper expressed the view that ending the binary line would enhance the development of higher education by promoting 'efficient expansion' through institutional competition. It set a target of one-third of young people entering higher education by 2000, together with increased participation by mature students (though there was not to be concomitant funding). The polytechnics were to be allowed to adopt the title of universities (which they did), and the CNAA was to disappear. The new funding councils would take responsibility for assessing quality.[48]

The 1992 Act, embodying these proposals, therefore reshuffled the organization of higher education in the names of competition, efficiency and quality. Reorganization of national systems and funding mechanisms was also taking place in other countries, with similar targets, including increased student numbers and greater institutional efficiency and accountability. Although United States higher education retained its essentially non-federal character, it also – both at federal and individual state levels – was consistently pressed in directions that served the same purposes as those of Britain and other countries. In 1966 James Perkins had indicated a strengthening American model of a 'national educational superstructure' consisting of agencies that performed functions universities 'could not perform individually and never got round to performing collectively'. He described the super-structure as 'the educational pyramid that is now emerging. Higher education is becoming a system that runs from the department through the college, the university, the state, the regional compact, the national association, and the international body.'[49] The details of this pyramidal picture did not precisely fit Britain at that time or later but it pointed to actual and prospective US developments that echoed British and other processes. The British pyramid of the 1990s can be described as a system that ran from the department through the faculty, the university and its administration and committee structures, the regional funding councils and the national government, its ministries and agencies. The developing frameworks of European policy and legislation and the international organizations and partnerships promoting, for example, distance education and 'e-learning', were also visible at the pinnacle of the British pyramid, but with different significance from that of the national power structures that were redesigned in the late 1980s and early 1990s.

'ACHIEVEMENTS SINCE ROBBINS'

The Conservative target of roughly a third of the age group participating in higher education was reached, and the target was then raised to 50 per cent by the incoming Labour government in 1997 – with what outcomes it is for the history of the twenty-first century to discover. By the mid-1990s, therefore, the total number of UK higher education students was in excess of 1.5 million. In 1996–97 of the 1.6 million students in higher education institutions, over 1.1 million were full-time or on sandwich courses, and there were 200,000 higher education students in further education colleges. Some 65 per cent of higher education students were full-time, 28 per cent part-time, and 7 per cent Open University students (also classified as part-time). By this period 51 per cent of higher education students were female, an increase from 26 per cent in 1962–63 and 37 per cent in 1979–80). Mature students (that is, aged 21 or over for entry to undergraduate courses and 25 or over for postgraduate students) now accounted for over 50 per cent, the majority of them part-time, including the OU).[50] At the end of the 1980s, before unification, the universities accounted for 36 per cent of students and the polytechnics and colleges (and their Scottish equivalents, the Central Institutions) accounted for 55 per cent (plus 9 per cent by the OU).

There are important features that these growth figures do and do not reveal. In 1996, a paper on 'Achievements since Robbins' was produced for the Dearing Committee on higher education by the government's Department for

Education and Employment (DfEE) together with the Scottish and Welsh Offices and the Northern Ireland Department of Education. In congratulatory terms the paper compared the Robbins expectations with transformations that had exceeded them. Higher education no longer catered 'just for a privileged elite but provides opportunities for a significant proportion of young people. In Robbins' day, just one young person in seventeen went on to higher education. Now it is approaching one in three'. There were five times as many full-time students as in 1963. Higher education was no longer just for young people 'and predominantly young men'. Females had reached parity with males and there were more mature than young entrants. Some commentators had suggested 'that the rapid expansion of higher education has allowed deterioration in the standard required for entry. But the evidence does not support this view.' The past 30 years had demonstrated 'the capacity of higher education for change', and there were changing needs ahead.[51] The content and tone of this account did not, however, reflect the often angry 'capacity for change' with which higher education had faced major funding difficulties (presented positively here as the virtue of 'competitive funding'). The Labour government at the end of the decade was also to realize that the figures concealed important social disparities, as many universities continued to under-represent state secondary schools in their selection procedures, as social class and ethnic minority background continued to influence access to higher education, and as gender and age continued to influence entry to particular programmes. At the end of the century, therefore, the government was criticizing, cajoling and developing financial and other strategies to combat 'exclusive' tendencies within higher education. Both the arithmetic of the system and the contours of the 'pyramid' conceal historical diversities and hierarchies. Oxford and Cambridge had to respond like other universities to salient aspects of national requirements, but they retained their unique character, prestige and influence. While the polytechnics had acquired the university title, most of the colleges of higher education that had emerged in the 1970s, mainly from the teacher training colleges, were removed from the picture through amalgamation or closure – with only a few left free-standing. Colleges of further education with substantial numbers of higher education students faced some of the ambiguities that the polytechnics had had to deal with in an earlier generation, complicated by the financial and status difficulties of the 1990s. Binary conceptions had not quite died.

One territory that more than others displayed the implications of withdrawal of trust was teacher education. Political dissatisfaction with the operation, funding and standards of schools in the 1980s and 1990s, and therefore plans for their reform, raised issues of teacher education that surfaced more and more sharply after the 1991 White Paper. Government intervention in this case was not simply one of direction and finance, it was also one of control of curricula, recruitment and the accreditation of colleges and university departments of education. Since government had direct interest in the numbers and qualifications of school teachers, the Secretary of State could adopt measures for teacher education in ways not accessible for most other parts of higher education. In fact there had always been considerable resistance to the inclusion of teacher education in the definition of higher education, even when provided by or in association with universities. Not only was 1992 a key policy year, it was also a key 'teacher training' year (policy makers steadfastly refused to call it 'teacher education'). In January a press release on a speech made by the then Secretary of State, Kenneth Clarke, announced 'far-reaching proposals to change the shape of teacher training'. Clarke's successor, John Patten, was described in another press release four months later as announcing 'far-reaching reforms of training for teachers in secondary schools'. The crux of Clarke's proposals was the enhancement of the role of schools in the training of teachers, doubling the amount of time students would spend in schools, and new accreditation criteria 'geared to the outcome of training rather than the process and content of courses'. His speech emphasized concerns about the training of new teachers and his intention to press ahead with

> the next stage of reform ... I want to see schools playing the key influential role in a much closer partnership between the schools and the teaching training institutions ... The college-based parts of teacher training must be fully relevant to classroom practice.

Patten announced that trainee secondary school teachers would be expected to spend at least two-thirds of their postgraduate course in schools under the guidance of an experienced teacher. The remaining third of such courses would be spent 'on school-focused activity'. Practising teachers were to be more involved in the design of courses. New criteria were to be issued, 'promulgating revised criteria for the approval of secondary PGCE [Post-Graduate Certificate of Education] courses'.[52] A Council for the Accreditation of Teacher Education provided advice to the Secretary of State and implemented policies. The details of school–higher education partnerships were published by the Council in June 1992, together with criteria for the accreditation of initial teacher training.[53]

We are concerned here not with the details or validity of these policies but with the operation of government in a field in which it could take initiatives affecting higher education outcomes, because it had a direct interest in the implications for the schools. The initiatives also sent signals for other fields about which government could have concerns, including preparation for employment in industry and commerce, and 'skills-based' or 'evidence-based' forms of professional and other preparation. They also extended the 'pyramid' diagram of higher education into a wider range of government-related agencies than we have so far suggested. The state was widening its reach, shaping the bodies that serviced its policies and provided advice. Teacher education was perhaps unfortunate in being the area of higher education from which government could most easily withdraw trust and take direct action.

MAINTAINING AND ENHANCING

Of all the issues that by the 1990s had become prominent in national organization and institutional operation that of quality was most resonant. As required by the 1992 Act a Higher Education Quality Council was established by the organizations of heads of universities, polytechnics and colleges of higher education, to control the procedures for *assuring* quality in the institutions. The funding councils were required to establish Quality Assessment Committees to *assess* quality. For the remainder of the decade a variety of changing procedures (different in England from those in Scotland and Wales) were adopted for both of these approaches. Teaching quality assessment (TQA) was paralleled by a regular national research assessment exercise, a major difference being the funding that was allocated on the basis of the latter. Institutions rapidly established or improved their own committees, units and procedures to prepare for and respond to external TQA visits. The nature and rate of development of these institutional bodies were not uniform, since the former polytechnics had traditions of such preparation and response for internal validation and external quality-related scrutiny by the CNAA, or to some extent by validating universities. Quality, elusive and difficult to define, was a function of the institution and its organization, curricula, teachers and their professional development, support services for teaching and student learning, the availability and use of new technologies, accreditation by professional bodies and relationships with employers, schools and others. There were uncertainties to be clarified about the criteria of assurance and assessment, as well as about the position of the system of external examiners that had grown up in Britain from the late nineteenth century. As the processes of maintaining and enhancing teaching quality became more public, so did strains intensify between the universities and the external agencies, as well as between the internal requirements of the institutions and the traditions of laissez-faire amongst teachers, particularly when strongly committed to research as the overwhelming priority. In universities and departments without the strong internal validation machineries of the former polytechnics, the intentions of the English quality assessment procedure meant something approaching a revolution:

An approach to quality which encompasses the breadth and depth of student achievement and learning experience, based on the institution's own aims and objectives, is one which will allow for consistent and rigorous quality assessment within a framework of diversity of institutional mission.

Although responsibility 'for maintaining and enhancing the quality of education properly rests with the institution', the 'rigorous quality assessment' was an external intervention of a kind that large numbers of academic staff had not previously experienced.[54] From the early validation procedures of the CNAA to the TQA visits in the 1990s the balance of external scrutiny and internal responsibility never ceased to provoke controversy.

One of the complexities relating to quality assurance was the modularization being widely introduced into the curriculum from the early 1980s. The primary intentions were to give students greater choice, to open up the curriculum to full- and part-time students, and to reduce the parallel provision of courses in different programmes. This could be seen, for purposes of sustained learning and suitable assessment, as too fragmented a recipe. Or it could be seen as focusing on 'students as *managers of their own learning* who need feedback to provide a basis for improving their own learning strategies, and as *decision makers* and *choosers* of learning programmes'.[55] Modular structures, under CNAA auspices, had been pioneered from the beginning of the 1970s.[56] From the end of the 1980s and through the early 1990s most universities to various extents adopted the system.[57] Related to this development was also that of credit accumulation and transfer in some institutions and regions enabling students to build awards on the basis of credits from an institution or group of institutions.

The importance of these developments lies in the new version of transformation taking place in higher education. The accumulation of changes gave higher education a profile quite different from what it had been in recent decades. Learning and teaching now assumed a priority in a transformed situation, shaped by changed student numbers and diversity, modular structures and the increased mix of full- and part-time students, student debt and substantial part-time paid work, the confused loyalties of academic staff, and the shifting priorities of institutions relating, for example, to funding and student recruitment. The transformation was one relating also to teaching strategies, such as work-based, problem- or resource-based versions of active learning and autonomous learning, with pockets of innovation around the system.[58] The Dearing report on *Higher Education in the Learning Society*, published in 1977, suggested that:

if the quality of students' educational experience is to be maintained or improved, innovative teaching strategies which promote students' learning

16. Ron (Lord) Dearing. (Council for National Academic Awards photograph.)

– many of which are already in place – will have to become widespread. This means that higher education institutions will need to continue to emphasise the centrality of learning and teaching in their work.

The report recommended that 'with immediate effect, all institutions of higher education give high priority to developing and implementing learning and teaching strategies which focus on the promotion of students' learning'.[59] In addition to overarching concerns about access to and the funding of higher education, the committee was here giving authority and focus to the rising tide of attention being paid to this issue. Universities were developing their learning support units and appointing senior administrators, for example pro-vice-chancellors, to oversee the implementation of institutional policies (which became a funding council requirement). Books by practitioners and others were proliferating in Britain and internationally on aspects of improving teaching strategies and student learning and motivation, and theorizing on the approaches and the issues. New journals were appearing and established ones were giving more space to articles on such topics. The Higher Education Funding Council for England (HEFCE), in 1995, announced the first stage of a Fund for the Development of Teaching and Learning (FDTL), inviting applications 'to support projects aimed at stimulating developments in teaching and learning in higher education and to encourage the dissemination of good teaching and learning practice across the sector' [60] This initiative followed its quality assessment of the first 15 subjects ('units of assessment') covered in 1993–95, and as further subjects were covered more stages of the FDTL were announced.

The mid-1990s also saw a surge of developments relating to the new technologies whose importance the . Dearing committee emphasized. The MacFarlane report on *Teaching and Learning in an Expanding System* in 1992 had stressed the need for significant improvements 'in the effectiveness and quality of teaching in higher education', and a 'vigorous programme of research and development in teaching methods and educational technology and radical changes in attitude toward technology-based learning'. Although a Scottish report, this had considerable resonance south of the border.[61] In 1993, Diana Laurillard, who was to be a member of the Dearing committee, published an influential book on *Rethinking University Teaching*, examining the new technologies and their implications for practice.[62] What such publications, British and international, emphasized was that important technologies were available, but that their uses had not been thought through. The National Council for Educational Technology in 1993 considered that if the technology already available were to be exploited in education generally, 'the impact on practices of teaching, learning and cultural transmission would be dramatic'.[63] Exploitation in the mid-1990s was indeed producing some dramatic changes. Universities, or individual departments or courses within them, were developing distance programmes, particularly at postgraduate level, intended for British or international student populations. Wye College, for instance, which amalgamated with Imperial College, London, in 2000, by then had some 1,000 students worldwide on a series of electronically based postgraduate programmes in such areas as biodiversity and sustainable agriculture. A consortium of 'Learning Option' organizations, including Suffolk

University College and British Telecom, was offering a range of short courses in the Eastern Region using a number of Internet tools and on-line learning through a 'Televersity'. An electronically based University of the Highlands and Islands in Scotland was being developed, and regional developments of a similar kind were in various stages of planning elsewhere. An international literature was developing rapidly, together with international conferences and direct contact amongst practitioners and innovators in the field. Multimedia and virtual reality experiments were gaining momentum. A project on innovation in teaching and learning in British, mainly English, universities in 1997–99 found the largest group of innovations to be computer-related (using the Internet, Intranet, computer-aided and computer-based learning and computer-mediated communication).[64] A Canadian contributor to a British conference in 1997 described two features of what was now becoming an international phenomenon. First, innovation in teaching:

> which has traditionally been associated with more fringe areas of the university, such as the distance education units or specialist R&D educational technology units, is now coming from the 'core': original and exciting technology-based materials initiated and developed by faculty themselves.

Second, however, although there had been widespread adoption of new technologies for teaching in recent years, 'they have yet to bring about major changes in the way teaching is organized and delivered. Without such changes, though, technology-based teaching will remain a marginalized activity.' Preventing new technologies remaining marginal meant structural changes and fundamental changes to the way teaching was organized.[65]

The importance here of such commentaries and developments lies in the strong links being established between new technology, innovation, the centrality of learning and teaching, the ways technologies could be used, interaction amongst users, support services, ideas and resources, the organization of teaching and the restructuring of the universities themselves. The book and the article, the conference and the network, articulated the development, announcing that the new situation required not tinkering but a revolution in the ways learning, motivation, teaching and outcomes were understood. These were new kinds of linkages between the interests and resources of the state, the direction-pointing or direction-confirming roles of committee and agency, the mounting emphasis on what was actually needed or happening in the institutions, and the responses of individuals to pressures and opportunities. Given other difficult contexts that we have discussed, these were not straightforward and uncontroversial, or uniformly understood and welcomed. They added, however, another dimension to higher education at the end of the century. One trajectory we have traced in the twentieth century has been from the creation of institutions to the dominance of the state. Another, however, has been from a concern about provision and access to a concern about quality and student learning. Since, en route to the late 1990s, there was a wide range of other crucial issues, these have not been the only trajectories, and none of them has been simple.

FIN DE SIÈCLE

The focus here is not on the correctness or otherwise of particular policies or strategies, but on the ways in which, and by which agencies, these were advocated. The focus is not the legitimacy of higher education as part of government's agenda for economic and social policy, for the improvement of schools or manpower provision. Access to higher education, standards and the employment of graduates are understandable government concerns. The point here is the cumulative impact of particular kinds of involvement and the ability of higher education to respond and reshape itself for the achievement of aims generally considered desirable and important by the higher education system, but also those – which may or may not coincide – of the society to which it relates. As we have noted in relation to the views of Moberly and others, the state needs higher education and higher education needs the state, in a fragile balance of reciprocity.

Throughout the twentieth century the system and its proponents confronted the changing interpretations of purposes and values. As higher education internationally became focused on the issues, problems or crises of the short term, it had decreasing incentives and opportunities to address values and visions. It was surprising to spectators in Europe, Australia and the United States, for example, that the Secretaries of State for Education and Employment, Scotland, Wales and Northern Ireland in 1996 appointed the National Committee of Inquiry into Higher Education, the Dearing Committee. The surprise attached to its broad remit to recommend

> how the purposes, shape, structure, size and funding of higher education, including support for students, should develop to meet the needs of the United Kingdom over the next 20 years, recognising that higher education embraces teaching, learning, scholarship and research.[66]

Higher Education in the Learning Society and its appendices were published in 1997. The committee's choice of title for the opening chapter of the report was 'A vision for 20 years: the learning society'. The concept of a developing learning society was central to the report, intended no doubt to avoid too sharp a focus on the technicalities of the immediate future and on the uncertainties of the distant future, and to offer a bridging, distinctive contribution for higher education across the two:

> The expansion of higher education in the last ten years has contributed greatly to the creation of a learning society, that is, a society in which people in all walks of life recognise the need to continue in education and training throughout their working lives and who see learning as enhancing the quality of life throughout all its stages. But, looking twenty years ahead, the UK must progress further and faster in the creation of such a society to sustain a competitive economy.[67]

Necessary characteristics for higher education included responsiveness, flexibility in provision, effective learning and teaching, rigorous standards, taking advantage of C&IT, world-class research, playing a part as 'the conscience of a democratic society', and sustaining a culture 'which demands disciplined thinking, encourages curiosity, challenges existing ideas and generates new ones'.[68] The main purposes of higher education were defined as similar to, but updating, those of the Robbins principles. The overall aim was to enable society 'to make progress through an understanding of itself and its world: in short, to sustain a learning society'. This was broken down into four main purposes:

- to inspire and enable individuals to develop their capabilities to the highest potential levels throughout life, so that they grow intellectually, are well equipped for work, can contribute effectively to society and achieve personal fulfilment;
- to increase knowledge and understanding for their own sake and to foster their application to the benefit of the economy and society;
- to serve the needs of an adaptable, sustainable, knowledge-based economy at local, regional and national levels;
- to play a major role in shaping a democratic, civilized, inclusive society.[69]

The committee proposed a comprehensive framework for different progression paths through the system, considered the needs of part-time students, emphasized the importance of a continued increase in participation in higher education, suggested a student contribution to tuition fees as one of the funding proposals to solve current financing difficulties, and focused heavily on C&IT and the improvement of learning and teaching (a phrase it preferred to teaching and learning).

The committee saw extended understanding and use of C&IT as strategically important for its vision of higher education and a learning society, believing that its 'innovative exploitation ... holds out much promise for improving the quality, flexibility and effectiveness of higher education'. It recommended that all higher education institutions should have overarching C&IT strategies in place by 1999/2000 and it made a series of related technical, financial and policy recommendations.[70] In general terms, it saw the next 20 years as 'a period of major change in the practice of learning and teaching in higher education' and gave the theme a salient place in the enunciation of its vision. What was required was the depth of understanding 'fostered by an active approach to learning'. Students needed access 'to more than just the articulation of knowledge in the form of books and lectures. They also need practical experience that rehearses them in the professional or scholarly skills of their field, and the opportunity to develop and express their own understanding.' This was not just a technical point – reinforced by discussion of work-based learning elsewhere in the report – but was presented as 'a vision [that] puts students at the centre of the learning and teaching process and places new challenges and demands upon teachers'. Such theories and principles had long been propounded in higher education but they were here given new national prominence. The committee advised that immediate steps were needed to provide all teachers with appropriate training and to create a national scheme of teacher accreditation through an Institute for Learning and Teaching in Higher Education.[71]

In these and other respects the Dearing committee translated its vision into a series of related directions or values. Higher education and lifelong learning required an organizational framework that would enable people of all kinds to find routes through it. Prompt measures were needed to improve teaching. The clarification and effectiveness of relationships between higher education, the state and employers made necessary what the committee termed a 'compact' amongst them:

> At the heart of our vision of higher education is the free-standing institution, which offers teaching to the highest level in an environment of scholarship and independent enquiry. But, collectively and individually, these institutions are becoming ever more central to the economic wellbeing of the nation, localities and individuals. There is a growing bond of interdependence.[72]

If the committee's overall vision was not radical, in the circumstances of the mid-1990s it would be difficult to picture how its vision might have been more so. Some of the themes and recommendations were indeed radical in their moment, launching or reinforcing feasible directions in which a momentum for the learning society might be increased. The report addressed the financial difficulties of the system, the increasing demands on staff, and long-continuing dilemmas relating to the fact that 'while traditional but still-relevant values must be safeguarded, higher education will need to continue to adapt to the needs of a rapidly changing world'.[73] What had been expected of Robbins was clear, but there were few clear academic or popular expectations of Dearing, indicated by the surprise generated by its major emphasis on learning and teaching. There had been neither extensive debate nor passionate interest to underpin any elaboration of vision. Its terms of reference had in fact grown out of a consultation on the aims of higher education arranged by the DfEE in 1994, 'with a view to determining its appropriate size and shape'. Some 100 responses had been received, mainly from higher education institutions, professional bodies and other organizations. This was an exercise limited in every sense, by the number and nature of the respondents, and by the purpose of the consultation. Most respondents seem to have been content to support the Robbins broad objectives, subject to some changes since 1963: the shift from elite to mass higher education; technological advances and an information revolution; global markets, which 'had all led to an increasingly uncertain labour market and the end of "a job for life" '. A summary of this DfEE consultation for the Dearing committee covered, for example: economic and social purposes; lifelong learning ('several organisations' identified this as of 'growing importance'); enhancing performance in the international market; various kinds of balance – such as between initial and continuing education, teaching and learning; assessment, quality ('widespread concern that it should be maintained'), funding, and student demand.[74] Against this background the Dearing report seems almost visionary.

The Labour government's response in 1998, in the context of its emerging emphasis on lifelong learning and the learning society, was directed towards participation and access, quality, the economy and employability, C&IT and professional development, and funding issues. *Higher Education for the 21st Century*, the government's response, was therefore concerned with the initial implementation phase of the committee's recommendations. The government was committed to what it now called 'the learning age', and it highlighted part of the committee's vision:

> The Committee set out a vision of a world class higher education system combining rigour and economic relevance. At the heart of this vision is the idea of a compact between universities and colleges, individual students, the world of work and society itself. The Government shares the Committee's vision.[75]

Little remained of vision, however, in the immediacy of the funding, quality and other targets of the response. A parallel government document, *The Learning Age*, placed higher education in a wider consideration of the new age, defined at the outset as one of 'information and of global competition'. It considered how the 'learning age', also described as a 'renaissance for a new Britain', applied to individuals, business, communities and the nation, with a focus on learning – most frequently represented as skills. Higher education enabled young people and mature entrants to study full- or part-time and 'works with employers to provide them and their employees with the skills they will increasingly need, and with high quality strategic and applied research which benefits both the economy and our national life'. Higher education needed to enhance its role, for example, by providing more places to meet demand; ensuring high standards, which would enhance the employability of graduates; offering opportunities to those who had missed out earlier in life; contributing more to the economy and being responsive to the needs of business; making itself more accessible by exploiting new technology and flexible delivery. Critics were to suggest not that these were unworthy targets, but that they were insufficient and narrow, and ignored important implications of what was meant by 'learning'. Conservative and Labour governments in the 1980s and 1990s variously pursued commitments to the values of a competitive society, community needs or the 'inclusive society', and had views (not always clear and consistent) about the contribution higher education could and should make. The Dearing report itself was the nearest any government or 'official' statement came in the 1990s to linking analysis with vision.

As their relationship to the patron state grew more complex and strained, the institutions themselves generated no sustained concern for the values of the 'university' or of 'higher education'. The university – not only in England or the United Kingdom – was perceived by some as having been betrayed by concessions to state or student demands, whether for expansion or changes in governance or the organization of curricula and assessment. For others, the reverse was the case: higher education in general and the universities in particular had failed to respond adequately to the pressures for change – academic, social, economic, technological, national, international. Betrayal was a conception, generally expressed passionately, of the values of a socially and academically elite past. The claim of failure to respond was an often puzzled awareness of the reality or inevitability of a mass higher education for a mass society, with profound implications for the shape, funding and behaviours of the system. Twenty-five years after the publication of the Robbins report, Sir Claus Moser, who had been statistical adviser to the committee and was now Warden of Wadham College, Oxford, criticized the universities for post-Robbins failures. They had failed to use the 'boom years' of the 1960s (followed by a 'more chilly' climate) as they might have done by working constructively with Westminster and Whitehall. Public relations generally were poor. Too often the universities – collectively – seemed to be on the defensive ... the UGC and the Committee of Vice-Chancellors and Principals, must bear some responsibility.

The universities had not responded to all of 'the Robbins challenges':

Organisational reforms were not pursued as actively as they should have been. Nor were links with industry, though the fault here lies on both sides. Universities were not quick off the mark in seeking non-government finance, though Lord Robbins himself had warned in the strongest terms of the dangers of excessive dependence on state funding.

Moser's main hope was that 'we might recapture the high ground of serious-ness that characterised the Robbins Report and the subsequent public debate'.[76] In 1990, in a report on widening access to higher education, Sir Christopher Ball described post-compulsory education as in 'a muddle', underlined that there was 'as yet no shared vision of a better future' and that 'the traditional model of university-education is itself an impediment to expansion – as also are many typical features of English culture'.[77] In 1992 Tapper and Salter, in an account of *Oxford, Cambridge and the Changing Idea of the University* placed the two universities in the context of national financial, organizational and policy changes, which revealed the weaknesses of higher education as a whole. The book ended with what might serve as a memorial to this period of lamentation about opportunities lost or spurned. There had been no attempt to formulate 'a new model of the English university', and universities were now probably left with nothing but 'competent leadership and managerial efficiency'. Nevertheless:

one would have hoped for a concerted attempt to escape the confines of nostalgia and damage limitation. Surely the most profound criticism of the universities has been their failure to create their own vision of the future? One that, because it was based upon a political reality combining the best of the past with the recognition that universities were going to be very different kinds of institutions in the future, could be sold to the public at large. The age needed a Newman, or even a Moberly; it conjured up a more assertive CVCP.[78]

Concern with values, purposes and vision had not disappeared entirely in the final decades of the century. There was indeed no Moberly, and no Truscot or Ashby or Lindsay. It was not a time for the kind of influence sought by the Moot or the Christian Frontier Council. Moberly's *The Crisis in the University* had brought together a group of academics who shared his search for ways to develop an approach to higher education. This group, through various changes and an amalgamation, became the Higher Education Foundation (HEF) at the end of the 1980s. From 1988 the HEF published a journal, *Reflections on Higher Education* , and its annual conferences in the 1990s discussed such themes as 'academic community', 'the crisis in knowledge for higher education', 'university teaching' and 'lifelong education'. Many of the members, participants in conferences and contributors to the journal were senior figures in higher education, and some, like Roy Niblett and Marjorie Reeves had played a long and prominent part in the discussions that followed *The Crisis in the University* (and Niblett, as we have seen, took part in the prior discussions and was a member of the group that persuaded Moberly to write the book).[79] This was a tradition of concern kept alive in difficult times, given also that there had been a substantial reduction in the number of Christian colleges of education from the 1970s. Although a tiny number of Christian colleges remained, and some of those that amalgamated with other higher education institutions retained a Christian presence there, the Anglican, Roman Catholic and Methodist Churches and their colleges had lost much of the base on which to influence higher education models or visions.

The most extensive attempt in Britain in the 1990s to analyze the situation in higher education was a sequence of books by Ronald Barnett, each one looking for a deeper or redirected way into the issues. *The Idea of Higher Education*, in 1990, basically asked the question: 'Can the idea of a liberal higher education be recovered, and be implemented?' Higher education as 'emancipatory', 'a freeing of the mind' had been undermined, including by having become 'a pivotal institution in the apparatus of the modern state'. The 'emancipatory' nature of higher education could be 'reinstated', despite the absence of any educational theory of higher education – any 'recognized way of conducting a serious educational discussion of higher education'.[80] Barnett's theoretical framework was designed, therefore, to make such an analysis possible. The recovery was to be by questioning every aspect of the developments that had displaced the critical nature of a liberal higher education. Vocational emphasis on skills, for example, was acceptable only if it could be *educationally* justified, that is, if it could be 'the object of critical appraisal on the part of the student'. Critical questions were not being asked about 'learning'.[81] Higher education was no longer a dissenting voice but an accomplice in the social mainstream. Its role as critical commentator needed to be 'restored ... the idea of higher education as a fulcrum for critiquing can be resurrected – *must* be resurrected'.[82] The future was defined in a vocabulary of 'recovering' or 'regaining' a liberal higher education, 'restoring' or 'resurrecting' its emancipatory condition and critical role.

Within and outside the book sequence Barnett attacked the adoption by higher education of concepts and vocabularies such as those of competence, capability, enterprise, transferable skills, experiential learning and problem-based learning. He opposed the proposal for vocational qualifications to be extended to higher education as a Trojan horse of skills, explicit outcomes and higher-level competences.[83] The second volume in the series, *The Limits of Competence* in 1994, explored more fully the burden of this critique. If higher education was to play its part in expanding a 'sense of rationality' in society 'it cannot do so by complying uncritically with the agendas presented to it', but by itself becoming 'self-critical' and 'self-informing':[84]

> Competences and outcomes cannot provide guidelines for a higher education curriculum. It is the business of higher education to develop critical capacities, which must include the evaluation and possible repudiation of contemporary competences.

The latter were inevitably *'behaviour and capacities to act as desired and defined by others'* (my italics). It was not only the state and its agencies who constituted the 'others'. It was unlikely that 'corporations in the world of work have in mind the kind of emancipatory critique sketched out here'.[85] The attack also extended to wider vocabularies and practices, such as modularization, credit accumulation, open learning and 'the student experience'. Underlying them all he saw a process of 'reproduction, not transformation'. 'Outcomes', for example, were 'a response to a given situation … a *re*processing of presented sense data'.[86] All of these undermined the 'emancipatory critique' crucial for higher education. Teachers should cease to be defined as facilitators of learning, curriculum managers or counsellors, but as educators. The 'idea of educator' also needed to be 'recovered'.[87]

The third volume, *Higher Education: A Critical Business* in 1997, further elaborated the concept of a critical higher education, though he now proposed abandoning the notion of 'critical thinking' in favour of 'critical being, which embraces action and the self together with thought'. The student as 'critical actor' was the aim. An understanding of what was needed had to begin by asking whether there were tendencies 'that will thwart the development of criticality'. It would not be impossible to achieve this, but it 'demanded strategies and actions that are little in evidence. The university as a centre of and for a critical life is an endangered species.' The university itself was 'at best indifferent or even, *sotto voce*, somewhat hostile to the encouragement of critical thought in its students'. Such modes of critical thought might have their sponsors in the wider community, the professions, or in the business and commercial sector. There were shifts of ground in Barnett's argument, but the main theme remained transparent – the reconstruction of the critical university. He rejected the notion of vision (as well as leadership and inspiration) as dangerous, because they 'run against the concepts of genuine community and critique'.[88] The first three volumes in the sequence therefore represent a number of *fin de siècle* turning points. He was essentially addressing an internal higher education audience – although he did not take account of the fact that the vocabularies and processes he attacked were often far different and more 'critical' in their *implemented* content than within the theoretical discourse. Outcomes defined for particular courses and programmes often displayed the emancipatory characteristics that Barnett espoused, as did nationally generated programmes such as Enterprise in Higher Education (EHE) and the Teaching and Learning Technology Programme (TLTP), which were considerably transformed in the implementation process. These rarely constituted the domestication in higher education of structures and objectives accepted uncritically from outside, 'defined by others'.

It is also important that much of the history of the twentieth century that we have discussed has been, of course, one of creation, expansion, modification, change emanating from 'others' – many of whom, like Moberly, Ashby, Crosland and Robbins were both outsiders and insiders. The difference when Barnett was writing lay in the content and degree of rigidity of what was on offer to or required of higher education. The voices of earlier decades of the century were largely arguing *for* something, while in the 1990s Barnett was arguing *against* what he saw as the principal causes of the essence of the university being undermined. Seeking a basis for the 'serious educational discussion of higher education', his philosophy and argument were responsive to the interventionist state and its ambitions, but neglecting the responses that 'educators' inside the institutions were often able to make.

A fourth volume in the sequence, *Realizing the University*, appeared in 2000. It was a different book for a new century. His own confidence in restoring the critical higher education for which he had argued was gone. In its place was a portrait of the 'supercomplex' world in which the university as it had been known was at an end, but with the prospect of a totally new one, renewed in the inner city, more open, more diverse, with collapsed boundaries, global and new local opportunities. Old approaches to knowledge, democracy, critique and emancipation could not be a foundation on which to rebuild the university, which more than anything had to 'live with incoherence'.[89] The argument was structured round the 'conditions of uncertainty', 'multiple uncertainties'. A university that was to be appropriate for 'an age is a university that is itself chaotic'. The very concepts of management, organization and leadership had to be abandoned, except in order to bring about conditions of uncertainty or chaos. The university needed forms that would enable it 'to respond and to prosper amid radical uncertainty'. A new form of university was one that 'requires construction, but, thereafter, it will acquire an internal dynamic of its own'. The book concludes:

> Amid supercomplexity, the university has the dual responsibility not only of compounding uncertainty but also of helping us to live with uncertainty; even to revel in it. This is the task in front of the university. In a world where everything is uncertain, there is no other task.[90]

This was a long way from anything advocated over the previous century – and from anything propounded in the final moments of the twentieth century by Barnett's contemporaries or in his own previous work. This peroration argument might surface as a starting point for a history of higher education in the twenty-first century.

NOTES AND REFERENCES

1. Secretary of State for Education and Science, *Education: A Framework for Expansion* (London: HMSO, 1972), p. 38.
2. Niblett, W.R., 'Higher education: one system or two?', *New Society*, 25 January 1973, p. 177.
3. DES and Scottish Education Department, *Higher Education into the 1990s: A Discussion Document* (London: HMSO, 1978), pp. 1–2, 10–11.
4. David, P., 'Ups and downs of finding a way over the hump', *Times Higher Education Supplement*, 19 May 1978, p. 7.
5. Edwards, E.G. *et al.*, 'Into the 1990s – projection or policy?', *Times Higher Education Supplement*, 27 October 1978, p. 13.
6. Hoggart, R., *After Expansion: A Time for Diversity'* (Leicester: Advisory Council for Adult and Continuing Education, 1978), pp. 5–6.
7. Secretary of State for Education and Science and Secretaries of State for Scotland, Wales and Northern Ireland, *The Development of Higher Education into the 1990s* (London: HMSO, 1985), sections 1–2, 6–9.
8. Speech reprinted in University of Reading, *Bulletin*, no. 180, February 1985, p. 7.
9. Speech in Conference on the Green Paper, Society for Research into Higher Education and *Times Higher Education Supplement*, July 1985, pp. 9–10.
10. Marris, R. 'Why Sir Keith should be impeached', *Times Educational Supplement*, 6 December 1985, p. 4; Marris, *The Higher Education Crisis: A Sermon for Conservatives and Socialists* (London: Suntory-Toyota International Centre, London School of Economics [1986]), p. 2.
11. Fairhall, J., 'Baker promises expansion of higher education', the *Guardian*, 24 September 1986.
12. Secretary of State for Education and Science and Secretaries of State for Wales, Northern Ireland and Scotland, *Higher Education: Meeting the Challenge* (London: HMSO, 1987), passim.
13. Sutherland, S., 'The idea of a university?', in National Commission on Education and Council for Industry and Higher Education, *Universities in the Twenty-first Century* (London: NCE, 1994), pp. 1–2.

14. Shattock, M.L., 'Financial constraints on universities: when the pips begin to squeak', in Flood Page, C. and Yates, M. (eds), *Power and Authority in Higher Education* (Guildford: Society for Research into Higher Education, 1976), pp. 62–70.
15. Christopherson, D., *The University at Work* (London: SCM Press, 1973), pp. 111, 118–22.
16. Niblett, W.R., 'Preface' to International Association of Universities, *Problems of Integrated Higher Education* (Paris: IAU, 1972), p. 7.
17. Pedley, R., *The Comprehensive University* (Exeter: University of Exeter, 1969), p. 19.
18. Pedley, R., *Towards the Comprehensive University* (London: Macmillan, 1977), pp. 84–5.
19. Edwards, E.G., *Higher Education for Everyone* (Nottingham: Spokesman, 1982).
20. Merrison, A.W., 'The claims of research, scholarship, and contemplation', *Universities Quarterly*, vol. 28, 1973, p. 45.
21. Jackson, R., 'Higher or further, that is the question', *Times Higher Education Supplement*, 15 October 1971, p. 16.
22. Ashby, E., 'The academic establishment: bottleneck or pump?', ibid.
23. Halsey, A.H., 'The idea of a university: the Charles Carter lecture, 1984', *Oxford Review of Education*, vol. 11, 1985, pp. 115–16.
24. Ashworth, J.M., 'Universities in the 21st centuries [sic] – old wine in new bottles or new wine in old bottles?', *Reflections on Higher Education*, vol. 5, 1993, pp. 47, 50.
25. Whitfield, R., *Academic Birth, Life, Death; and Resurrection?* (Birmingham: University of Aston, 1983), p. 2.
26. Brooke, P., 'Public expenditure constraints', in Jaques, D. and Richardson, J.T.E., *The Future for Higher Education* (Guildford: Society for Research into Higher Education, 1985), p. 73.
27. Secretary of State for Education and Science *et al. The Development of Higher Education into the 1990s*, p. 6.
28. Slee, P., 'A consensus framework for higher education', in Ball, C. and Eggins, H., *Higher Education into the 1990s: New Dimensions* (Milton Keynes: Open University Press, 1989), p. 63.
29. Lord Annan, 'The university in Britain', in Stephens, M.D. and Roderick, G.W., *Universities for a Changing World* (London: David & Charles, 1975), p. 25.
30. Joint CVCP/UGC working group, Performance indicators in universities, London, CVCP (typescript, 1986), p. 1.
31. Becher, T., *Academic Tribes and Territories: Intellectual Enquiry and the Cultures of Disciplines*, (Milton Keynes: Open University Press, 1989); Becher, T., 'Towards a definition of disciplinary cultures', *Studies in Higher Education*, vol. 6, 1981, pp. 109–22; Clark, B.R., *The Higher Education System: Academic Organization in Cross-National Perspective* (Berkeley, CA: University of California Press, 1983); Clark, B.R., *Perspectives on Higher Education: Eight Disciplinary and Comparative Views* (Berkeley, CA: University of California Press, 1984, containing chs by Clark and by Becher).
32. Ball, F. and Eggins, H., 'Introduction', in *Higher Education into the 1990s*, p. 1.
33. Kogan, M., 'The British experience', in Higher Education Group, *Governments and Higher Education – The Legitimacy of Intervention* (Toronto: Ontario Institute for Studies in Education, 1987), p. 173.
34. Niblett, W.R., 'An absence of outrage: cultural change and values in British higher education 1930–1990', p. 22.
35. Dainton, F., *British Universities: Purposes, Problems and Pressures* (Cambridge: Cambridge University Press, 1981), p. 2.
36. Darling, J., 'What were universities for?', in Jaques, D. and Richardson, J., *The Future for Higher Education* (NFER-NELSON, 1985), p. 120.

37. Ball, C. and Eggins, H. 'Introduction', in *Higher Education into the 1990s*, p. 1.
38. Quoted in Sheffield, E. *et al., Systems of Higher Education: Canada* (New York: International Council for Educational Development, 1982), p. 13.
39. Clark, B.R., 'Implementation in the United States: a comparison with European higher education reforms', in Cerych, L. and Sabatier, P., *Great Expectations and Mixed Performance: The Implementation of Higher Education Reforms in Europe* (Trentham, NJ: Trentham Books (English language edition 1986), p. 259.
40. Perkins, J.A., 'The drive for coordination', in Perkins, J.A. and Israel, B.B. (eds), *Higher Education: from Autonomy to Systems* (New York: International Council for Educational Development, 1972), pp. 1, 7–8.
41. DeVane, W.C., *Higher Education in Twentieth-Century America* (Cambridge, MA: Harvard University Press, 1965), pp. 125, 142.
42. Kerr, C., 'Foreword', in Cerych and Sabatier, *Great Expectations and Mixed Performance*, p. xv.
43. Dawkins, J.S., *Higher Education: A Policy Statement* (Canberra: Australian Government Publishing Service, 1988), p. 27.
44. Clark, B.R., 'The insulated Americans: five lessons from abroad', in Altbach, P.G. and Berdahl, R.O., *Higher Education in American Society* (Buffalo, NY: Prometheus, 1981), p. 292.
45. Hesburgh, T.M., 'Nature of the challenge' and 'Closing remarks', in Kertesz, S.D. (ed.), *The Task of Universities in a Changing World* (Notre Dame: University of Notre Dame Press, 1971), pp. 3, 489).
46. Moynihan, D.P.,'State *vs.* academe', *Harper's*, vol. 261 (1980), p. 40.
47. Trow, M., 'Managerialism and the academic profession: the case of England', *Studies of Higher Education and Research* (Council for Studies of Higher Education, Stockholm), vol. 4 (1993), pp. 4–7.
48. Secretary of State for Education and Science and Secretaries of State for Scotland, Northern Ireland and Wales, *Higher Education: A New Framework* (London: HMSO, 1991).
49. Perkins, J.A., *The University in Transition* (Princeton, NJ: Princeton University Press, 1966), pp. 72, 77.
50. National Committee of Inquiry into Higher Education, *Higher Education in the Learning Society* (London: NCIHE, 1997), pp. 18–22.
51. DfEE *et al.*, 'Higher Education: Achievements since Robbins', paper for the National Committee of Inquiry into Higher Education, typescript, 1996, pp. 1–2, 10.
52. DES, 'Clarke announces radical overhaul of teacher training' (typescript), London, 4 January 1992, press release 2/92 and speech paras 15, 18, 20, 21; DES, 'Patten announces expansion of school-based teacher training', typescript, London, 26 May 1992, press release pp. 1–3.
53. CATE, 'The Accreditation of Initial Teacher Training ... A Note of Guidance', typescript, London, November 1992.
54. Higher Education Funding Council for England, *Quality Assessment* (a consultation paper), October 1992, p. 1.
55. Young, M.F.D., *The Curriculum of the Future: From the 'New Sociology of Education' to a Critical Theory of Learning* (London: Falmer Press, 1998), p. 86.
56. Cf. Watson, D. *et al.*, *Managing the Modular Course: Perspectives from Oxford Polytechnic* (Milton Keynes: Open University Press, 1989), chs 1 and 2.
57. Davidson, G., *Credit Accumulation and Transfer in the British Universities 1990–1993*, London, HEFCE (n.d.), ch. 1.
58. Cf. Hannan, A. and Silver, H., *Innovating in Higher Education: Teaching, Learning and Institutional Cultures* (Buckingham: Open University Press, 2000).
59. NCIHE *Higher Education in the Learning Society*, p. 116.

60. HEFCE, Fund for the Development of Teaching and Learning, circular, December 1995, p. 1.
61. Committee of Scottish University Principals, *Teaching and Learning in an Expanding Higher Education System* (Edinburgh: CSUP, 1992), ch. 3 and p. 42.
62. Laurillard, D., *Rethinking University Teaching: A Framework for the Effective Use of Educational Technology* (London: Routledge, 1993).
63. NCET, Briefing paper no. 20, 1993, quoted in NCET, *Information Technology and Learning: Problem or Solution?*, Briefing Paper New Series 8, National Commission on Education, 1995. p. 1.
64. Hannan and Silver, *Innovating in Higher Education*, p. 151.
65. Bates, A.W., 'Restructuring the university for technological change', typescript, Carnegie Foundation for the Advancement of Teaching, 'What kind of university?', London, 1997, pp. 4, 9–10.
66. *Higher Education in the Learning Society*, p. 1. For commentaries from Germany, Sweden and the United States cf. Quality Support Centre, *The Dearing Report: Commentaries and Highlights* (*Digest Supplement*, 1997).
67. Ibid., p. 9.
68. Ibid., Ch. 1.
69. Ibid., p. 72.
70. Ibid., pp. 202, 206–7.
71. Ibid., pp. 114 and ch. 8 passim.
72. Ibid., p. 11.
73. Ibid.
74. DfEE, Scottish and Welsh Offices and Department of Education for Northern Ireland, Purposes of Higher Education, typescript, London, June 1996, passim (Annex A summarizes the responses to consultation).
75. DfEE, *Higher Education for the 21st Century: Response to the Dearing Report* (London: DfEE, 1998), p. 4.
76. Moser, C., 'The Robbins report 25 years after – and the future of the universities', *Oxford Review of Education*, vol. 14, 1988, p. 8.
77. Ball, *More Means Different: Widening Access to Higher Education* (London: Royal Society of Arts, 1990), p. 6.
78. Tapper, T. and Salter, B., *Oxford, Cambridge and the Changing Idea of theUniversity: The Challenge to Donnish Domination* (Buckingham: Open University Press, 1992), pp. 245–6.
79. For aspects of the post-Moberly developments cf. Reeves, M. (ed.), *Christian Thinking and the Social Order: Conviction Politics from the 1930s to the Present Day* (London: Cassell, 1999).
80. Barnett, R., *The Idea of Higher Education* (Buckingham: Open University Press, 1990), pp. x–xi.
81. Ibid., pp. 78, 161.
82. Ibid., pp. 172–4.
83. Barnett, R. (ed.), *Learning to Effect* (Buckingham: Open University Press, 1992), pp. 7–11; 'HE's national curriculum', *Times Higher Education Supplement*, 17 November 1955, p. 13.
84. Barnett, R., *The Limits of Competence: Knowledge, Higher Education and Society* (Buckingham: Open University Press, 1994), p. 24.
85. Ibid., pp. 81, 124.
86. Ibid., pp. 157, 173.
87. Ibid., pp. 192–3.
88. Barnett, R., *Higher Education: A Critical Business* (Buckingham: Open University Press, 1997), pp. 48–50, 58–9.

89. Barnett, R., *Realizing the University in an Age of Supercomplexity* (Buckingham: Open University Press, 2000), pp. 11–20, 57–8.
90. Ibid., pp. 130–4, 172.

11

PRESSURES AND SILENCES

ADAPTATION

The voices we heard at the beginning of the twentieth century, such as those of Haldane and Webb, considered existing university provision and called for more. By the time of Flexner's intervention in 1930 it was already important to explore and evaluate the different types of university, and the trends. In their separate ways, during and after the Second World War, Truscot and Moberly examined what was wrong in the operation of the university and its failure to position itself amid cyclonic social and international changes. Ashby took Moberly's understanding of the problem further, located the failure in the history of science and technology and confronted the relationship between tradition and adaptation. Robbins and Crosland widened further the understanding of 'higher education' and moved the state into a stronger position to influence and to co-ordinate. Governments increasingly determined directions, planned targets, related higher education to social and economic imperatives. The voices of higher education became concerned largely with response and the short-term. Change in the late-century included the national and institutional machineries for control of and quality in the system, and Dearing raised higher the already growing profile of student learning and the improvement of teaching. The story of twentieth-century higher education therefore includes policies and buildings, students and funds, the organization of the national system and of the curriculum, new institutions and the development of old ones, the community and the Internet, the book and the journal, the conference and the professional network, the parliamentary and the private debate, perplexity and protest, values and purpose, advocates and opinion.

The main focus has been the process of making and transforming a system of higher education, together with attempts to interpret it in massive contextual changes. Moberly most determinedly cleared a way into the territory and Ashby most directly penetrated it. The book that most clearly portrayed its contours in the late century was Ashby's 1974 *Adapting Universities to a Technological Society*, some of the argument having been inaugurated in *Technology and the Academics* and elsewhere. In the later work, considering the nature of a 'mass higher education', he looked carefully at the contemporary features of higher education systems and institutions internationally and placed them, as he had always done, in a conceptual framework derived in large part from biology. There is one passage which serves as an invaluable text for the discussion here:

> It is characteristic of higher education systems that they are strongly influenced by tradition. They display what a biologist calls phylogenetic inertia. This is not surprising, for one of their functions is to conserve and transmit the cultural inheritance. It is characteristic of them, too, that from time to time they adjust themselves – sometimes painfully – to the social environment which surrounds them ... There are, therefore, internal and external forces acting on higher education systems and when all is well there is an unstable equilibrium between these forces. At present there is a worldwide instability in higher education systems, and these systems are shifting, one hopes toward fresh equilibria which will be different for different societies. But while the movement is going on there are strains and anxieties; none of us know where the new equilibrium will lie. That is why it is disappointing that so much emphasis, by governments, by the press, and indeed within the systems themselves, is on how to expand, how to pay for expansion, and not on how to change.[1]

A good deal of this history has been about the painful 'strains and anxieties' of the changing equilibrium resulting from competing forces. At different times we have witnessed the unstable equilibrium under scrutiny, not necessarily in such a vocabulary, and by advocates who would not have known what 'equilibrium' could be achieved.

The changes of the earlier decades in the scale and variety of university education involved controversy, aspiration and sometimes disappointment. The variety, as Ashby pointed out in 1967, was in part a protest against the exclusiveness of Oxford and Cambridge, but 'by a process of social mimicry' the new institutions acquired some of the prevailing assumptions and characteristics of higher education.[2] In later decades against the backdrop of world war and cold war, social and economic tensions and rapid technological change, the strains became more acute and the universities and their advocates sounded more lost. From the 1970s particularly, critics pointed to the failures of higher education. Niblett declared in 1974 that 'universities are far from realising the extent of the change of outlook that is required of them: changes of assumption, changes of orientation, changes in the content of what they teach'. The expansionist pressures on universities had not yet 'caused them to think in any fundamental way about their new function in society'.[3] Lord Annan, the following year, as we have noted, thought it foolish not to realize 'that if a nation moves from small-scale to mass higher education, it must expect the customs, ideals, organisation and behaviour of its universities and other institutions to change'.[4] Others in these final decades, but also earlier, looked to forms of adaptation, perhaps involving, in Barnett's initial formulations, 'resurrection' or undermined values 'regained'. The book titles underlined conceptions of the processes at work. For Löwe in 1940 it was a case of 'universities in transformation', for Dent in 1961 they were 'in transition', as they were five years later for James Perkins, President of Cornell University. During the 1960s period of American student protest the books told of 'the troubled campus', or the university 'in turmoil' and in the following decades authors wrote of American higher education 'in decline' or the university 'in ruins'.[5] Although Moberly's 1949 *The Crisis in the University* continued to have echoes in some parts of the British literature, the titles were on the whole more measured, reflecting specific aspects of experience and change rather than deeper anxieties or an overall scenario.

Slowly, and under pressure, higher education had to change. In the final decades of the century it did so either by government behest or in anticipation of the consequences of inertia. For some institutions the effort was greater and more traumatic than for others. Although the responses of higher education in different countries were to historically different environments of social, economic, technological or other change, the voices articulating the needs were remarkably similar. Perkins talked in 1966 of the immensely complex task of 'university direction, stability, and growth'. It had to achieve 'not only an internal harmony, but a harmony that is in a state of constant adaptation to the outside world'.[6] Gavin Brown, the new Vice-Chancellor of the University of Sydney, Australia, argued in 1996 that:

it is only by constant re-appraisal and re-invention that universities can survive to flourish. Moreover, we are driving a vintage model largely designed in late 19th century Germany, with some modifications incorporating the Arcadian vision of Cardinal Newman and more recent body-styling and trim adapted to a down-market reinterpretation of the words 'research' and 'culture'.[7]

The language of change was relatively constant from the Moot to Ashby, from Cornell to Sydney, though the language did not always mean the same thing, and circumstances, emphases and directions differed. Systems of higher education worldwide, and the English system in particular, had spent the late twentieth century in Ashby's 'unstable equilibrium'. In spite of political and ideological certainties, what 'fresh equilibrium' lay ahead at the end of the century – none of us knew.

WHICH VOICES?

The advocates of higher education chosen for this discussion were not necessarily 'representative' voices. In some cases they were the only ones speaking aloud – especially in the earlier decades. In others they seemed to be of two kinds, either aiming to encapsulate what was known or needed to be known, or confirming deficiencies and postulating futures. Not surprisingly, the most vocal advocates of system building, the vice-chancellors or the writers of influential tracts or books have been male, since for most of the century women did not have access to the positions of power and influence. From the end of the nineteenth century they did have positions as heads of women's colleges on the margins of Oxford and Cambridge, and as heads of teacher training colleges well beyond the margins of the university system until the second half of the twentieth century. One of the difficulties in the story has been the way threads of public attention have come and gone – including the education of women, advanced technological education, adult education and quality. Others, of course, have been permanently at the surface or not far from it – state funding, privilege, size, student numbers, autonomy. The most important voices for this story have therefore been those that spoke of the present and sketched a future, whether these were individuals, journals or committees. This was the case with the increasingly dominant voice of government, minister, commission or agency.

The advocates we have heard fall into categories. Some came from outside the system – Haldane, Webb, Simon, for example – though these were often participants at the level of university court or government committee. Others were senior insiders, vice-chancellors or others (Moberly, Livingstone, Ashby), who may or may not have continued to participate in teaching or activities other than administration or institutional leadership. Others might be described as 'cross-overs' (Robbins, Crosland, Joseph) who left or temporarily stood outside the academic system and led a committee or a government department. The members of the two rough, basic categories and the occasional cross-overs frequently, of course, strayed into one another's company or behaved untypically. Only at the end of the twentieth century did a third category emerge, one that had a clear public voice – though in different locations and exerting a different kind of influence. They appeared in the story mainly in the last quarter of the century. They were practitioners, trying to understand, implement and adapt pressures for change and oppor-tunities available, the practicalities, potential and limitations of teaching strategies and the ways in which students learn. They wrote articles and books and were consulted about programmes and possibilities, not about purposes and futures. They were course and project leaders, active in their own and others' professional development, researchers, and above all teachers concerned about students and the impact on them and on themselves of policies and funding decisions. They grappled with skills, outcomes, types of assessment, modules, interactive technologies, group projects and other approaches to student learning. The first two categories of 'senior advocates' were heard through the variety of forums and media that we have discussed. This third category tended to speak to one another, in workshops and conferences about teaching strategies and curriculum change, the assessment of prior learning, modular courses – the minutiae of the management of change. Their journal articles, books in series targeted at higher education teachers, conference papers, Internet and intranet papers and materials or reports on their own pedagogical research, represented a changing map of the present. The map reflected what was happening, what was wrong and what was possible, how things worked and might work, and with what ends. The map was constructed of elements generated inside and outside institutions, but elements that became the focus of a new pattern of professional relationships. Not all teachers, of course, took part, but the public voices added to the variety of experience and opinion available in higher education. The other two categories of advocate knew about the *intentions* of changes to the map, but from their distance were aware about the actual changes (when they were aware of them) through the survey, the research, evaluation or other commissioned report. Reports reached steering groups or limited audiences in funding or other bodies, but were mostly forgotten by national organizations or commissions or government departments when the next intentions were formulated.

Since the outcomes of these descriptions and analyses of experience appeared in the professional conference and in publications with defined professional audiences, they reflected the move towards an emphasis on learning and teaching that the Dearing committee confirmed. It would be possible to interpret the history of twentieth-century higher education in terms of teachers' practices, student learning behaviours (including those influenced by gender, class and minority differences), lecture and seminar effectiveness, examination and assessment models – that is, 'internalist' features. Our focus here has been essentially on the phases of growth and change of a higher education 'system' and on attempts to define and amend its purposes. The nature of 'practice' and 'experience' is an essential part of the total landscape of higher education, but to situate it adequately in the story of the relationship between higher education, the state and opinion would also mean considerably extending the story and the discussion to include these and other contingent elements.

One such element is the persistence in all aspects of higher education of the combat between processes of change and attitudes of inertia or conservatism. This was a combat that Flexner found in the emergent system (including some changes that he felt, both in the United States and in Britain, to be profoundly wrong), and which Ashby detected at Belfast and in his later writings as associated with faculty frontiers and professorial oligarchies. It was a combat that Truscot portrayed vividly in *Redbrick* and in the confrontation between old and new in his cameo of 'A redbrick tea-party'. Much of the higher-education literature of the late twentieth century reflected this combat internationally. One image was an American one in 1968: 'the university has been – with the possible exception of the post office – the least inventive (or even adaptive) of our social institutions since the end of World War II'.[8] There is nothing exclusively American about such judgements on university systems, or about the difficulties of organizational change in universities. In the book where this judgement was quoted the possible sources of change were preceded by a list of such difficulties:

> Organizations are inherently passive ...consist of patterns of repetitive and continuing interaction patterns of coordinated and ordered behavior ... organizations are hierarchical ... Organizational activities and procedures tend over time to assume a sacred quality ... these practices – whether they be lecturing or rain dancing – may come to be ritualistically continued without an evaluation of their effectiveness ... most organizations experience some difficulty in adapting to new conditions. Academic institutions, however, appear to have particular problems in addition because of their own distinctive characteristics: their purposes and support are basically conservative ... academic institutions are deliberately structured to resist precipitant change.[9]

There were, of course, commentators who would not have seen most of these as criticisms, but they are footnotes to many of the difficulties perceived at times in the English system. The failure of higher education to recognize the kinds of change to which it needed to respond was the burden of much of the argument we have considered. This provided a 'surface' motive for some of the 1980s and later political intervention in higher education – 'surface' because of the co-existence of deeper political motivation.

None of this suggests that higher education institutions are always incapable of self-directed change. 'Higher education' has been the home of immense variety, including variety of attitude and initiative. The suggestion is that to locate the voices of professional practice in the discussion, it would be necessary to disentangle attitudes to structural, curricular and other aspects of the institutions. It would also be necessary to pursue further the issues surrounding individual, professional initiative and innovation, and the times and conditions in which it has been more or less possible for these to override the 'passive', 'hierarchical' or 'ritualistic' environments in which teaching and other professional activities take place. While it is important to view these aspects of a system, the institutions and their inhabitants in their complexity, it is also useful to be reminded that some of the foundations on which these rest can to a considerable extent be national and international, and the voices that have to be heard speak within institutions and systems, and across national frontiers.

OPINION

In considering advocates and voices it has never been possible accurately to gauge audiences. Who read the book, how interested or responsive the conference was, how widely the messages of the Moot or the Christian Frontier Conference were carried into other circles, what response there was to a leaflet or a speech in Manchester or Bristol or Hull ... these are other things 'none of us know'. Counting a magazine's or a newspaper's circulation helps little or not at all, and the relationship between advocacy and the laying of the first brick or the appointment of the first professor is a matter for great conjecture. Occasionally there is light. The persistence of local politicians and the Workers Educational Association, the strong support of A.D. Lindsay, Lindsay's friendship with Moberly and the eventual support of the UGC for the creation of what became a University College and then Keele University are clear. So are the Simon campaign for a national review of higher education, his presentation in the House of Lords, responses in the debate and in the press, the views of particular Conservative ministers, the adoption of policies by the Labour Party in opposition, and the establishment of the Robbins committee. Most of the time in this story, however, the focus has had to be on the wishes and intentions of protagonists and what their views and actions reflected, in parallel with demonstrable developments in the emergent and actual system. 'Opinion' cannot be reliably judged in relation to what has been written or proclaimed; nor can the general response and influence of wide constituencies.

Many of the commentators that we have discussed attempted to capture in a sketch or a more detailed portrait the state of public attitudes towards the universities or higher education at different times. Deller, for example, in his 1933 lecture on *Tendencies in Higher Education*, thought that universities were 'increasing in public esteem and respect', though not necessarily praised for what was 'truly praiseworthy'. Praise was accompanied by criticism, and it was said, for example, and 'perhaps not without some justification, that the English universities are too complacent ... They are accused of being oblivious of the change in the spirit of the age ... They are remote, unfriendly, melancholy, slow.' Critics from outside, he suggested, do not always know of 'the constant criticism which begins at home, of the continuous process at Boards and Councils and Senates of examination and discussion and debate'.[10] That was a mixed a message about public esteem, and clearer ones only really began to appear in the upsurge of popular interest in education after the Second World War, and particularly in the period leading up to and following the Robbins report. In 1961 Sir Charles Morris reflected that 'for a good many years now the universities have enjoyed a very good press; and public and professional opinion have been hardly less favourable'. Surprising though this was to the hard-pressed universities, 'on balance this period of indulgence and sympathetic friendliness by the public has been a good thing for the universities'.[11] Such press-watching and sensitivity to public mood offer no systematic analysis, but commentary on public opinion and the reputation of higher education was rarely able to do more. In 1963, after the publication of the report, Robbins told a Home Universities Conference that he spoke 'as one who tries to listen in to what is being said in different quarters about universities (particularly now that this subject has become the centre of conversation)'. He identified what he called an 'animus against universities – do not deceive yourselves: there *is* an animus', that was a result of the complicated ('"unduly complicated", as the outside world sees it') nature of universities' entrance requirements.[12] On this and on other higher education topics, Robbins and his colleagues on the committee had received over 150 memoranda of evidence from organizations and nearly 200 from individuals, and they had interviewed at some length 120 or so individuals and groups of organizational representatives. Most of these were from education or fields closely related to it, but many were from the professions and industry, religious and political organizations. The fact that Robbins had listened to what was being said was no doubt an understatement, but the fact that universities (he was addressing a university conference) had become 'the centre of conversation' was not.

Looking back over the couple of years following the Robbins report, the Vice-Chancellor of the University of Leicester thought that 'in a few months the honeymoon was over', building grants had been cut and a crisis of confidence existed in the universities, partly as a result of 'the ineptitude of the U.G.C.'. The universities were 'getting a bad press', with achievements overlooked and the universities' problems far too complicated for writers about them to understand.[13] The position from this point on was one of what Shils in 1975 called 'public ambivalence' – the universities esteemed for their practical value or ideals, but condemned as elitist or for the behaviour of their students – though there was also some support for students' criticisms of their institutions. Opinion outside the universities was 'complicated and heterogeneous'.[14] The Vice-Chancellor of the University of Durham described the Robbins report as a 'watershed ... It marked the arrival of an altogether new level of public interest in the universities.'[15] Public interest, however, can be indicative of support, hostility or both in a continuing 'ambivalence'. In fact, from the mid-1960s the reputation of the universities undoubtedly declined. Their 'monastic seclusion' or 'ivory tower' mentality was under attack from government and media, student militancy was pilloried, academics were criticized for joining the 'brain drain' to the United States or taking part in 'unprofessional' strikes and other action.[16] Mistrust and uncertainty (in some quarters including, from the early 1970s, about the status and effectiveness of the polytechnics) went together with other sentiments generated by increased student access and wider family experience of higher education. It is not easy to generalize about public 'opinion' or 'interest' in the complex relationships of higher education with a wide variety of constituencies, but that there had been a considerable change for many people with regard to many issues is evident across these later decades. Sir Frederick Dainton commented in 1981 on a decline in 'public esteem', which universities needed to reclaim: 'there is some public disillusionment with higher education itself', because it did not meet public expectations and did not increase the country's prosperity.[17] A writer in *The Economist* in 1994 assailed what he called 'Towers of babble' (not only in Britain). Universities that 30 years before had been 'arguably the most pampered institutions on earth' and had been seen by Robbins as part of a symbiotic relationship with the economy, enabling both to grow:

> This mood has vanished. Universities are on the defensive everywhere, distrusted by governments, worried about losing income and influence ... in Britain, the government treats higher education like an inefficient nationalised industry ... Nothing less than a populist backlash against academia appears to be under way ... Two complaints are especially prominent: that universities have been hijacked by 1960s radicals, more intent on pandering to minorities than advancing knowledge, and that academics rarely give value for money.[18]

What this picture (and the cartoon of 'Ivory Tower University' accompanying it) represented was one important element in the changed balance of ambivalent attitudes, particularly at the level of government opinion and policy. The 'populist' backlash, however, can easily be misinterpreted as a 'popular' one.

Important in all of this is the distinction between 'opinion' and 'audience'. These fragments of insight into popular or political opinion suggest little or nothing about the relationship between advocate and audience. The 'publics' to whom they addressed their plans or visions were of the many kinds indicated by the medium of their messages – the 'gentlemanly' magazine or the professional conference, book or parliament. Their audiences were potential sponsors, pressure and interest groups, the intellectual elite, academics, university-related constituencies (Court, Council and so forth), the 'public', the interested citizen. The institutions themselves and their collective presence were therefore both audience and advocate, listening and responding, defending, appealing or reaching out. The CVCP and the CDP, the AUT and to some extent the UGC at various times, spoke for the system and were addressed by Moberly or Simon or the *Universities Quarterly*. The collective presence was always subject to disruption. Truscot spoke from within for the redbrick universities but bluntly attacked important features of them. The replacement of the UGC by new funding arrangements completely changed the pattern of who could speak for the universities. Advocate, audience and system were instruments for shaping opinion, but they were also part of it and its outcomes.

EQUILIBRIA

For whom did this whole complex system and set of interactions operate? Four constituencies have presented themselves clearly at different times. First, the institutions of higher education and what developed across the century into a system. The universities and new entrants to the definition of 'higher education' combined their own aims, needs and aspirations with aspects of higher education traditions, and the organizing and representative bodies of the system defended, articulated and promoted its operations and requirements. Second, the state. At the beginning of the century, and particularly from 1919, the state was involved in the financing of the universities and the fledgling university colleges, and from the 'climacteric' of the mid-1940s was a majority paymaster. It was engaged from the early 1960s in extending its co-ordinating role and thereafter in directly influencing and shaping the system, its direction and its values. Third, the participating individuals – students, teaching and support staff, and to a lesser extent external members of university governing bodies. Students and teaching staff were both, particularly in the second half of the century, in the ambiguous position of being independent of the state at the same time as receiving state support (in the case of students) or state-funded salaries. Both operated in environments (buildings, libraries, research and teaching resources) dependent on state funding. Higher education, as many of the voices we have heard have reminded us, existed primarily for the students, though as some others argued, primarily for the purposes of advancing knowledge. Whether as teachers or researchers, however, the system of higher education and its funding mechanisms served them. Fourth, the wider society – employers, the professions, parents, the media, social organizations and processes requiring research and development outcomes, or inputs to community activity. Some of the outside constituencies became increasingly present within the institutions themselves in the later century – not only through governing bodies, but also as members of committees, advisers, involved in projects, supporting sandwich courses and work-based learning. Professional body accreditation and preparation for employment were more part of the polytechnic tradition, but as new curricula developed in the older universities and national pressures for attention to the employment market increased, institutions generally sharpened their employment-directed mission. No one constituency held a monopoly of the answer to the question 'who is higher education for?' though the balance of interpretation changed – most prominently as national economic and ideological considerations came to dictate policies more explicitly, especially from the mid-1980s. Nor was any one of these four constituencies self-contained. Employment affected all of them. Research and scholarship were not a matter solely for staff. Funding and resources were of general concern. Reputation and esteem were the product of interactions amongst them all.

'Who is higher education for?' was replaced as a priority question when the Research Assessment Exercise (RAE) was born in 1986. A focus in higher education, in both sectors, had already been established on issues of quality (often translated into 'excellence', or lack of it) but the RAE was new in offering all the constituencies data on which opinion could be shaped and funding could be allocated. In 1986 and 1989 the RAE was conducted by the UGC and then by its replacement, the UFC, and it therefore covered only the 'old' universities. HEFCE, acting on behalf of all the funding councils, took over the exercise from 1992, therefore also including the 'new' universities and colleges of higher education. The same policy enthusiasm for comparative data and league tables that had penetrated the schools and was to extend to other public bodies had now begun to penetrate the universities. Ashby's 'equilibrium' was being transformed not only between institutions and between them and the funding bodies as state agencies, but also among subjects, within institutions as well as nationally. The outcomes of the RAE and TQA assessments were in fact not just 'data'. They served as impressions, hunches and guidance for parents, students present and potential, schools and employers, as well as academics and institutions in relation to one another. Hierarchies were being reinforced. The long-established but often re-balanced relationships amongst the constituencies were undergoing a different level of transformation.

What we have encountered in the story of these relationships has been a sequence of warnings given about the equilibria at different times:

- There were boundary lines not to be overstepped, mainly regarding the boundaries of state responsibility and intervention (most commentators until the boundaries were removed altogether in the mid-1980s).
- Autonomy was important but not without its own boundaries (for example, Moberly).
- Universities policy and decision making were not just for the professoriate (Truscot and Ashby).
- Universities should not live within frontiers, and should relate to the community in a variety of ways (Haldane, Lindsay, Truscot).
- It was wrong not to address higher technological education, but it was wrong for technology not to be seen as humanist (Ashby).
- The curriculum was not inviolate (Ashby, Robbins).
- There were aspects of the curriculum that had to be safeguarded (Flexner, Livingstone).
- Hierarchy and privilege were unacceptable (Truscot, Simon).
- The system was incomplete (all commentators from Webb and Haldane to Robbins and Crosland).

In stages, the system was steered towards greater spread, scale and complexity. It became a 'good' not for an 'elite' but for a 'mass'. A mass higher education, like higher education itself over the whole century, was also 'for whom?' It was for the population at large – for families, students, the wider society, for lifelong learning, all of which raised questions of access and inequalities. However, it was also for the economy, the professions, jobs, the institutions themselves – not all of the last with unmitigated enthusiasm. A mass higher education was also increasingly 'globalized', notably crossing frontiers electronically and in other ways.

AN ABSENCE OF VOICES

The kinds of voices that interpreted equilibria and advocated change in the first three-quarters of the twentieth century were absent in the final decades. The silence obviously has to be related to the dominance of the state and confusion in the system, but those references and judgements must not be oversimplified. External pressure is not necessarily to be criticized. At times in the century such pressure was necessary if new institutions were to be created and existing ones to be modified and reformed. The state and higher education's external communities had legitimate concerns about access, institutional direction, effectiveness or outcomes. Institutions and academics are not necessarily conservative or inert, and the abandonment of all aspects of tradition is not a necessary condition even for the most basic forms of adaptation. Perhaps what the century most clearly demonstrates is therefore the possibility of change when there is not just an 'unstable equilibrium' but also a purposeful dialogue about reaching beyond it. The danger is not in pressure but in *unremitting* pressure and beleaguered institutions and individuals. The beleaguered may reform, but they may also remain unrepentantly conservative. From the early 1960s, and most particularly from the mid-1980s, higher education became an instrument to be used explicitly for national economic regeneration, and pressure therefore became unceasing and as fluctuating and unpredictable as economic policy itself. Beleaguerment related to the constant pressure of requirements for expansion, skills, new types of degrees or the kaleidoscopes of market orientation and accountability. The argument is not that these were *wrong*, it is simply that they were frequent, incessant and paralyzing. The conditions of higher education (not only in England and the United Kingdom) in the late twentieth century – and at the beginning of the twenty-first – were not conducive to the forms of dialogue and advocacy that were central to higher education in the earlier twentieth century.

If individual, institutional, community, state and international interactions are capable of producing creative, unstable equilibria, it is clear at the beginning of the twenty-first century that the growing inequalities amongst the partners have led to what can only be described as an uncreative stable *dis*equilibrium. In these conditions it is difficult within the institutions and the higher education system to see the possibility of influential advocacy or opinion making. The voice, the potential opinion maker, is silent when dominant partners and their publics will not be listening. Decade by decade until the late twentieth century higher education found its advocates, its representatives, its voices (not only its Cassandras and specialists in trench warfare). What became less available to it in the often intrusive, unfamiliar circumstances of the last decades were voices offering messages of new equilibria, of practical vision. Such voices did not appear, to interpret the present as practitioners knew it, to examine the state and its crumbling mansions, to help to create a different kind of ferment, and to persuade – as Ashby and others had done – that there were possibilities of redesign and a new equilibrium.

NOTES AND REFERENCES

1. Ashby, E., *Adapting Universities to a Technological Society* (San Francisco, CA: Jossey-Bass, 1974), p. 136.
2. Ashby, E., 'The future of the nineteenth century idea of a university', *Minerva*, vol. 6, 1967, p. 5.
3. Niblett, W.R., *Universities Between Two Worlds* (London: University of London Press, 1974), p. 2.

4. Annan, N., 'The university in Britain', in Stephens, M.D. and Roderick, G.W., *Universities for a Changing World: The Role of the University in the Late Twentieth Century* (London: David & Charles, 1975), p. 25.

5. Löwe, A., *The Universities in Transformation* (London: SCM Press, 1940); Dent, H.C., *Universities in Transition* (London: Cohen & West, 1961); Perkins, J.A., *The University in Transition* (Princeton, NJ: Princeton University Press, 1966); Atlantic *Monthly, The Troubled Campus* (Boston: LittleBrown, 1965); Wallenstein, I., *University in Turmoil: The Politics of Change* (New York: Atheneum, 1969); Ashworth, K.H., *American Higher Education in Decline* (College Station, TX: Texas A&M University Press, 1979); Readings, B., *The University in Ruins* (Cambridge, MA: Harvard University Press, 1996).

6. Perkins, *The University in Transition*, p. 59.

7. Brown, G., 'The University – Past, Present and Future Organisation Structure' (Inaugural address, September 1966), typescript, p. 1. (Cf.www.usyd.edu.au/about/vcinaug.shtml).

8. Kristol, I., 'A different way to restructure the university' (1968), quoted in Hefferlin, Lon, J.B., *Dynamics of Academic Reform* (San Francisco: Jossey-Bass, 1969), p. 6.

9. Hefferling, ibid., pp. 10–15.

10. Deller, E., *Tendencies in University Education* (London: Oxford University Press, 1933), pp. 16–17.

11. Morris, C., 'Some reflections on the conference', *Universities Quarterly*, vol. 15, 1961, p. 189.

12. Lord Robbins, 'Universities and the future pattern of higher education', *Home Universities Conference Proceedings 1963* (London: Association of Universities of the British Commonwealth) pp. 21–2.

13. Noble, T.A.F., in a symposium on 'Who killed Cock Robbins?', *Twentieth Century*, vol. 174, 1966, pp. 47–8.

14. Shils, E., 'The academic ethos under strain', in Seabury, P. (ed.), *Universities in the Western World* (New York: Free Press, 1975), p. 32.

15. Christopherson, D., *The University at Work* (London: SCM Press, 1973), p. 5.

16. Cf. Silver, H., 'From great expectations to bleak house', *Higher Education Quarterly*, vol. 41, 1987, pp. 207–24.

17. Dainton, F., *British Universities: Purposes, Problems and Pressures* (Cambridge: Cambridge University Press, 1981), p. 11.

18. Wooldridge, A., 'Towers of babble', *The Economist*, 25 December 1993–7 January 1994, p. 54.

INDEX

For Product Safety Concerns and Information please contact our EU representative GPSR@taylorandfrancis.com Taylor & Francis Verlag GmbH, Kaufingerstraße 24, 80331 München, Germany

T - #0101 - 270225 - C0 - 234/156/16 - PB - 9780713040494 - Gloss Lamination